Warp Shoals

Barsuvian

Zayth
War

Valcetti's
Salvation

Egarian
Dominion

Burnscour
Death

WINTERSCALE'S REALM

Lucin's Breath
Frontier

Bastion

SCREAMING VORTEX

RAGGED
WORLDS

The Temple

PORT WANT
Orbital

FOOTFALL
Orbital

The Battleground

Hermitage

Witch-Cursed
World

THE KORONUS PASSAGE

N'S ABYSS

THE CAULDRON

Dolorium

Rain

Grace

FOUNDLING WORLDS

OD-EMPEROR'S
SCOURGE

VOID DANCER'S ROIL

Iniquity

Corpse Stars

Septagonic Void

Sidereus
Pluaeron

Coreward

ROGUE TRADER
THE KORONUS BESTIARY

ROLEPLAYING IN THE GRIM
DARKNESS OF THE 41ST MILLENNIUM

CREDITS

LEAD DEVELOPERS
Tim Huckelbery with additional concepts by Sam Stewart

WRITING AND DEVELOPMENT
Owen Barnes, Matt Boles, Max Brooke, Lester Crow, John Dunn, Craig Gallant, Jordan Goldfarb, Jeff Hall, Tim Huckelbery, Sam Stewart, and Michael Surbrook

EDITING AND PROOFREADING
Alex Davy and David Johnson

GRAPHIC DESIGN
Evan Simonet

COVER ART
Daarken

INTERIOR ART
Erfian Asafat, Ryan Barger, John Blanche, Alex Boyd, Matt Bradbury, Anna Christenson, Paul Dainton, Vincent 'Yogh' Devault, Wayne England, Dave Gallagher, Mark Gibbons, Zach Graves, Jason Juta, Chun Lo, Brynn Metheney, Ameen Naksewee, Neil Roberts, Sept13, Jasper Sandner, Douglas Shuler, Adrian Smith, Nikolay Stoyanov, and Emerson Tung

MANAGING ART DIRECTOR
Andrew Navaro

ART DIRECTION
Andy Christensen

PRODUCTION MANAGEMENT
Eric Knight

EXECUTIVE GAME DESIGNER
Corey Konieczka

EXECUTIVE PRODUCER
Michael Hurley

PUBLISHER
Christian T. Petersen

LICENSING & DEVELOPMENT COORDINATOR
Deb Beck

GAMES WORKSHOP

LICENSING MANAGERS
John French and Owen Rees

HEAD OF LICENSING
Jon Gillard

HEAD OF LICENSING, LEGAL, AND STRATEGIC PROJECTS
Andy Jones

HEAD OF INTELLECTUAL PROPERTY
Alan Merrett

SPECIAL THANKS
Playtest Coordinator Ronald DeValk; "Veterans of a Psychic War" Benn Williams with Chris Lancaster, Scott Philips, Aric Wieder, Rebecca Williams, and Eric Young; "You Bid Babies?!?" Jordan "Milly" Millward with Keri Harthoorn, Kyle Harthoorn, Kieren Smith, Julia Smith and Malcolm Douglas Spence; "Unrepentant" Lachlan "Raith" Conley with Brad Twaddell, Mark McLaughlin and Jordan Dixon; "The Librarians" Pim Mauve with Gerlof Woudstra, Keesjan Kleef, Jan-Cees Voogd, and Joris Voogd; "Furnace of Destiny" Ryan Powell with Max Hardenbrook; "No Guts No Glory!" Sean Connor with Stephen Pitson, Adam Lloyd, Simon Butler, Steven Cook, Charmaine Thornton, Ben Newman; "Roll Perils…" Matthew 'H.B.M.C.' Eustace with Mike "Rosie's Husband" Madani.

FANTASY FLIGHT GAMES

Fantasy Flight Games
1975 West County Road B2
Roseville, MN 55113
USA

ISBN: 978-1-58994-801-3   Product Code: RT11   Print ID: 1260MAR12

Printed in China

For more information about the Rogue Trader line, free downloads, answers to rule queries, or just to pass on greetings, visit us online at

www.FantasyFlightGames.com

CONTENTS

INTRODUCTION

"Do not waste your fear on the unknown, for in Koronus we have known terrors aplenty to fill your nightmares."

–Seneschal Venton Tiebolt

Humanity may have settled untold worlds in the Koronus Expanse, but only the most audacious of Rogue Traders would dare claim that it asserts any true dominion over this lawless region of space. For every conquered planet there are dozens more under the control of natural predators, foul xenos races, or other enemies ready to contest mankind's rightful destiny to rule. Explorers operating in the Expanse are sure to encounter these threats in their journeys, either by accident or design, and must be ready lest their ship and their profits be lost.

WHAT'S IN THIS BOOK?

THE KORONUS BESTIARY is a compendium of the dark creatures and xenos races awaiting Explorers in their travels through the Expanse. Some of the confrontations might be part of planned Endeavours, but others are likely to be chance encounters with lethal monsters or hostile powers. Also included are commentaries from Arch-Militant Lorayne Thornhallow. Her current employment as bodyguard to Rogue Trader Tallen Alberse is perhaps her most hazardous position yet, as Alberse is in constant pursuit of new trophies and glorious adventures. Thornhallow's role is to keep him alive in these ventures—something she is evidently very good at, having weathered countless lethal encounters in the service of her patron. Her observations on the creatures and races should be taken seriously, as they represent the first-hand knowledge of someone who has survived to tell the tale.

The enemies detailed in this book are accompanied by adventure seeds and other hooks that GMs can use to import these new dangers into ROGUE TRADER games. Each of the following chapters concentrates on one type of threat, ranging from bestial monsters to predatory alien races to the terrors that lurk beyond reality. The final chapter offers the GM a system for creating new and unique threats for Explorers to face in the Koronus Expanse.

CHAPTER 1: BEASTS AND MONSTERS

Chapter 1 examines some of the more dangerous creatures found across the Expanse. Each is commonly associated with a single planet, though some have become scattered across systems due to mysterious causes.

CHAPTER 2: ALIENS OF THE EXPANSE

Chapter 2 covers the major sentient xenos races in this lawless region of space. These represent perils much greater than any single creature, for here the Explorers face powerful fleets, mighty armies, deadly weaponry, and other dangers that could not only imperil their lives but also their very dynasties. This chapter includes information about the devious Stryxis, the brutal Orks, the treacherous Eldar, the ferocious Rak'Gol, and other enemies that the Explorers face in their pursuit of profit and glory.

CHAPTER 3: DENIZENS OF THE WARP

Chapter 3 presents a different sort of threat, that posed by the Enemy Beyond. Xenos creatures merely destroy an Explorer's body, but the forces of Chaos can rend his very soul.

CHAPTER 4: XENOS GENERATOR

Chapter 4 introduces a system to create new random xenos creatures for ROGUE TRADER games. GMs can use this generator to produce unique beasts to provide profits or threaten the Explorers (usually both), as well as dangerous plant life and even primitive sentient races ripe for exploitation and possible introduction into the Imperium, either willing or unwilling.

NPCS AND WEAPONS/KNOWLEDGE

All NPC creatures and characters are also assumed to have the appropriate Weapon Training Talents for any weapons that appear in their profile, unless otherwise noted. It is up to the GM to determine what other weapons the NPC might be capable of using if a special situation arises. Similarly, it is assumed these beings also are versed in the knowledge necessary to perform their livelihoods, and the GM may also deem that they have other knowledge or lore depending on the adventure.

ENEMY PROFILE PRESENTATION

In all the entries presented in this book, the characteristics, movement values, and weapon damages have been presented with all modifications included. Weapon damages include the effects of the enemy's Strength Bonus and Talents that always apply to damage such as the Crushing Blow Talent. Talents, Traits, and special rules that have a variable effect or only apply in particular circumstances have not been combined into the profiles presented here. It is also important to note that these creatures and NPCs are not necessarily bound to follow the same strictures for their profiles as Player Characters.

NEW TRAIT: IMPROVED NATURAL WEAPONS

Some creatures have teeth as sharp as the finest hunting dagger, or claws able to crack apart carapace armour like a cheap Amasec bottle. Their Natural Weapons no longer count as Primitive.

NEW WEAPON QUALITY: RAZOR SHARP

The edges of these claws or blades are honed to an unnatural degree and can slice through most armour with ease. When an attack made with this weapon results in two or more Degrees of Success, the weapon's Penetration is doubled.

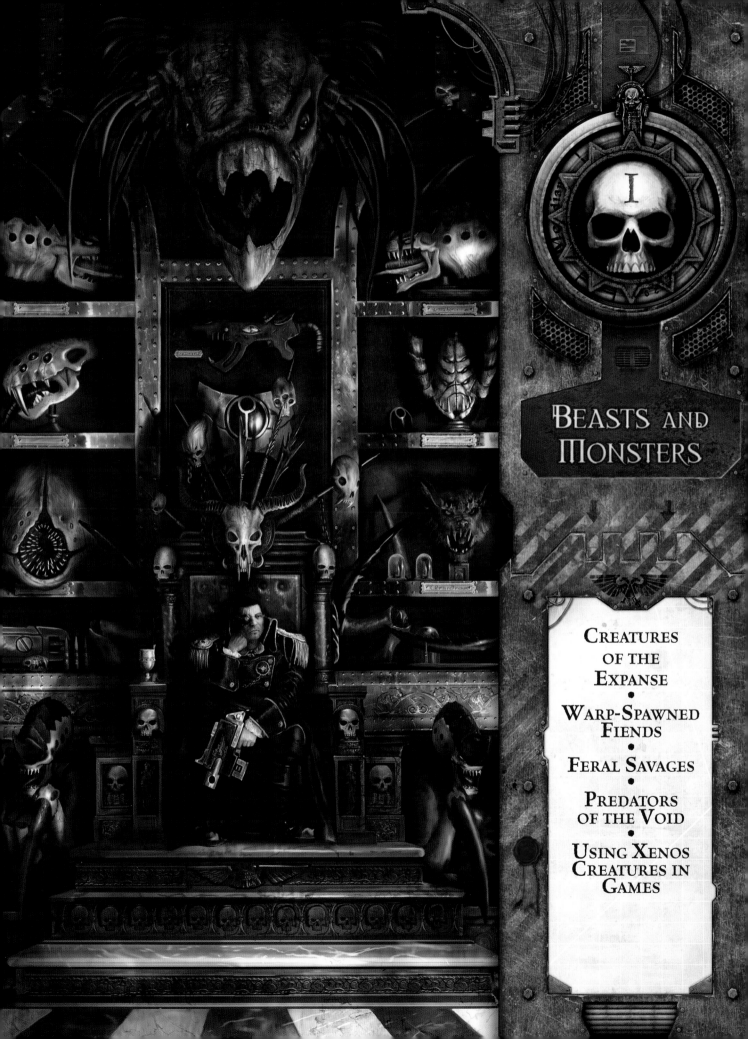

BEASTS AND MONSTERS

- CREATURES OF THE EXPANSE
- WARP-SPAWNED FIENDS
- FERAL SAVAGES
- PREDATORS OF THE VOID
- USING XENOS CREATURES IN GAMES

CHAPTER I: BEASTS AND MONSTERS

"You think those Orks were bad? Wait till you land on Burnscour, or some of the other worlds out here. You'll be wishing it was just greenskins coming after you."

–Arch-Militant Pel Lakken

The Koronus Expanse is home to a great many worlds that have been settled by humans, to various degrees of civilisation. As it is technically beyond the Imperium, it exists in a lawless state where the only rule is what bolter and lance can establish, and property is held for only as long as it can be aggressively defended. Xenos races roam freely, preying on humanity and denying its rightful destiny to rule the void. This is an extremely dangerous region, yet for a Rogue Trader its open nature makes it ripe for exploitation and profit. Those who would make their means in the Expanse must deal with more than just these threats, however. The Expanse is filled with all manner of bestial creatures, and while these do not present the same kind of dangers as hostile xenos, they are no less hazardous. Each poses new perils for Explorers, as unique as the world it occupies. Many also offers tremendous potential for profit and glory, often of a personal nature impossible when dealing with merchant trading or combat in the void.

Every planet across the Imperium offers its own range of flora and fauna peculiar to that habitat, along with those breeds previously imported by design or accident. As mankind spreads its dominion across a planet, these life forms often become beaten down into more manageable forms, the better to serve their new masters. The Koronus Expanse, however, knows no masters. Much of the region is still unexplored, and humanity has only properly surveyed or settled a fraction of its worlds. New planets are uncovered on what seems a daily basis, each filled with new life forms that offer the possibility for profit and ruin, usually in equal measures.

These newly-discovered worlds often have not seen human presence for millennia, if at all, or worse yet have only known the foul touch of the xenos to disturb their natural biology. Here animals, plants, and things as yet unclassified dominate, despite the best efforts of humanity to eradicate them or simply just slow their growth. Those planets most hostile to human life are termed Death Worlds. These generally host countless horrific species, each aggressively evolved to survive against their environment and fellow life forms, all of which are often lethal in the extreme. These can range from nearly-invisible insects that silently implant toxic eggs to mammoth beasts larger than Imperial tanks that simply swallow anything that fits into their enormous maws. Plant life can also show extreme lethality, with fast moving carnivorous flora or fungal spores that can kill in moments. Generally, the life on such

worlds is clearly dangerous, though some offer threats of a more subtle nature that only careful analysis from Magos Biologis researchers can uncover.

Even the worlds assumed to be fully under control, however, may offer up dreadful new surprises. Settlers, miners, researchers, agri-toilers, and others often disturb hidden creatures or bring forth long-slumbering beasts from what were thought to be relatively safe environs. The implantation of Imperial manufactorums and hydroponic bastions into some biospheres can also result in the introduction of chemical effluent and other sewage, creating monstrous mutations and causing some flora to erupt into deadly new variants. Other creatures seem to have been deliberately introduced onto certain planets, in what could be attempts to hinder efforts from competing Rogue Traders or merchant interests. Radical xenologists speculate that specially bred beasts have been implanted into some native biospheres for sport or other less commercial reasons as well, including simply to eliminate humans from a world. Certainly, the introduction of immature megafauna or even especially carnivorous beasts into a new environment can be devastating.

In some instances, these new threats can destroy a once-successful mining facility or devastate a thriving colony. More often, though, they simply become part of the local living conditions, with workers constantly on their guard against bestial invasions or plant infestations. As long as the planet remains profitable, even with additional costs for such defences, no Rogue Trader would countenance shutting down a venture for mere local troubles. Despite the dangers xenos creatures pose, to be a Rogue Trader is to deal with the unknown and alien, and the

Koronus Expanse offers both aplenty. Most would not have it any other way, and pride themselves in their ability to properly confront (and profit from) such encounters. Exploration is where new profits are to be found; those that stagnate into safe and easy trading patterns in the Expanse do not last long, as here the more aggressive develop greater riches. Across the Expanse, there are countless examples where hazardous life forms have been turned into increased revenues, even if just as new attractions in illicit beast houses. The nobility in the Calixis Sector has an insatiable appetite for unique creatures from the Expanse, as the enticing degree of danger makes them all the more attractive, and many Explorers make handsome livelihoods supplying this demand. Some prefer this to the Cold Trade, as the hazards are generally more obvious and there is less danger from the Inquisition or slighted xenos races.

Some Explorers even seek out these perils, to test themselves against the Expanse itself. In a place and a calling where one can die at a moment's notice from attacking xenos, failed technology, or other hazards too numerous to list, such a distilled confrontation is perhaps a welcome change. Here the outcome all comes down to a man and his skills. The only view most have of xenos creatures might be behind plasteel barriers at jaded spire parties or at the bottom of Beast House fighting pits, and they can never know the exhilaration of combating these creatures in the wild. Most call this behaviour reckless and even suicidal, but it is well known that wearing the newly-tanned skin of an exotic creature when striding across Port Wander is usually enough for many rounds of free drinks in the taverns.

CLAWED FIEND

"Each time I think I have seen the worst predator on any Death World, that is when I know I am about to see something even more horrific."

–Arch-Militant Roland D'Vrexe

Damage to the *Aureus* from the greenskin ambush was worse than we originally thought; after only a short journey through the warp, we had to emerge back into blessed real space to give her Gellar Field a rest while the machine spirits recovered. We found ourselves near Molokov, a Death World known for its armoured predators. With little to do while we waited, Alberse of course jumped at the chance for a hunt, especially when he learned several previous expeditions had gone lost there. We were having little any luck finding beasts worthy of his attentions, but did find the remains of what had once been a proud gun-cutter. Heavily corrosive precipitation had taken its toll on the wreck and there was little more than a pitted hull and shattered glassteel. As we began to scout around the wreck, a storm that had been threatening to pour on us for hours finally opened up, as if on cue, and the deluge began falling. We quickly got inside the torn cargo hold and waited for the storm to end.

We relaxed a little in our hideaway from the cruel rainfall, when suddenly a terrifying cry brought us to our feet and to arms. Something was out in this weather, but the cascade and steaming mists obscured any view beyond a few metres. Without warning, a huge bulk of muscled fur and claws rushed into the now-cramped space under the wreck, spattering us all with acidic water as it ripped and clawed at us. The awful precipitation ran like little rivers down the thing's face and horrible maw. The creature's brutish arms tore through our

retinue, eviscerating two of our group before we could even adjust to its presence. The hideous thing lashed its barbed tail across Alberse's armour, knocking him to the ground and thankfully to a degree of safety as I drew my Locke to fire.

The retorts were deafening in the enclosed space and the smell of the bolts' exhaust blended quickly with the horrid aroma of the creature. I hit the thing twice, sending it piling end over end and knocking three armsmen to the ground in its spasms. It reared up again and this time it seemed even angrier than before. It took Ecclesiarch Karoline's head clean off with one still-smoking arm while trying again to punch its tail through Alberse's abdomen. By now what was left of our party had taken up arms and we began to pump bolter shells and lasrounds into the crazed xenos beast, barely slowing its attacks but driving it back into the rain. Finally, the thing slumped into the smoking mud and moved no more.

After we returned to the ship, Alberse had it cleaned, stuffed, and placed on display in his state room. It is quite impressive, and certainly didn't hurt his negotiations with those Calixian fops a week later. There are even rumours saying it comes back to life during the evening watches and stalks the halls looking for lazy crewmen to devour. Just stories, but remembering how many it killed when you're looking at the beast makes it hard to dismiss them quite so easily.

UNSTOPPABLE FURY

The body of a Clawed Fiend is an amalgamation of the most predatory aspects of nature. Its size is tremendous and it can move that bulk of muscle and claw at almost preternatural speeds. The arms are long and muscular, giving it a tremendous reach. It also sports a long corded tail of bone and sinew, ending with a deadly spike of bone. The Fiend gets its name from the ferocious tips on each of its fingers and toes. Each claw is larger than an Ork's finger and is cruelly shaped. The curved mass of chitin that forms each talon comes to a dangerous point and the edge is almost as sharp as a mono blade.

The head of the Fiend is frightening yet also perfect for its predatory role. The creature's face is flat and bereft of hair, and protective leathery skin stretches thickly over its skull. Long fur surrounds the rest of the head, trailing to lengths along the back, arms, and legs. Its multiple eyes can see in several spectrums and its large ears can pick up the slightest of sounds no matter its environment. Beast House hunting reports (as well as recordings taken from pit fights) seem to indicate that it prefers a moving target, but these also show it is not fooled by a creature keeping absolutely still.

Even apart from its heightened senses, the Clawed Fiend's combat prowess is truly remarkable. Stories of the creature's strength amaze even the most jaded of xenologists and savants of the Expanse's myriad fauna. Reports abound of the creature tearing through the largest of herd animals and slaying even the best-armoured of opponents. It is rumoured that a Fiend can even claw through ship bulkheads given time. A single swipe from this xenos has been known to literally take the head from a man's shoulders.

While the exact reasons are as yet unknown, it has been proven that after a Clawed Fiend is wounded (no easy feat on its own) it enters an even more furious state. This has become a feature highlight in many a pit fight, with some gamblers wagering not only on when it makes its kill but also when it enters this condition of supreme frenzy. Some xenos researchers believe this is nothing more than a physical reaction to the creature's injury as it strives to defend itself from attack, though most dismiss this as few other creatures display this behaviour to this extent.

Another theory is that a Clawed Fiend enters a hyper-aware state when injured, releasing extreme amounts of endorphins, adrenaline, and other chemicals to course through its body and initiating such terrifying carnage. Some studies of recovered corpses suggest that the creature is actually angered by the scent of its own blood, which contains a series of pheromones that enrage the creature. More disquieting studies go so far as to wonder if this behaviour is even due to natural evolution, or perhaps the result of careful breeding or gene-engineering. Veterans of encounters with a Fiend know simply to strive to kill it with the first shot and, if that fails, be prepared for fury beyond imagining.

The beast's habitat is a matter of some dispute to those in the Expanse. While many assume that it originally came from Burnscour, given the famously deadly nature of both the beast and that world, variants of the xenos have also been found on several other planets including Gallant and Vaporius. A white-furred Fiend was even killed on Lucin's Breath and its pelt sold for a small fortune. There are numerous theories as to how this might have happened, such as the creatures being left on various worlds accidently during transport to Carnivoriums throughout the sector, or perhaps an unknown xenos menace has been using the creature to pacify targeted planets by killing off any native threats, be they sentient or bestial. There is even talk of them being able to warp-walk to other planets, although this theory is given no credit by any serious Biologis. Few know the truth, that the creature actually hails from the remote Donorian sector, far away from the Expanse or even the Calixis Sector. This secret is known only to a handful of xenologists, senior Rogue Traders, and others who guard the deepest mysteries of the Expanse for their own hidden reasons.

What is known about the Clawed Fiend and its role in its ecology is certain. This creature, no matter where it is, rapidly rises to the position of an alpha predator. It eats anything when it is hungry, and it kills or destroys whatever gets in between it and its chosen prey.

Clawed Fiend								
WS	BS	S	T	Ag	Int	Per	WP	Fel
43	—	(10) 59	(10) 53	47	16	(10) 54	23	04

Movement: 5/10/15/30 **Wounds**: 48
Armour: Toughened Skin (All 4). **Total TB**: 10
Skills: Awareness (Per), Climb (S) +10.
Talents: Berserk Charge, Bestial Fury†, Blind Fighting, Combat Master, Crushing Blow, Iron Jaw, Nerves of Steel, Swift Attack, Takedown.
Traits: Bestial, Brutal Charge, Dark-Sight, Fear (2), Natural Armour, Improved Natural Weapons, Size (Hulking), Sturdy, Unnatural Strength (x2), Unnatural Toughness (x2), Unnatural Perception (x2).
Weapons: Claws (1d10+10 R, Pen 1; Razor Sharp, Tearing), Tail Spike (1d10+2 R; Pen 0; Tearing).
†**Bestial Fury**: If the Fiend suffers one or more Wounds in a previous Round, it automatically gains the Frenzy and Lightning Attack Talents for the remainder of the combat.

CREEPING STALKER

"Lucin's Breath—where the ice comes alive and swallows men whole."

–Lajos Gelei, Thermal Processing, Winterscale Mine C-74K

Alberse had initially landed on Lucin's Breath to conduct some highly unofficial business with the Shrivs, a group of rather dubious local scavengers with some rare items for trade. Things actually went well; we got to trading stories and mention was made of something called a "Creeping Stalker." Alberse, naturally enough, had to find one. Thus, we ended up marching across the landscape with our local guides (for an extra fee), looking for something a few metres long and wide, with translucent flesh and an irregular hide. The Shrivs seemed fearful, but I had to wonder how dangerous such a creature could be, considering I'd been told life on this iceball moved at millimetres per day to conserve energy. This was before I saw one in action.

Standing amid a glassy forest of crystalline boulders and towering ice spires, any doubts I had as to the danger of a stalker were quelled when I saw the snow ripple behind a man. I barely had a chance to shout a warning over the vox before the thing had him. What had seemed to be a layer of water ice and methane frost now revealed itself to be a flowing mass of semi-transparent flesh and writhing tentacles. The luckless Shriv's patchwork void suit dissolved wherever the tentacles touched, venting air that froze almost instantly. I pulled Alberse away with one hand and drew my Locke with the other. Another in the party pointed a hand flamer at the monster but the frigid temperatures meant the promethium failed to ignite. His fumbling attempts to make the weapon work resulted in his being the next to fall. For a supposedly sessile creature, the thing was moving awfully fast.

Having shoved Alberse to what I hoped was a safe location, I turned my attention back to the beast. With two men's screams no longer crowding the vox I was able to make myself heard, and told Alberse (and everyone else) to get back. I then braced and opened fire. At such close range, each round barely had time to ignite before they slammed home, splattering the creature (and what was left of its two victims) over the frozen landscape.

As I cautiously looked around for any more (and noticed the Shrivs had disappeared from the scene), Alberse recovered from his initial shock. His first act was to complain that my bolter had rendered the animal's skin useless as a trophy. His second was to declare that we had to find another of the creatures. He simply had to have a skin for his trophy room. Fortunately, the frozen forest about us seemed to be home to several and we were able to dispatch a second one with a single well-placed Hellgun round.

Once the animal was dead, I had to admit the skin was a rather interesting sight, seeing as it was nearly transparent in some areas and covered in a speckled pattern of blotches in others. On the other hand, it took an effort of will not to laugh (or retch) when it turned out the ship's trophy room was far too warm to properly display Alberse's newest prize. The skin stank like underhive drops and began decaying once we had ignited our drives to leave the system, going from glassy flesh to a leathery goo before we had even entered the warp.

ICEWORLD TERROR

Life on Lucin's Breath is uniquely adapted to the planet's freezing temperatures. Creatures (including some mobile flora) there move very, very slowly—if at all—in an effort to conserve as much energy as possible. Creeping Stalkers, being one of the planet's apex predators, normally move at a blistering rate of nearly a metre an hour, while lesser animals such as the rotund Ice-Eaters might cover the same distance in a week or more. The Stalker's lack of speed and natural coloration can make it very hard to detect as most look like just another mottled patch of frost and ice. They are also virtually silent as they move, like most life on the planet. This behaviour allows them to approach unseen and unheard, and more than one miner, distracted by a piece of balky equipment, has been taken unaware by what he assumed to be just another patch of snow.

Stalkers—and all life native to Lucin's Breath—have vastly reduced metabolisms, with life-spans that can might be measured in centuries, and their body temperature registers as just barely above the ambient freezing conditions. Even digestion is accomplished at a reduced pace, with locals reporting Stalkers taking months (if not longer) to fully consume a meal. In the rougher camps outside the Wrecks, some have taken to capturing a Stalker then placing bets as to which parts dissolve away first from the swollen stomach. As food is so hard to come by, even when engorged a Stalker is more than willing to attack new prey if they have the energy and opportunity presents itself. Stalkers are never truly sated, and always hungry for more sustenance.

The average Creeping Stalker is a flat, vaguely diamond-shaped creature two to three metres long by one to two metres across. However, as Stalkers never stop growing, it is possible larger ones exist and apocryphal tales on Victory Station tell of creatures dozens of metres wide eating entire vehicles, crew and all. A Stalker's skin and flesh is mostly translucent, except where mottled patches serve to break up the featureless covering and aid in camouflage. The hide is surprisingly tough, considering its fragile appearance, and can stretch greatly to accommodate meals. The creature is without skeleton or internal structure; the only rigid parts are the rings of ripping transparent teeth set around the wide, jawless mouth. Four long, whip-like tentacles surround the mouth as well, and serve to drag anything the Stalker comes in contact with, be it an ice-eater or a luckless miner, into its mouth.

GLACIAL PREDATION

In order to conserve energy, Creeping Stalkers remain motionless while hunting, lying in wait for days on end, until they are covered with a layer of frost and drifting snow. They are lacking eyes and most xenologists in the Expanse believe they detect the approach of prey through the faint electrical fields most living creatures generate. Humans, being larger and far more physically active than most life forms native to Lucin's Breath, have extremely intense fields even when shielded by layers of protective clothing and armour. When it detects prey the Stalker slowly closes in on its prey until it is within killing range. Once properly positioned, it bursts into activity, burning decades worth of stored energy in a matter of moments and moving so quickly its body steams from the exertion.

As the Stalker flows from its hiding spot under the snow and ice to attack, its primary weapons are the lashing quartet of tentacles. Victims hit by a tentacle are quickly wrapped up and pulled back to the mouth, which secretes acidic enzymes to absorb as many nutrients as possible. Struggling targets are lashed by additional tentacles until they are sufficiently weakened. Once the target stops moving, it is crammed into the mouth with one pair of tentacles, while the other pair quest for additional prey. If none is available, the Stalker settles down, becoming one with the landscape and building up energy reserves as it digests its prey. If the meal is of sufficient size, the Stalker may reproduce through binary fission, taking a year or more to divide into two smaller but fully-grown Stalkers.

STALKERS ON OTHER WORLDS

While the Stalker seems uniquely suited to the impossibly cold biome of Lucin's Breath, other disturbingly similar creatures have been found on other worlds. Adapted to far warmer climates, they prowl underhives, the lower decks of void ships, the fetid swamps of feral worlds, and similar locales. There is much debate as to whether this represents parallel evolution or artificial breeding programmes by parties unknown. The skins of Creeping Stalkers, provided they are kept at reasonable temperatures, are of value to collectors of exotic lifeforms. Even more so are the Stalker's crystalline teeth, which are in great demand among the aristocracy of certain planets as ornaments and art objects.

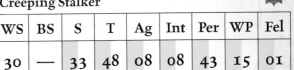

Creeping Stalker								
WS	BS	S	T	Ag	Int	Per	WP	Fel
30	—	33	48	08	08	43	15	01

Movement: 1/1/1/1 **Wounds:** 12
Armour: Tough Hide (All 2). **Total TB:** 4
Skills: Climb (S), Concealment (Ag) +20, Silent Move (Ag) +20.
Talents: Fearless, Hardy, Resistance (Cold).
Traits: Bestial, Blind, Burst Of Speed†, Cold Dweller††, Multiple Arms, Natural Armour 2, Natural Weapons, Size (Enormous), Sturdy, Strange Physiology, Toxic, Unnatural Senses.
†**Burst Of Speed:** By releasing stored energy, a Creeping Stalker is capable of bursts of surprisingly quick movement, adding +20 Agility and updating its Move to 4/8/12/24 for 1d10 Rounds.
††**Cold Dweller:** Whilst stationary in ice or snow, the Creeping Stalker gains +20 to Concealment Tests. It also ignores penalties for moving over ice, snow, and other difficult terrain. Energy weapons, however, do an extra 1d10 of damage to the creature.
Weapons: Teeth (1d10+3 R; Pen 1; Tearing, Toxic), Whip Tentacles (1d10+3 I; Pen 0; Flexible, Snare, Toxic).

KHYMERA

"They came through the walls. We fought them with all we had... but they came through the walls."

–Sgt. Nestor Roderic, Sceadu Angel 9th Regiment

It had seemed a real distress call, a common occurrence in our current region. Eldar raiders had attacked another colony near Bannon, and Alberse personally knew one of the magisters well enough to verify things (and also knew he was capable of richly rewarding our efforts). We followed the signal to a seemingly deserted landing pad far inside the high bastions surrounding the main complex. Not too far away were the ancient remains of some xenos vessel, mutely standing watch over the area. We searched but could find no trace of them, or even from where the signal was originating (which made Tech-Priest Algon even more irritating than usual). As daylight faded, we could also see flickering lights in the wreckage, but the wild, inhuman cries gave us little hope they indicated the missing colonists.

At that point I had to suspend our searches to prepare for possible assault, recalling our people while the lander was readied for likely takeoff. Shapes were seen darting among the distant shadows, gathering in number until a pack of fast-moving felinoid beasts came racing across the open plain. We opened fire, but they proved too quick. Curses were hurled about as some on the walls exclaimed they hit their targets but that the las-bolts simply passed on through. The creatures were upon the perimeter faster than could be believed, but I knew we could pick them off once they had to stop below us against the surrounding prefabricated rockcrete and plasteel.

That wasn't the case. The beasts didn't break stride, and simply galloped through the structure below us, entering the complex perimeter in moments. They moved with huge leaps, slashing out with long spiked arms, ripping apart those on the ground readying the lander and dragging down some on the walls to be devoured. I'm sad to say fire discipline vanished as we were thrown into an absolute panic, caught totally unawares by this attack. Some fired wildly, others ran away to hide, while a few called upon loudly for the Emperor's aid. It wasn't coming, and these things were rapidly chewing through our people. One of the creatures sprang up at me and I managed to get a bolter hit to its midsection. Instead of

the bloody carcass I expected to land messily on me, though, the thing fractured into dark red smoke and was gone.

I dropped to the ground and searched for Alberse, finding him for once ably dealing with another of the beasts with an artful slash of his xenos sword. The creatures were all finally dead, leaving behind only unnatural wisps of grainy smoke, but we paid a great price in blood and lives ourselves. We could now hear more activity from the wreckage in the dimming light, and knew we had been too late for the colony and Tallen's friend. We reclaimed our fallen and made for the lander, lifting into the air as quickly as possible. Below us, the xenos wreckage was covered with dancing lights. Alberse had the site torpedoed from orbit.

NIGHTMARE HUNTERS

Khymerae are terrifying creatures, literally born from a person's nightmares. They spawn in the warp, coalescing into existence like malignant cysts around the psychic energies that fear and terror leaves in the Immaterium. They do not form at the whim of the Chaos Gods nor do they appear to be fragments of these powers. Taxonomists of the Ordo Malleus classify them not as actual daemons but as warp creatures, one example of the many unnatural flora and fauna existing in the Immaterium, though this distinction is usually lost on those facing the beasts. Khymerae lack a proper corporeal form, allowing them to flicker between real space and the Sea of Souls at whim, appearing momentarily before a foe and then vanishing suddenly to launch an attack from an unexpected direction. Their phasing powers also mean Khymerae can appear inside areas thought secure—such as locked rooms or the fighting compartments of armoured vehicles. They have even been known to appear inside of moving void ships, meaning they were either drawn by on-board psykers or were directed in the attack by agencies unknown.

Those Khymerae encountered in the Expanse usually have a huge, roughly feline form, best likened to a skinned hunting cat. Each appears a slightly different assemblage of skinless flesh, mighty jaws, grasping talons, and powerful limbs. The bright red muscles glisten wetly no matter the level of illumination, while the bare bone of the skull sports several pairs of flat black eyes. The long black tongue appears segmented, as if it was an immense worm extending from the Khymera's mouth. Two great raptorial arms sprout from the shoulders, some linked by thin strips of red muscle and white sinews and lined with impaling spikes. Others have more tentacle-shaped whips of serrated flesh, and can lash out with blinding speed to catch prey. Much smaller talons are found on the chest, where they are used to rip small bits of flesh from a downed victim, while the tail is a fleshless series of bone links. Some attack survivors have reported even more bizarre shapes with bulging eyes and tusked jaws lacking the dorsal talons; it is supposed these may be immature variants or creatures formed from unnatural xenos nightmares. The entire effect, though, is always one of noisome unnaturalness and cannot be mistaken for anything but a warp-spawned creature of Chaos.

Khymerae are pack hunters and are often found in small groups of four to eight, but in areas of great psychic disturbance can appear in vast hordes of forty or more. They fear little and normally view everything, even other warp creatures, as prey. While they do not display any actual sentience, they do show great cunning in their actions while hunting. Their usual tactic is to rush in as quickly as possible, leaping over or phasing through any obstacles they encounter. Once a Khymera closes with a desired target, it quickly lashes out with its raptorial arms, seeking to snare its prey with the sharp spikes. The Khymera then drags its victim within range of its long-fanged jaws and smaller chest talons. However, the Khymera does not spend too much time on any one target and quickly moves on to a fresh victim, seeking to spread as much fear and terror as possible within a short period of time.

It is in this way they reproduce, using these terrifying attacks to spread new nightmares and other strongly emotional reactions, from which new Khymerae can emerge. Once they have glutted themselves on their kills, the Khymerae fade away, rejoining the warp which birthed them.

While often found in the vicinity of open warp gates and similar manifestations, Khymerae can also appear far from any known Chaos incursions. There are many tales throughout the Expanse of cruel Eldar using these creatures as part of hunting packs or raiding parties, somehow controlling the unstoppable ferocity the beasts normally display. Some even quietly speculate these xenos may actually capture Khymerae in the depths of the warp or other shadowy realms, conquering their will and enslaving them to their new masters. Regardless of how they came to be under Eldar control, in these situations the beasts are even more dangerous than usual as their handlers can direct their fury to best advantage. Where they might normally rampage in wild pursuit, here they can be aimed at the foe so as to cause maximum carnage and casualties. They can also be used as tracking and hunting animals, loping across huge distances and warping in and out of real space with a tremendous pace. It is nearly impossible to hide from a Khymera on the hunt, as walls, bastions, bulkheads, and even voidship hulls do not slow them in their quest.

Khymerae can also be found in the Expanse wherever powerful and long-lasting psychic impressions have been formed. Battlefields, places of massacre and slaughter, torture chambers, and similar locations all may have seen sufficient fear and suffering to cause the creation of one or more Khymerae. Some Inquisitors who covertly roam the Expanse have also reported tales of powerful psykers, especially those unstable nascents still lacking full control of their abilities, accidentally summoning newly-formed Khymerae from the warp. The psyker's nightmares that resulted in the spawning of the warp creature are trivial compared to the actuality of the Khymera, now given physical form and eager to meet its creator.

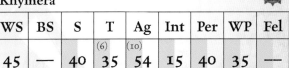

Khymera								
WS	BS	S	T	Ag	Int	Per	WP	Fel
45	—	40	35 (6)	54 (10)	15	40	35	—

Movement: 12/24/36/72 **Wounds:** 21
Armour: None. **Total TB:** 6
Skills: Awareness (Per), Dodge (Ag), Tracking (Int) +20, Silent Move (Ag).
Talents: Furious Assault, Hard Target, Heightened Senses (all), Swift Attack.
Traits: Bestial, Daemonic (TB 6), Daemonic Presence†, Dark Sight, Fear (3), From Beyond, Multiple Arms, Natural Weapons, Phase, Quadruped, Size (Enormous), Unnatural Agility (x2), Warp Instability.
†**Daemonic Presence:** All creatures within 20 metres take a −10 penalty to Willpower Tests.
Weapons: Teeth and Claws (1d10+4 R; Pen 0; Tearing), Raptorial Arms (1d10+4 I, Pen 1; Tearing or Flexible).

KILLIAN'S BANE

"Sure, I'll guide you there. You go find it, and I'll be sure to let your House know how you died. You also pay up front before we leave."

–Beastmaster Avon Tearl

Every now and then I get reminded that Alberse is very good at his own job, mine of course being only to keep him alive so he can do it. We were on Burnscour, accompanied by Rogue Trader Rogol Marloux and his retinue. He and Alberse were rivals—not to the point of outright ship-to-ship combat, though just about anything else seemed acceptable. It was all part of some game I think they enjoyed playing. Marloux had invited us to a joint hunt on this Emperor-forsaken world, and Alberse of course could not refuse any opportunity to prove his skills.

I spent most of my time on that oddly clear day watching Marloux's people, to prevent any "accidents" from happening, while they did the same to me and mine. Our leaders were actually paying real attention, though, and noticed a wide depression meandering through the firegrass. We walked along the flattened foliage, weapons ready as the ground turned to marsh and then emptied into a wide swamp of deep murky water. We searched the dank vista, unaware that something had already made us into prey.

It came from behind, a huge snake covered with plated scales and lumps of moss and weeds. The mouth gaped open, far wider than imaginable, and simply swallowed Marloux whole as it moved quickly into the water. We all opened fire, hammering its rear length with punishing bolter rounds that left thick carmine blood spurting into the swamp. Alberse was already safe off to one side, a slight smile behind his visor, so I grabbed his prized sword and leapt onto the stunned thing's wide back. Not one of my sanest moments, but the shimmering xenos blade sliced a wide enough length for me to reach in with my bionic arm and drag Marloux out, dripping with viscous ooze but still alive. I pulled him to shore just in time, as the snake-thing came back to life and reared back towards us, maw again spread wide to reveal masses of teeth. I threw Marloux at Alberse, knocking them both away as it struck. Despite heavy fire across its head, it managed to take the upper half of one of Marloux's combat servitors back into the dark water. Nothing surfaced again except more blood.

Despite several broken ribs, Marloux argued with Alberse the entire way back to the shuttles. They must have settled things eventually, though, as they grasped arms before we departed for *Aureus*. Something about the beast stayed with me, and sure enough I found Killian's tale in an old slate lying out in Alberse's office, with special details concerning the creature's movement patterns. Alberse would only say that it had all worked out even better than he had hoped, given the extremely profitable debt Marloux now owed him.

I had to take it as a something of a complement that he thought I was able to protect him against one, and the rather large bonus Alberse paid didn't hurt either. I don't often see his ruthless streak, but that's why he's successful and many other traders out here aren't heard from once they leave Port Wander.

HORROR OF THE SWAMPS

This gigantic beast is one of the most fearsome predators of the infamous Death World's scattered wetlands. It was simply known as the Burnscour Wyrm, one of many dangers of the planet, until Rogue Trader Augustus Killian made the species legendary across the Expanse. Most of these snake-like creatures are at least ten metres in length, although tales relate of ones much longer including the truly monstrous specimen Killian encountered. Each recorded specimen is massive in size and covered with protective scales that are proof against the caustic rains which seem to pour nonstop across Burnscour. The scales along the back are rougher and thicker, with many sporting short chitin spikes.

These dorsal spikes are often covered with clumps of moss and other vegetation, giving the serpent a more shaggy appearance than other scaled creatures possess. Adepts of the Xenos Biologis have observed specimens deliberately diving through thick flora to drag away clumps. These plants provide a natural disguise, enough to help them stalk their prey and fool most of the larger arboreal predators. The mouth is perhaps the beast's most distinctive feature though, as the jaws are only connected to the rest of the creature's skeleton with long elastic bands of sinew and muscle. This allows the beast to open its maw extraordinarily wide, letting it swallow even the oversized creatures of Burnscour. Those it cannot swallow, it bites apart with rows of powerful fangs, each strike able to tear away huge swathes of flesh.

The Bane is amphibious, preferring areas with calm water, though some have been sighted along deep rivers. It can breathe underwater for extended durations, but maintains most of its life either floating across swamp lakes or slithering along the ground. Beastmasters from the Sector have tracked some Banes several kilometres from wetlands either stalking prey or moving to new habitats, indicating that they can survive out of the water for long periods as well. For a primarily water-based creature, it can move with surprising speed across dry land and is fast enough to run down many beasts. Most Banes are relatively sedentary, however, calmly gliding along the stagnant waterways with occasional dives to search for prey swimming beneath them.

A Bane normally attacks in a swift motion, ideally attempting to engulf the quarry in a single stroke. The attack is terrifying, as the Bane can rear up in to a towering height as part of its lunge. If near water, it also endeavours to swallow as much liquid as possible at the same time. This accomplishes two things, helping drown its victim but also allowing the Bane to settle rapidly to the bottom of the swamp, safely obscured from other predators. If on land, or attacking aquatic life, the Bane's powerful musculature steps in to help crush the life from its prey. Once subdued sufficiently, the Bane regurgitates the remains to rip them into more digestible chunks and then swallowed again.

Luckily for those creatures sharing its habitat, a Bane feeds relatively infrequently, and a single large meal lasts it for many days. Banes reproduce by releasing huge swarms of tiny offspring mere centimetres in length into the swamp, where most are quickly eaten by other predators. Even these miniature Banes are dangerous though, as if they are not killed when consumed, they continue growing and eventually bore their way out via the masticating serrated teeth. The small progeny often attach onto larger creatures, leaching off blood and flesh until large enough to drop off and eat on their own.

THE DEATH OF AUGUSTUS KILLIAN

The creature gained its now infamous name many years ago, when Rogue Trader Augustus Killian, the beast hunter famed across the Calixis Sector and into the depths of the Expanse, took his leave on Burnscour to show off his prowess to a gathering of the Sector's nobility shimmering behind protective power fields. He claimed to possess a new archeotech discovery to unveil, though exactly what it was he would not say other than it would result in a spectacular display.

Killian confidently strode to the nearby water's edge, wielding only his family's heirloom power sabre. He then produced an oddly shaped crystalline object, which shown with a blue-white light as he waved it over his head to the crowd's delight. Vid-captures recovered later show faces quickly turning to terror as a wyrm larger than ever seen before rose out of the swamp and far above the trees. For a long, dreadful moment, nothing moved except for the swamp water dripping onto the stunned trader, then it fell to take Killian between jaws now stretched wide enough to swallow a lander.

Theories vary if the mysterious device had somehow summoned the beast from the depths, or was designed to help him vanquish it, or perhaps protect him somehow. He was simply gone in a moment as the beast dove back into its dank home, the massive tail carelessly shattering the power field generators and plasteel tents surrounding the panicked crowd. Some insisted that Killian glowed an unearthly metallic sheen in the brief moment before he was engulfed, but this was never substantiated in the vid-captures.

House Killian was suddenly ruined in a single day, losing not only their master but also the ancient and invaluable Warrant of Trade he had always famously carried in a small stasis cylinder on his wide sash as a point of pride. Many Explorers have since also lost their lives attempting to find the creature, knowing that inside is not only what could be a priceless device but also an actual Warrant, which would allow them to establish their own dynasty.

The tale spread through Port Wander's many taverns and from there into the Calixis Sector, and soon the notoriety made it a creature in high demand for the illicit fighting pits and beast arenas across the region. Seeing their favourite gladiators eaten alive, and then betting if they can escape before perishing, is often the highlight of many such affairs.

Killian's Bane								
WS	BS	S	T	Ag	Int	Per	WP	Fel
43	—	(8) 46	(10) 53	47	22	36	33	—

Movement: 6/12/18/32 **Wounds**: 41
Armour: Scaled Skin (All 5). **Total TB**: 8
Skills: Awareness (Per), Climb (S), Concealment (Ag), Silent Move (Ag), Swim (S) +20.
Talents: Fearless, Hardy.
Traits: Amphibious†, Bestial, Crawler, Fear (3), Gulp Attack††, Natural Armour, Natural Weapons, Size (Immense), Unnatural Strength (x2), Unnatural Toughness (x2).
†Amphibious: This creature survives equally well on water or land, and can Swim at its full Speed (see page 267 of the **Rogue Trader** Core Rulebook). It may also breathe underwater for six hours.
††Gulp Attack: If the Bane's attack succeeds and gains three or more Degrees of Success, it may instead swallow its target whole rather than determining damage. The prey must be of a Size at least one level smaller than the Bane (for example, Hulking for a Bane of Enormous Size). The victim is now inside the belly of the beast and immobilised as if struck by a weapon with the Snare quality until he frees himself (by making an **Arduous (–40) Strength Test**), or is rescued. Any subsequent attacks that do Damage to the Bane's Body location deal a quarter of that Damage to the victim as well. Whilst interred, the victim suffers from Suffocation (see page 261 of the **Rogue Trader** Core Rulebook).
Weapons: Extendable Jaws (1d10+8 R; Pen 4 R; Tearing).

MEDUSAE

"I've seen giant leeches, Taladar Grave Ticks larger than your hand, and even that poxy head lice I picked up in the bilges, but I ain't never seen anything like that thing."

–Rating Limcuando, aboard the freighter *Argentum*

We were on Lathimon's Death in the well-named Accursed Demesne, where Alberse had taken us to search for an Explorator team that was late for its check-in. We reached the surface and the chill environment and inhuman structures put me on edge before we even started searching. As we were walking towards the last known location of the team, the ancient halls were just too silent. I remember the smell of age, of dust and mould, and a hint of spice that unnerved rather than comforted me. Our lumens seemed to be having trouble in the winding corridors, and were sending flickering shadows dancing across the pale stone.

According to Alberse and the men who were with us, the thing drifted down from above a doorway, gliding out of the shadows to alight on top of me. The only thing I knew was that my hat was knocked away and suddenly the top of my head was covered with a fleshy substance. Sound was muffled and I felt stirrings through my hair. I reached up to grab the thing from my head when everything went to hell.

I felt the oddest sensation, like icicles sliding into my head. There was no pain, really, just a coldness and numbness unlike any I have felt before. My hand stopped and instead of reaching for the creature, it curled into a fist and I screamed, but I did not scream, we screamed. My sight became hazy, as if seeing through a red haze. Our mouth was pulled tight into a rictus-like grin and we burned with feelings, too powerful and intense to fully describe.

According to Alberse, Missionary Ventrise came up to my side and applied his oh-so-holy mallet upside my head. We fell to the floor unconscious, but thank the God-Emperor, my thick skull stayed intact. I woke up in the Medicae Ward some thirteen days later. It seems that our chirugeon was a learned-enough man to be able to remove the thrice-cursed alien from atop my cranium. He seemed surprised I had survived such an attack and the surgery. He said I was blessed, but I am not so sure. Alberse did retrieve my hat, though, for which I was indeed grateful.

Alberse now keeps the hopefully dead thing in a bloodlocked enviro tank in one of his main trophy rooms aboard the *Aureus*. The bronze and plas-glass enclosure is ancient enough to be trustworthy, but still always feels too fragile to hold such a thing should it awake. It now hovers in the tank, its tendrils moving obscenely in the circulating air. I sometime go in at night with my bolt pistol and stare at it for long minutes, wondering if it is truly dead or if it still feels those terrible emotions. Many times I imagine putting a round right through the creature, Tallen's leave be damned, just be sure.

Of the Explorator team, nothing was ever found aside from some mechadendrites ripped into shards of bronze and steel. Their base camp was empty of bodies. I pray they died from something else before the Medusae found them. Any death would be better than what those things could inflict.

TENTACLED LEECH

The true horror from a Medusae is not due to the creature itself, for while it is clearly an unnatural creature, it does not seem to pose any direct threat. A Medusae's main body is no more than a bag of flesh, not much larger than a human head. The flesh itself is not unusual, except for the fact it carries a high concentration of neural pathways and receptors. Some theorise that this unusual neurology resembles the brain of a sentient species, but most knowledgeable biologis wave off such thoughts. Its eerie hovering, though, is perhaps the most disturbing feature. While several savants have studied the creature, none can determine how it floats effortlessly without any visible means of propulsion.

While the Medusae has no limbs as such, it does have a surprising number of thin, whip-like tentacles, numbering in the dozens. They seem to look like bare spinal cords, free of bone or chitin. This is not so far from truth, as the Medusae's main form of attack seems to be inserting these tentacles into the brain and nervous system of a creature and melding with it. The Medusae has somehow become the ultimate parasite. It does not just live off of the vital fluids or flesh of its host. It actually becomes one with it.

The Medusae's unique neural structure allows the foul xenos to inset itself into the mind of its host and take over the host's body, all the while allowing the host to remember and feel everything. Those few victims who have survived an encounter with a Medusae tell tales of feeling as if they can take in all of the emotions around them with exceptional clarity. Others have mentioned that they felt as if they were storing that emotion, intensifying it and holding onto it like an obscene sponge. Worse, those attempting to rescue their victimised comrades from the creature are often struck senseless by overpowering waves of powerful anguish, seemingly emanating from the very eyes of those they would save.

Along the sides of its body are also a series of thicker tentacles, often sprouting larger growths. These growths form in a series of ploin-sized tubers, folding over one another like a cluster of ripe fruit. The body of the Medusae seems to have no need for these growths and they appear to be completely extraneous to the Medusae itself. There are even reports of these growths coming off the Medusae during an attack without causing the creature any real harm, like the tail of a lizard. It has been noted, however, that as the creature attacks and uses its host, these growths seem to enlarge and new tubers seem to form.

Studies of these growths have been inconclusive, though this has not prevented Cold Traders from doing a brisk business in them. They feature in tales of sordid gatherings where the debauched and debased dare each other to actually consume these growths. Even the smallest nibble is enough to send these foolish cads into paroxysms of either agony or ecstasy, it being difficult to tell the difference in their faces. The experience is too much for even these jaded degenerates, as they collapse into coma-like states, their brains unable to process such intense emotional power. Spire-gossip says that none have ever recovered, but this has not stopped others from such temptations, such is the reputation for the experience.

Scholars of xenos in the Expanse are stymied by what little information there is about these creatures and how contradictory the reports appear to be. This has hindered efforts to pin down

their home world, and many hold they are not native to the Expanse. The creatures do not seem to favour any one climate and, other than their attack upon victim sentients, they do not seem to require any sustenance, assuming this attack is indeed needed for survival. They have been sighted in the company of Eldar raiders, latched onto what appear to be slave-caste beings, leading some to believe the creatures could be pets or even a food source for that race. Some psykers have also provided accounts saying they had encountered Medusae whilst in states of dreamlike meditation, but the very nature of these reports make them dubious at best.

Medusae

WS	BS	S	T	Ag	Int	Per	WP	Fel
35	—	25	20	47	28	36	58	—

Movement: 4/8/12/24   **Wounds**: 6
Armour: Unnatural Skin (All 2).   **Total TB**: 2
Skills: Awareness (Per) +10, Concealment (Ag), Dodge (Ag), Psyniscience (Per) +20, Silent Move (Ag) +20, Tracking (Int).
Talents: Fearless, Hard Target, Lightning Reflexes, Step Aside.
Traits: Fear (1), Flyer (2), From Beyond, Hoverer, Improved Natural Weapons, Regeneration, Size (Puny), Strange Physiology, Unnatural Senses (Emotional Resonance), Unnatural Speed.
Weapons: Tendrils (1d10+2 R; Pen 2 R; Tearing), Medusae Eyeburst†.
†Medusae Eyeburst: When hosted, a Medusae can make a ranged attack by staring into the eyes of an opponent. The Medusae and the target make an **Opposed Willpower Test**; if the target wins, then nothing happens, but if the Medusae wins, then the target is Stunned for each Degree of Success (to a minimum of one) as they emotionally vomit forth overwhelming agony and grief.

Special Rules

Parasitic Attachment: If the Medusae is able to make an undefended attack on a target due to Surprise or for other reasons, then the Medusae may instead attach itself to the target. The intended host must make a **Difficult (–10) Toughness Test**. If he succeeds the Medusae was not able to attach to the target; if he fails then the Medusae has attached itself and now the target is under its control.

Removal of Medusae: Explorers can try to remove the Medusae from its host with a **Hard (–20) Medicae Skill Test**. On a Success, the Medusae is removed from the host, but the host suffers Damage equal to half his wounds, reduced by 1d5 for each Degree of Success on the Medicae Test. If the Test is failed, the host suffers 1d5 Damage for each Degree of Failure beyond the first, and the Medusae is remains attached to the host.

Medusae and NPC Hosts: NPCs already hosting a Medusae should use the given profile for the host and switch its Intelligence, Perception, and Willpower with those of the Medusae. As the two individual creatures have now become a new single organism, it is impossible to remove the Medusae without killing both it and the host.

MUKAALI

"Not of our world, but surely created for it."

—Nadueshi nomad saying

I'm generally not enthusiastic about expeditions. You leave a city, you lose control over your surroundings, and then something tries to control (or eat) Alberse and bolter fire ensues. Naduesh was no different, despite being a not unpleasant place to berth. I had thought perhaps we had laid over just to relax a bit and restock on basic supplies, when of course it turned out there was other business, out in the far deserts away from the cyclopean ruins covering the planet. Alberse's mystery rendezvous was some days away and, despite my objections, we used local mounts instead of our regular ground vehicles to better "blend in" with the natives. The beasts were huge things, with long necks and thick, leathery hides. Docile enough, and ponderous with their gait. It was a long trip through dry sands to the rocky destination, but we packed heavily and the Mukaali as the natives called them didn't seem to need much to survive.

We finally arrived, and our attempt at subtlety seemed a failure. Someone else must have also heard about the cache, as hidden gunmen ambushed us on arrival, quickly shooting our mounts from under us with harpoon-like spears. We were surrounded, but all they did was strip our supplies, weapons, survival gear, and even my hat. Then, with a roar, they sped off on massive bikes, leaving us to die in the endless heat. Alberse surmised our deaths were to look like just another hunting party gone bad, leaving the true architects behind the attack safe from suspicion (though we both had our suspicions). We awaited nightfall, in order to attempt to walk the huge dunes back to the city, but the beasts turned out to be tougher than we thought.

Each began stirring, only wounded, it seemed, and still able to stand and carry our now much-lighter weights. Even their wounds seemed to close, with only dribbles of blood leaking before the solid hide condensed around the jagged tears. They were magnificent, maintaining pace across the wastelands despite their injuries. They needed little guidance, so we lashed ourselves to their backs and tried to conserve ourselves. The dry winds and scorching sun were brutal, yet the Mukaali trod on without stop, heads rocking as they navigated the unsteady dunes. It seemed though they would be carrying our dead bodies soon when we came across bike tracks. That night, we slowly came upon their camp, the Mukaali silent except for muffled panting. It turned out Alberse had chosen wisely, as we noticed the smoking bikes, overwhelmed by the heat and sand. He cocked an eye at me, which I studiously ignored as I planned out our own attack on the sleeping thieves. Amateurs.

We later dragged them back to the lander, where others went to work extricating knowledge of their employers. We recovered our belongings, including the mysterious cache and, more importantly, my hat. It took us a few days to fully recover from the ordeal, but the Mukaali could probably have marched to the other side of Naduesh and back, Emperor bless them.

PASSAGE THROUGH THE DESERT

Also known as sand pacers, Mukaali are large animals that thrive in dry environments and are known on several worlds as excellent modes of primitive transport. They are oddly shaped, with forelegs slightly taller than the rear set, but their uneven stride manages to produce steady movement for their riders. Uniformly hairless, the bodies are covered with a dense skin which folds like heavy cloth along their musculature, and are usually in mottled neutral tones along the top and softer pale coloration below. Its head is almost an afterthought at the narrowed end of the neck, more a termination than a separate shape, with a lipless, rubbery mouth. Their eyes protrude from the sides of the head and provide strong peripheral vision, allowing the beast excellent means to detect predators along its flanks. They have trouble seeing directly ahead, however, so the creatures are continually rocking their heads from side to side in a slow but steady rhythm so as to gain a better view in that direction. Their feet are wide and padded, giving them solid traction on soft terrain and preventing them from sinking into desert sands.

Mukaali are supremely adapted to these desert environs. The species originates from far away Goru-Prime, where vast herds roamed the vast scorched wastelands covering the equatorial regions. In these arid regions the beasts thrive like no other, able to live for long stretches without either food or water. Their skin is exceptionally condensed and acts both as an insulator from external heat and a barrier to prevent interior moisture from escaping. The hide protects powerful muscles, designed more for duration than sprinting but still capable of reaching good speeds over short distances. Unlike other creatures that metabolise stored fats to provide energy, the Mukaali's metabolism is acutely efficient, and can extract nourishment to an extremely thorough degree. Their traditional thin diet has always been tough shrubs and other sparse vegetation, which they chew and regurgitate through multiple stomachs and digestive organs, some beginning in their bulky necks. Each organ extracts more and more moisture and nutrients, allowing the creature to sustain itself far longer on far less than would be expected for its size. One of the major dangers in caring for the creature is overfeeding, for their digestion can be easily overwhelmed with unpleasant results. A Mukaali can easily outlast a human or even the sturdiest of pack animal, though, especially as the temperatures rise well into threatening levels. They fare poorly in colder climates, however, and collapse and die quickly when temperatures drop below freezing levels.

VALUED PACK BEAST

Their endurance would not be of import if it were not for their superb transport capabilities. A Mukaali can bear a prodigious load with no break in stride, easily capable of carrying not only a rider but also a full set of packs as well. Some have even been used to tow wheeled cargo containers. This capacity for heavy transport, along with their generally docile temperaments, has made them ideal mounts in many desert locations and for many desert riders. In these harsh conditions, they often outperform mechanised transport, and certainly require less maintenance and upkeep. Riders need little or no training, as the beasts respond well to direction and can keep to a directed course for long hours without correction.

Mukaali soon began appearing on numerous other planets with similar climates as local tribesmen struck deals with Rogue Traders to export the beasts for many uses, including combat roles—most notably with the Imperial Guard mounted regiments hailing from Tallarn. Lacking any sense of aggression, Mukaali have no actual offensive strengths other than accidentally trampling their enemies as they stride forward. Unless actively controlled, the animals quickly run from almost any perceived danger and must undergo strong training to be able to gallop forward towards enemy lines. Despite this, the beasts take part in many operations where their tough skin, strong muscles, and survival characteristics keep them and their riders alive and fighting longer than many other mounts.

THE MUKAALI OF NADUESH

Mukaali have existed on Naduesh for many generations, imported long ago by a clever Rogue Trader who realised they were a perfect fit for the wide areas of dry, desert climate on that world. Here they quickly became part of the native culture, acting as personal transport, beast of burden, and even food should conditions demand the desperate act. Overall they have adapted very well, creating a slightly new strain unique to the world. Breeders on Naduesh discovered though that if their Mukaali were not allowed to breed in the wild they are even more cowardly and timid than usual, barely suited for anything but the mildest of burden duties, and even then they may run away when startled. For this reason, many herds are allowed to breed in the open plains, with herdsmen deployed to watch over them to protect from poachers or other dangers. As needed, stock is culled from these wild herds for training and resale to buyers across the Expanse and beyond.

The beasts are a common trading item and source of income for many Nadueshi tribes. Many experienced hunters travel from the Calixis Sector to pick steeds to carry them on their latest expeditions, and colonists purchase entire herds as they prepare to immigrate to the drier or hotter planets they intended to make home. They have also been seen in several planetary forces in use as military mounts, but less frequently in mercantile or mercenary bands. One infamous Brontian Longknives platoon even somehow arranged for a herd to stampede into enemy lines, shocking their foes long enough for the guardsmen to overrun their flattened enemy.

Mukaali								
WS	BS	S	T	Ag	Int	Per	WP	Fel
21	—	(10) 55	51	23	14	36	08	14

Movement: 8/16/24/48   **Wounds:** 21
Armour: Toughened Hide (All 2).   **Total TB:** 5
Skills: Awareness (Per).
Talents: Iron Jaw, Hardy, Resistance (Heat).
Traits: Bestial, Desert Dweller†, Natural Weapons, Pacifist††, Quadruped, Size (Enormous), Sturdy, Unnatural Strength (x2).
†**Desert Dweller:** Mukaali are supremely adapted to desert conditions, and can last for great periods without water or food. The beast only takes one level of Fatigue for every five levels accumulated due to dehydration or starvation, but take twice as many against the effects of extreme cold.
††**Pacifist:** The creature has no temperament for attack, and only defends itself in combat. When not under a rider's control, it always attempts to flee an area where fighting is underway or there are clear dangers.
Weapons: Hooves (1d10+5 I; Pen 0).

RAZORWING

"It is not only mono-edged feathers that make a Razorwing."

–Michel Soppe, First Illuminator of Hive Sibellus

We had come to the surface of Oradum, a large moon in the Marwolv system, where Alberse had arranged a rendezvous. Discussions with a local trade baron quickly went bad though, with unpleasant rumours that other agencies also interested in the merchandise, and we were soon moving as fast as we could to reach our scheduled pick-up spot. The locals were now out for our heads, and our tech. We were about halfway into a large herd of massive herbivores to use as cover across the clearing, when Armsman Tzebartis called attention to the reddish-brown skies above. It seems a flock of birds had caught his attention as they wheeled and dove along the edge of the herd we were hiding in.

I watched as the flock suddenly dived down, but instead of aiming at a dying turf rat or some carcass, the flock was focused on one of the beasts that stood several paces away from the main herd. Before I could fully comprehend the creatures' strange actions, they were down and around the male, and that is when the blood started to fly. At first I thought the huge beast had begun swatting the smaller ones out of the air and what I was seeing were the remains of the avians. All too quickly we realised it was the beast that was in trouble, not the flyers.

The herd around us began to quickly stampede away from the attack. I tried to watch what was happening, fascinated despite myself by the carnage, but our need to keep to our feet and not be run over made that difficult. The birds, now covered with blood and tissue, were fast and precise in their attack, more than a match for the slow herbivore. In less than a minute, these xenos avians reduced their target to bloody flanks of flesh and skin. As heavy slabs of meat and sinew struck the ground, the flock absconded with their prize, the still somewhat-intact skeleton. They literally took those bones into a nearby scrub tree and began to crush and devour them. The skeleton was gone in less time than it took them to flay the poor creature in the first place. The squadron then spun about in the air and began emitting high-pitched, undulating tones. That is when we realised that was not the only group of these avians in the area.

Two more flocks were now wheeling and fluttering around the skies above the pastureland. The herd was now in a state of panic, blindly running in any direction that they felt was away from danger. In our efforts not to get run over, we found ourselves without any cover at all. Now the locals were not our only concern, and we had to split our gaze between the threats on the ground and the new threats in the air.

The locals proved to be the lesser of the threats, and scattered away once they emerged into the open. When the predatory birds attacked again, this time directly at us, we realised those chasing us knew these avians better than we did. It took massed firepower just to keep the

flyers away, and any that breached our cordon of las-blasts did terrible damage. They also seemed to recognise when they were under attack, quickly veering away when one of us attempted to take careful aim at their rapidly moving forms.

We finally managed to get to the other side of the clearing and safety, where we patched up our wounded before finding our lander. Rising back into orbit, we saw down below us the creatures still circling over the clearing. Alberse had that familiar look in his eye, one I've seen all too many times, and I was certain we would be returning to this planet.

DEATH FROM ABOVE

The size of a mythical Terran hawk or eagle, the Razorwing is a particularly effective and vicious aerial predator. The creature is known to be an incredibly fast flyer; vid-captures show flocks of Razorwings actually out-pacing Chiropteran Scouts and other low-flying craft for short periods of time. While the creatures have tremendous speed, they rarely use it except for the initial dive, as otherwise they would overshoot their target.

Razorwings can also float in thermal updrafts, their wings locked to create a larger lifting surface as it scans for a tempting prey with small but powerful eyes. Once it has such a target, a powerful dive of the Razorwing slams it quickly onto its victim, allowing the many offensive abilities of the creature to come to the fore.

The claws and beak of the Razorwing are strong enough to cleave through the mass of its prey to get to the bones inside, but these are not the only weapons the Razorwing employs. The feathers of the avian, from its filoplumes on its head to the rectrice feathers on its tail, are as sharp and as durable as a mono-blade. Imperial scholars think this may be due to the excessive amounts of calcium in the Razorwing's diet, as the beasts are known to especially delight in crushing and eating the bones of its victims as well as the flesh. It is believed that it uses this calcium to strengthen and sharpen the feathers into tough and incredibly sharp tissue, like oceanic coral. This means the entirety of the Razorwing is a weapon, with such speed in its dive that it is akin to firing a bullet at its target, allowing the creature to slice or, in some cases, tear completely through a victim's body.

AVIAN PREDATOR

Whilst Imperial Biologis savants have studied the flock mentality of many avian xenos species across the Expanse and the Calixis Sector, the group tactics of the Razorwing are still something of a mystery (or at the least subject to much dispute). While many flyers hunt apart from the flock or exist as solitary predators, the Razorwing always seems to prefer hunting in a group. The flock seems to be lead by one primary flyer, similar to the way Fenrisian wolf packs operate.

This leader always pulls ahead of the main group in flight and is the first to try to strike a target when on the hunt. This alpha flyer seems to choose the target and also gets the largest share of the meal should their hunt be successful. Tales once taken as tavern nonsense were later verified in independent reports, showing the avians slick with blood and offal as they carry their calcified meal to some kind of foliage, there to eat and parade their kills.

What is more disturbing than its hunting patterns are reports that the Razorwing may be far more intelligent than any xenos researcher has realised. One such communiqué from a xenologist in Winterscale's Realm told of an unknown xenos giving what appeared to be verbal signals and hand gestures to a flock of Razorwings. Later vid-captures indicated the huntsman had trained the Razorwings to attack on command and bring the skeleton of their target back to him. Many seem to think that such incidents are more in the realm of fancy rather than reliable witnesses' testimony, but if such information can be verified, then these creatures could become quite a commodity, and even more dangerous to attain. It may also mean that those Razorwings displaying such behaviour are either previously-trained creatures that have escaped, or that their masters were nearby but out of sight for reasons unknown.

While a skilled predator, the Razorwing is also eerily beautiful. Its plumage takes on a multitude of colours from deep purple to light grey and is streaked with reddish brown hues. The eyes of a Razorwing are golden in colour and can spot a Teklese mouse from one hundred metres or more. The call of a Razorwing is somewhat melodic, but the xenos is known more for the shriek of its victory call than it is for its mating warble. Extended studies in field conditions are hazardous though; few have been lucky enough to witness a flock of Razorwings for long periods without being attacked themselves.

RAZORWING SIGHTINGS

Razorwings were first reported in the Expanse by the inhabitants of Oradum only some sixty years ago. They have been sighted on other worlds since, and most savants believe they have actually existed in the Expanse for a much longer time. It is assumed that they are carried to new planets by those who use them in hunts, and that many of those flocks sighted represent specimens either released or that have successfully turned on their masters and escaped.

Wherever they are, Razorwings become major threats to most of the native fauna, especially slow-moving grazing beasts. They seem to prefer hunting fresh prey instead of scavenging for meals, and as such, when a flock goes on a hunt, the bloodsoaked remains of their dining can soon be found dotting the landscape. On some worlds, small packs of scavenging vermin follow the Razorwing flocks to dine on the scant remains the avians leave behind.

Few planets have other species that can compete with these predatory avians once they establish a foothold in a compatible ecosystem, and Razorwings often become apex predators within a few short generations. Their presence has severely cut into the profits of many merchants who rely on meat-supplying beasts on several worlds, leading to many attempts to cull this xenos harshly and investigations as to if they are being used as biological weapons by rival traders. Most agree that should this invasive species continue encroaching onto further planetary environments, they could wipe out whole foodstuff species that the Sector needs to survive.

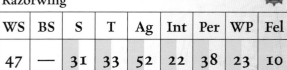

Razorwing								
WS	BS	S	T	Ag	Int	Per	WP	Fel
47	—	31	33	52	22	38	23	10

Movement: 4/8/12/24   **Wounds:** 10
Armour: Toughened Feathers (All 2).   **Total TB:** 3
Skills: Dodge (Ag), Silent Move (Ag).
Talents: Frenzy, Furious Assault, Lightning Attack, Lightning Reflexes, Step Aside, Swift Attack.
Traits: Bestial, Flyer (8), Natural Armour, Improved Natural Weapons, Size (Scrawny).
Weapons: Beak & Claws (1d10+3 R; Pen 2; Tearing), Wings (1d10+3; Pen 0; Razor Sharp, Tearing).

SAND TIGER

"Just what we needed. Something else to kill us in this Emperor-forsaken desert."

–Howin Smythe, Huntmaster

After our misadventures on Naduesh, the *Aureus* set course for Vaporius. A dry, desert world, it possesses two things in abundance: rocks and sand. Yet it plays host to a human culture—scattered cities of glass and copper built around springs and ruled by self-styled "Priest-Kings." Each claims to be the sole source of water for their city, so it came as no surprise when after our scheduled transaction was accomplished and the cargo loaded, Alberse announced he would travel to the surface to meet one of them. I'm sure he was curious to meet an ego that rivalled his own. I must admit I was curious too, so despite the lack of any realistic threats the meeting represented I decided to accompany his caravan transport.

We travelled to the city of Meh'phi and received an audience with its Priest-King, Heris. Even though it was clear there were few trade possibilities to be had, I should have known the Alberse and the Priest-King would get along famously. Over the course of an evening of entirely-too-long tales, Heris told us stories of his hunting exploits in the deep deserts. As soon as he mentioned "creatures of rare ferocity" though Alberse's eyes began to get that familiar intense focus. I was happy that, as always, I had packed my Locke and had arranged for Alberse's Nomad to be brought as well, along with plenty of ammo.

The expedition was everything I both feared and treasured. There was little apparent danger, and anything that could attack us would be seen kilometres away across the flat sandy plains. Alberse and Heris travelled in lavish style, and overall this seemed more an excuse to wallow in luxury than a hunt. As long as nothing actually happened, I was content enough; my time with Alberse allows all too few opportunities to be bored.

Heris and Alberse kept themselves entertained, so I was left to deal with the Priest-King's servants, none of whom spoke Low Gothic. On the evening of the fourth day, Alberse wandered from the caravan. Before I realised he was gone, I heard a panicked and all-too-frequent yell.

I found Alberse sinking into a large conical pit in the sand. At the centre was some sort of creature, a thrashing fleshy monstrosity with bristly hair and a gaping maw. Its movements were agitating the sand, loosening Alberse's footing and speeding his descent into its mouth. I was about to riddle the creature with bolt shells when Alberse shouted not to "damage the trophy!" I fired a few shots into the sand near it, sufficiently driving it away, then had to slide down the pit and help pull Alberse out of danger while one of the servants brought a power spear. By the end, I was sorely tempted to push him the rest of the way in and wish him the best of luck. As it turns out, the creature (a "Sand Tiger" in Vaporius' rude dialect) makes a fine display. Their bones are almost entirely crystal, and now the creature's skeleton occupies one of his trophy rooms on the *Aureus*. Of course, Alberse hasn't stopped complaining about the spear-sized hole in the thing's skull.

CLAWS IN THE PIT

Sand Tigers are native to the world of Vaporius on the far edges of the Heathen Stars, a parched, bronzed world dotted by brilliant (and poisonous) turquoise and cyan seas. The world is mostly desert, vast stretches of sand and dust broken by jagged mountain chains. The Sand Tiger makes its home amongst those inhospitable stretches of wasteland dunes.

Roughly half again the size of a man, the Sand Tiger is a ferocious and solitary predator. Its semi-silicate physical composition allows it to survive the nearly waterless environment it lives in, going for months or even years without any liquid besides that which it can take from its prey. The Sand Tiger is an ambush predator, burying itself in dunes two to three metres below the ground. Once it has dug its burrow, it agitates the sand around it with its powerful digging claws, loosening it. Then it waits, using a multitude of bristling hairs along its back to sense minute vibrations in the desert sands. If an individual is unfortunate enough to walk over the place where the creature is buried, it sinks into the loose and shifting sands, the Sand Tiger hastening its descent with further frantic digging. Soon the prey finds itself in a conical pit with the Sand Tiger's hungry maw at the bottom. The creature descends on its prey and shreds it with its claws and circular, tooth-ringed orifice, draining it of bodily fluids before eating the choicest bits of meat and leaving the rest to rot beneath the sands.

The Sand Tiger prefers to wait for its prey to fall into its trap before attacking. It ferociously fights anything that ends up in the pit it has dug, only fleeing if severely wounded. If the prey escapes the pit trap, a hungry or enraged Sand Tiger pursues them away from its nest. In this case, it prefers to burrow underground to attack from beneath the sands, but runs on open ground if need be. Prey is often scarce in the desert, so a Sand Tiger may pursue a target for dozens of kilometres before giving up. If, on the other hand, the Sand Tiger's prey attacks it from a particularly advantageous position (for example, from the lip of its own pit with ranged weaponry), the creature flees quickly, burrowing into the sand to escape attack. The Sand Tiger is an ambush predator primarily, and prefers to avoid a straight-up fight.

FLESH AND CRYSTAL

Despite the ferocious and elusive nature of the creature, the real draw for game hunters and adventurers is rooted in the Sand Tiger's semi-silicate nature. The creature's skeleton is made entirely of translucent, rose-tinted crystal, comprised of a molecular structure that no member of the Adeptus Mechanicus has been able to replicate. The haunting beauty and utter rarity of a Sand Tiger's skeleton makes it an exquisite and highly-valued trophy. A single tooth or claw is incredibly valuable—a complete skeleton could buy a Fury Interceptor.

The risk one takes to kill these beasts while leaving the skeleton intact only increases their value. Even if the skeleton is unharmed in the effort, removing it from the flesh is also an effort as the two bond on a near molecular level, possibly part of how the crystalline bones are formed. Attempts to grow the creatures in captivity have failed so far, even those done on Vaporius to ensure nothing is remiss in the special sands or atmosphere. The beasts grow normally, but never form their signature silicate endoskeleton, only soggy bones that easily break into segments of pulpy flesh.

TALES FROM VAPORIUS

One of the more popular stories told by voidfarers well in their cups is the tale of Magos Du'Bane. The Thulian Explorator is said to have travelled to Vaporius, where he became enthralled by the biological makeup of the wildlife there. The semi-silicate nature of certain native creatures such as the Dwellers in the Heights interested him, but the crystalline skeleton of the Sand Tiger truly fascinated the Magos. He spent weeks in the cities of various Priest-Kings, boring them to no end with his experiments and postulations.

Finally, desperate to be rid of the tiresome Tech-Priest, one of the Priest-Kings sponsored an expedition into the deep desert, so Du'Bane might find specimens. The tales all agree that Du'Bane found Sand Tigers, and became convinced that he could use a sonic amplifier to resonate with their crystal bones, drawing them from great distances to the machine. The last anyone heard about him, he was travelling into the deepest dune seas, seeking a suitable site to test his device. His arranged transport finally departed without him, but curiously was later paid the balance of the agreed on fee along with a substantial bonus.

Of course, most assume this is simply a story, designed to prise a few free drinks from the gullible in the Calixis Sector eager for tales of the fearsome and dangerous Expanse. Some hold it contains a measure of truth, however, and several expeditions have nearly been organised to seek out Du'Bane's last resting place. A Sand Tiger lure would seem to be a guaranteed way to make immense profit—if one ignored the danger of hundreds of ravenous predators converging on his location.

Sand Tiger								
WS	BS	S	T	Ag	Int	Per	WP	Fel
44	—	55	72	21	14	50	30	02

Movement: 3/6/9/18 **Wounds**: 18
Armour: Tough Hide (All 1). **Total TB**: 7
Skills: Awareness (Per), Concealment (Ag) +10.
Talents: Frenzy, Resistance (Heat, Psychic Techniques).
Traits: Bestial, Burrower (4), Improved Natural Weapons, Quadruped, Size (Hulking), Unnatural Senses (100 metres).
Weapons: Two Burrowing Claws (1d10+5 I; Pen 0), Tooth-filled maw (2d5+5 R; Pen 3; Tearing).

Special Rules
From Below!: If the Sand Tiger is burrowed in a sandy environment and remains undetected by its opponent, when that opponent comes within 5 metres of the creature they must make a **Hard (–20) Agility Test**. If they fail, they fall into a rapidly growing pit of sand roughly 5 metres across and 5 deep, with the Sand Tiger in the middle. It takes another **Hard (–20) Agility Test** and a Full Action to scrabble out of the hole once the victim is in it (the GM may modify this based on the victim's size and environmental factors). In addition, the victim counts as Surprised during the first round of Combat.

Berserker: The Sand Tiger may, as a Full Action, attack with all of its weapons instead of just one, launching itself in a fury of teeth and claws to claim its victim before it can escape. If it does so, it takes a –10 penalty to all attacks.

Crystal Skeleton: The true value of the Sand Tiger is its unique crystal endoskeleton, which is exacting to retrieve intact. A character may make a **Difficult (–10) Survival Test**, with an additional –20 modifier if the creature was killed by weapons dealing Impact or Explosive Damage (the GM may impose additional penalties if the means of killing was even more egregious, such as driving over the Sand Tiger with a Rhino APC). An intact Sand Tiger skeleton has an Availability of Unique. This decreases by one step for every Degree of Failure on the Survival Test.

SHADOWKITH

"The dead? Sure, but they always prefer to eat while the bodies are still warm."

–Tomas Leigh, Captain, *Light of Koronus*

The deal was just too good, and it was a lean time for us. Haggart seemed a decent enough sort, for a spire prince, and his claim that he wanted Alberse's aid in recovering his family's lost treasures, including the irreplaceable signet ring, checked out through independent inquiries. When he said they had been lost on Grace, however, Tallen's eyebrows and our price both rose much higher.

Grace had once been Chorda's very well-kept secret. Some who had barricaded themselves away managed to finally get rescued, but by then they were little better than the foul things that now roamed outside the walls. Those who returned called the sub-humans "Shadowkith" now, rather than proper men, and I was hoping we would manage to sneak in before these creatures could act against us.

Based on Haggart's information, Pilot Pharres skillfully landed us inside the wreckage of one of the many pleasure-palaces that dotted the grey landscape. It was cold and wet, and lightning burned through the dark clouds. I assigned armsmen to secure the compound while the prince and my trader lead the search. It was even darker inside the once-opulent mansion sporting Haggart's crest, and we risked firing up lumens. The smell hit us just as the scene appeared, though there couldn't have been enough flesh left on the bones to produce it all. Not a good sign, and things just kept getting worse when we heard cries pleading for help ahead of us.

Haggart rushed forward, and with a curse I ordered the others to go with him while I held Alberse back to guard the rear. Sure enough, behind us wide eyes appeared in the darkness far along the massive hallway, growing in number until I fired a few bolts in their direction. Las-cracks sounded ahead of us, and Alberse drew his glistening xenos blade as we moved cautiously forward. Ahead of us, only Haggart remained on his feet, a fancy duelling pistol barely holding off hordes of the pale things hunched in the shadows but ready to attack. Their voices were ragged but still human, taunting him by repeating those cries for help we'd heard earlier.

Our arrival drove them back, but we knew more would be coming. Suddenly, Haggart dove for one of the Shadowkith, too fast for us to stop him. We did our best to defend him, riddling the horrid things with bolter fire, but the prince was quickly lost under masses of clawed limbs and biting teeth. I saw him grasping for an ornate ring on a golden chain that hung from the emaciated neck of one of the creatures before he disappeared. I fired directly into the bloody mass of monsters and they finally scattered back into the darkness. They left nothing behind, not even their own dead.

We killed several more on our way out, perhaps in vengeance to some degree. By the time we were in the lander and ready to depart, there were dozens clambering all over the hull. We quickly lit off, burning away anything still below us with a scream of engines that drowned out any other cries.

Soon after, Pharres reported several wide vox-hails, some clearly automated distress calls but others actually carrying what sounded like genuine cries for help. I'd now heard how well the Shadowkith could still talk, and was relieved that Alberse acted wisely for once and quickly ordered Pharres to continue to the *Aureus*. We didn't speak again till we were finally aboard.

EATERS OF THE DEAD

There are many tales concerning the fortunes of those who attempt to tame one of the Foundling Worlds. Many are mere tavern tales designed to intimidate those venturing into the Expanse for the first time, but there are enough true ones that few can recount them all. It speaks volumes to the cursed nature of this region though that the horrific fate of Grace is barely a footnote to these annals.

The origins of Grace are shrouded in mystery and controversy, due to the nature of its founding. The Rogue Trader Aspyce Chorda had located a perfect world, and for a huge price ferried some of the wealthiest individuals of the Sector to the planet, far from regular warp routes and kept off most charts. Here they could safely retire in an extremely comfortable exile, away from Imperial Judgement or, worse yet, the retribution of their rivals. Surrounded by countless slaves and protected by layers of void shields, they could indulge their every whim in opulent palaces of the finest imported crystal and marble. Each estate contained the plundered wealth of numerous worlds, enough to sate even their enormous appetites. Numerous others followed, all eager to escape their previous lives (and ensure their own continued), and Chorda was always ready as long as each could meet her incredibly steep fee.

Now known as Grace, the planet held a stark beauty but offered little outside the protected bubbles around the palace compounds. It is wracked by near-constant storms, with lightning providing the only illumination in many areas. Little can grow there except simple fungi, so the fugitives were forced to rely on Chorda for all their food and other essentials. When devastating warp storms crushed supply vessels and sealed off the planet, they were slow to realise the repercussions. Years passed, and the inhabitants grew more and more desperate for food. As the technology broke down, they took to raiding each other's estates; when that failed to assuage their cravings, they turned first on the fallen, then on their slaves, then on each other. Those who were once the princes of the Calixis Sector, who ruled planets or vast criminal enterprises, were reduced to the most profane of existences. In time, their bodies altered to reflect their degraded lives, and became what are called Shadowkith today.

HUMANOID BUT NO LONGER HUMAN

The Shadowkith are still mostly human, though barely so, and many of the Magos Biologis would name them mutant. Their lean forms are emaciated sinew and lean muscle, stretched thin under leathery skin. Their eyes have become wide and furtive under the darkened clouds, as if they seek to hide their shame from the very skies. While it has been a relatively short time since Grace became isolated, this slide to degradation is more pronounced than would be expected, certainly more than would be expected simply from an unsavoury diet.

Some retain most of their intelligence, especially those who get meat in their bellies, but many more are scarcely sentient from poor diets consisting only of watery fungal growths. Xenos savants have undertaken analysis of this native flora with inconclusive results, despite suppositions that these fungi might have something to do with the accelerated morphic and cranial drift shown in the more primitive Shadowkith. As low as these wretches might be, life in some ways is worse for those who remain sane, knowing it is only a matter of time before they too fall to that state. For some, the awful knowledge of what they have done to survive means they no longer wish to rejoin humanity.

Grace is an unforgiving planet, and the hungry survivors roam the storm-ridden lands amidst the freezing hail in search of food. Their once-prized weapons having fallen into disrepair, as few had the knowledge to maintain them. The Shadowkith hunt in packs using numbers against their foes. These are now rumoured to include small feral Ork tribes, the remnants from some forgotten battle somewhere in the system and dangerous

enemies even for well-equipped humans. Most estates are now ruins, picked clean of edibles by the hordes that dwell in the darkness. Some still remain intact though, fighting desperately to keep the Shadowkith at bay, and continue to broadcast calls for aid with all the power their fading generatorium systems can provide. The æther surrounding the planet is often filled with multitudes of plaintive appeals, all hoping to reach any nearby ships or other pockets of humanity.

Many of these hails, though, are from those Shadowkith with access to the few functioning vox-casters still intact on the planet outside the intact estates. The terrible wretches are perpetually eager to lure unsuspecting meals, and these cries for assistance work surprisingly well even given the planet's reputation. Devious Shadowkith also use greed against their rescuers, promising them the legendary gilded treasures and more spoken of in the tavern tales, and even showing off some of the riches to tempt them even further. Those landing with hopes of vast fortunes soon learn, as those who became the Shadowkith did long ago, that Grace is especially good at crushing all hope.

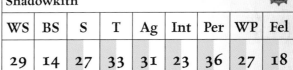

Shadowkith								
WS	BS	S	T	Ag	Int	Per	WP	Fel
29	14	27	33	31	23	36	27	18

Movement: 3/6/9/18   **Wounds**: 9

Armour: Thick Rags (Body, Legs 1).   **Total TB**: 3

Skills: Awareness (Per), Climb (S), Concealment (Ag), Deceive (Fel), Dodge (Ag), Forbidden Lore (Criminal Networks or Hidden Secrets of the Nobility) (Int), Search (Per), Silent Move (Ag), Speak Language (Low Gothic, High Gothic) (Int), Survival (Int) +20.

Talents: Blind Fighting, Hatred (Rogue Traders).

Traits: Fear (1), Wretch†.

†**Wretch**: When hunting, the barely human Shadowkith behave more like vermin than honest men. They eat anything or anyone, but always flee if outnumbered rather than fight. They also seek at all costs to keep their shameful dietary history a secret, and gain +30 to any Tests made to protect that information.

Weapons: Primitive Weapons (1d10+3 I; Pen 0), Salvaged Lasgun (Basic; 40m; S/2/—; 1d10+3 E, Pen 0, Clip 10, Rld Full, Unreliable), Teeth (1d5 R; Pen 0).

Gear: Assorted trinkets and mementoes, most worthless and broken but some perhaps priceless in nature.

GM Note: Unlike many of the beasts presented in this chapter, the Shadowkith may exhibit a wide range of behaviours and intelligence levels. The profile above represents an average Shadowkith, but the Bestial Trait can be added for an even more animalistic specimen. At the other end, those who have kept their faculties can be better represented by adopting elements from the Renegade profile (see page 373 of the **ROGUE TRADER** Core Rulebook). These latter might only appear as mindless as their lesser kin, perhaps through deliberate subterfuge, but are possibly as dangerously cunning as even the finest Rogue Trader.

SPECIES X-10198.RK

"Whatever is down there, it's best left alone."

—Armsman Kul T'Asdo

I won't claim to be an expert on the Adeptus Mechanicus. It's difficult to read someone when there isn't much left of their face, let alone eyes. One of them hired Alberse for aid on his expedition to Orn, despite the warnings about what lived there. I made the mistake of trying to ask why Lorum wanted to go there when his own people said not to. I got a very long reply, mostly in chattering cant, which he claimed mathematically proved the Disciples of Thule were incorrect. I stayed away from him the rest of the voyage.

After landing, we armed up and departed, Lorum accompanied by a retinue of heavily-armed combat servitors. The wrecked craft we saw in the distance was a welcome break from the endless thorns we were hacking through. It was massive, maybe the size of a small Warsphere, and I swear Lorem's bionic eyes seemed to grow brighter as we approached. In a nearby crater we found a huge section that must have broken off on impact. Lorum dove into it, his mechadendrites snaking around him to examine the tech strewn inside it, handing off interesting bits for his servitors to stow. We were all paying too much attention to the salvage.

They assaulted through the thick brush, not caring about the thorns slicing their fur. Humanoid enough, but more frenzied than even the wildest beast I've seen. I couldn't tell if they were animal or xenos; they wore tattered rags but displayed no signs of intelligence. We used the hull fragments as cover, not even needing to carefully aim as there were so many. The things attacked wildly, waving what looked like rifles but thankfully only using them as clubs.

The servitors alone cut them down by the dozens, but they didn't slow. Corpses began to pile up and still they kept coming, some insane imperative driving their fury at our very existence. The creatures had no real fighting skills, but their sheer mindless savagery more than made up for that lack. I hated to think how we would have fared if we had been caught defenceless.

One Hellgun failed, and the things quickly overcame its owner and dragged him away in bloody sections. We needed to run, and I yelled for a retreat. Lorum simply said that this "sum was unacceptable," and that he would chart his own path. His servitors moved to his side, and a blue flare lit up around them all. It was some sort of force field, and it kept the things at bay. He wasn't going anywhere, and I spat a curse as I knew we were on our own. I glanced at Alberse; he knew it as well and we both looked for the best path out of the crater.

Lorum must have calculated we would not make it, though I still don't know how he planned to get off the planet. We proved him wrong; it was hellish, but most of the creatures remained behind with Lorum and his servitors. Maybe they hated him as much as I did.

Some time later at Footfall, I encountered a Disciple who somehow knew of our visit. He assured me we had not stayed long enough to be in any danger. I had to disagree, saying the ferocity of those creatures made those few hours dangerous enough. He replied in a level tone that they were not the true danger and glided away. I was left wondering what we missed, and feeling glad that we had.

THE SAVAGES OF ORN

Precious little is known about the planet of Orn. Most comes from the Disciples of Thule, widely thought to have first discovered the planet. Despite their normally-merited reputation for obsession in the pursuit of knowledge, they made only one report of the planet and then departed. It stated they detected the crashed wreckage of a colossal spacecraft, infested by an unknown xenos race. Servitors examined the ruined vessel and sent back pic-captures showing the towering structure, still mostly intact within the even larger crater it made on impact. Multitudes of the xenos crawled all over its surface and swarmed through the interior, their actions unclear but seemingly reverential as they carried parts of the ship and other equipment through the ship's exposed walkways. Then the xenos noticed the servitors. The pic-captures transmitted back images that evoked emotional responses even amongst the most pure of the Disciples. Hundreds of the creatures descended screaming onto the scene. They tore into the servitors, ripping them into awful strands of flesh and wiring and devouring the still-twitching meat and viscera. The transmitting devices functioned long after the servitors were dismembered.

The Disciples marked Orn as Intransigent Omega, a world abhorrent and unwelcome for further investigation, and moved on to the next system in their endless archeo-quest. Those who know of the Disciples and their unquenchable thirst for ancient human technology assumed that the combination of lack of such relics and the lethality of the natives would make any visitations unprofitable, and likewise gave Orn wide berth. These assumptions might have been valid, but did not take into account that there could be other threats on the planet, threats that might pose a severe risk to mankind itself.

That is not to say the species, catalogued as x-10198.rk, is not dangerous enough on its own. The Disciples recognised it as clearly capable of intelligent behaviour, given the way they treated their mechanisms. Indeed, they acted much in the way Adepts of the Machine God properly revere holy technology. The xenos, however, never displayed proper usage, treating the units more like icons than devices to be used in the name of the Omnissiah. This was the worst failing the species displayed, but even the Disciples, despite their well-earned reputation for failing to properly observe the immediately evident, could not ignore the ferocious and bestial attacks the creatures made against the servitors. Additional research led them to investigate what could drive such behaviour and, by accident, they uncovered the planet's terrible secret.

Something about Orn's biosphere, perhaps due to ancient exposure to devastating warp storms or an intrinsic quirk in its sun's radiation, is anathema to certain types of neurological patterns. Lesser beings are not affected, but the brains of higher sentients are slowly eroded. With time, those exposed find their cognitive abilities faltering and memories fading. Each day is a tortuous experience, as more and more of the essential self is lost, until finally even the ability to recognise this is lost as well.

This species must have arrived on the planet long ago, possibly to establish a colony, and must have unknowingly stayed too long. As the planet's terrible alterations took place, they realised their danger and attempted to quickly depart. Their ship crashed after an aborted liftoff, though, perhaps because too many had already lost the necessary skills to operate the vessel. The xenos knew their only hope was to attempt to find a cure, and relentlessly strove to rebuild their ship's technology to aid in the effort. As time passed, one by one each descended into a feral existence, horribly aware of their fate but helpless to prevent it.

Now they only remember their final imperatives as imprinted behavioural patterns. Their desperate attempts to repair their ship and achieve a cure have become a worshipful devotion to their vessel and its technology. They gather about their ship as others might a chapel, making offerings and chanting with mangled speech that was once repair instructions. Defending their compound from what was conceivably a prelude to attack was twisted into murderous hatred of all other species, terrible in its extreme, and to hunger for their destruction. They have long forgotten how to use their own weapons, and carry the remains of extremely powerful energy rifles to use as simple mallets.

Now the species, its true name long forgotten and undiscovered, is a woeful shade of its previous state. Clothing is worn out of barely-remembered habit, if at all. Their bodies are covered in fur, though this could either be due to Orn or part of their natural form. The radiation from the ship's failed drive engines infests their bodies, but generations of exposure have left them relatively immune except for patches of furless skin that reveal scarred tissue. They are fast and aggressive, using their large ears to help locate prey, which they attack in artless waves of teeth and claws. In combat, they exist only as pure hatred, living only to kill anything they face.

Clearly this world was not for man, even those blessed by the Machine God. Calculations predicted even their protected cranial augmentations might not be proof against Orn's malignant blight. Thus the world was simply marked as unsuitable for mankind; the feral creatures themselves proved enough to dissuade almost all from further investigations. Orn still receives visitors, but few leave. Some perhaps are still alive, roaming the planet as new packs of feral creatures.

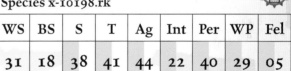

Species x-10198.rk

WS	BS	S	T	Ag	Int	Per	WP	Fel
31	18	38	41	44	22	40	29	05

Movement: 4/8/12/24   **Wounds:** 14
Armour: Furred Hide (All 1).   **Total TB:** 4
Skills: Awareness (Per), Climb (S), Concealment (Ag), Survival (Int).
Talents: Berserk Charge, Chem Geld, Die Hard, Fearless, Frenzy, Hatred (All), Hardy, Heightened Senses (Hearing), Iron Jaw, Leap Up, Rapid Reaction, Resistance (Psychic Techniques, Radiation), Sprint, Swift Attack.
Traits: Brutal Charge, Improved Natural Weapons.
Weapons: Xenos "Clubs" (1d10+3 R; Pen 2; Unwieldy), Claws and Teeth (1d5+3 R; Pen 0; Tearing).
Gear: Xenos trinkets.

TERRORAX

"The rain may dissolve your goggles, but trust me, you want to keep looking up. That's where the worst of them come from."

–Krellen Fosse, Calixian Beast House Procurer

Burnscour. When everything on a planet, including the weather, is actively trying to kill you, you have to constantly be watching for anything. Alberse, of course, only has eyes for further trophies for the mantelpiece above his new firewell. It had been a relatively quiet trip, though, meaning for this world there were relatively few casualties and serious injuries. We made eight drops over the course of the mission, and it was on the seventh that I nearly lost Alberse yet again.

He was in the mood for size on this hunt, and looking back it was probably the successful nature of the earlier missions that allowed this confidence. We had been hiking through the thick terrain, burning pathways with heavy flamers, when we heard the screaming over the vox channel. It came out of the wet darkness above, huge but totally silent, with spider-legs that stretched metres across and a shell that blended with the foliage. It was fast, too, grabbing Turv with wide claws and cracking open his armour like I would a grubnut. He was still screaming as it dragged him back into the trees. I shouted for the men to maintain vigilance on the ground even as I was firing my Locke, my shots only breaking off chunks of plated skin. The screams suddenly stopped as the creature disappeared into the heights, blood now falling along with the constant drizzle around us.

I watched for any sign of the thing, and even then barely detected a second creature as it rapidly ran down a trunk and leapt after Alberse. Throne, it was fast! It speared Alberse through the shoulder with one long foreleg, slowly bringing his wriggling form up to its claws and reversing back up the stalks. We opened fire again as best we could. Its body was large enough to make a safe target, but again its armour was able to withstand our weapons. I saw a softer-looking head emerge between the claws, however, and muttering a fast prayer made careful aim and took my shot.

His Eye was with me though, and the bolt exploded inside the toothed mouth. Alberse's helmet was splattered with gore as the creature shuddered and fell; thankfully he landed on top of the massive bulk as they both crashed to the ground. Other than his punctured shoulder he was well enough to argue with me when I called for immediate retrieval, but his bloody wound was going to draw even more unwanted attention and was likely already infected, knowing this planet.

It was called a Terrorax, and Alberse was delighted to add it to his collection of trophies. I had not heard of them before, but there are so many threats on Burnscour that it is hard to keep up with what seems a constant parade of nightmares. The scooped-out shell evidently can perfectly serve as a new firewell in his stateroom, thus opening up space for even more trophies. I shall have to keep the shapes of such creatures in mind from now on lest each new kill multiply into more hunts in this manner. Perhaps heavier fragmentation rounds would break similar shells nicely.

STALKER IN THE HEIGHTS

Burnscour does not breed weakness in any form; even the lowliest of prey are more deadly than the alpha predators on many other worlds. The Terrorax is literally one of the higher predators in this hellish environment, living in the verdant canopies of the thick jungles that cover much of the planet. It can grow to huge sizes, with legs spreading six metres across, and is strong enough to carry a fully laden Imperial Guardsman into the arboreal heights with ease. Its bulky reptilian body is protected with heavy chitin plating, as are the six long spider-like legs and two huge pincer claws mounted at the front of the body. This thick armour is sufficient to withstand the frequent corrosive downpours as well as most small weapons fire.

Typically, the creature uses its powerful fore-claws to grab and hold its prey, either crushing or tearing the doomed creature into submission. Witnesses have reported these claws able to cut off the limbs of Ogryn warriors and rip apart suits of heavy power armour. That there are few who doubt such reports speaks to the creature's ferocious reputation amongst veteran xenographers operating in the Expanse. The head is covered with a lesser layer of toughened skin, but some reports indicate it can be retracted into the central carapace when the rains or larger predators become too threatening. The wide jaw contains rows of serrated fangs, used to devour its exclusive diet of fresh meat, and extends far along both sides of the head allowing it to make huge, devastating bites from captured prey. The eyes are large and featureless underneath protective rims of chitin, reflecting slightly in a soft gleam in the shadowy lower areas of the jungle.

The multiple lower legs, however, are the primary method for locating new meals. Each of the long, stalk-like limbs contains powerful sensory nerves and can detect minute vibrations transmitted through the ground and trees. The creature can pick up signals indicating far-away prey in the dense jungle merely by resting a leg on a tree branch. This detection system is superior in many ways to visual or even olfactory senses, given the cluttered nature of Burnscour's landscape and multitudes of camouflaged lifeforms, many of which have disguised scents.

The sharp spikes at the end of each of these legs also make for deadly weapons, and can stab into flesh as easily as they stab into tree trunks to anchor the Terrorax as it moves across the foliage above the ground. While not as powerfully muscled or armoured as the fore-claws, they can punch out with surprising speed in many directions, striking at any creatures seeking to surround the beast.

DEATHLY SILENCE

The Terrorax is a quiet and patient hunter, scuttling without any sound across the foliage in constant search for prey. It is also incredibly agile, and is able to dart up and down jungle limbs as well as leap from one tree to the next with ease. Most of the time the fleshy head is almost totally retracted, protruding just enough so it can see. When not needed the heavy fore-claws are also rolled back so they do not interfere with the hunt.

It alternates rapid movement, ranging from a short distance along a branch to dozens of metres to a new tree, with short pauses to sense any nearby prey. Each pause allows it to use its sense of touch, via the nerves in each leg. Its highly-evolved sense of touch filters out rainfall and other natural patterns, allowing the creature to seek out any animal life moving below on the ground. Once a new victim's location is approximately determined, it moves closer until the prey is in sight.

When the quarry is visible, the Terrorax freezes into stillness to observe. The armoured plating has a mottled green and brown coloration and blends into the surrounding plant life, along with a rough texture that aids in the camouflage. Each of the long legs can easily be taken for a tree branch unless closely examined. It can remain in this state for long periods, preferring to wait until the prey moves into a location suitable for the attack. If the target is moving, the Terrorax slowly stalks the unknowing victim, keeping it in sight and patiently waiting an opportune moment.

Once the quarry is in an ideal location, the Terrorax slowly moves into place, one leg rising and falling at a time with deliberate and unnerving grace for a creature of its size. When it is ready, it springs down with speed and agility that belies its bulk. It can run down a stalk faster than it would fall, but can also simply leap down if the prey is too far from a trunk. Sometimes it refuses to wait for the prey to attain such a position, especially if it is overcome by hunger or an especially worthy morsel presents itself. In such cases, the Terrorax simply accelerates and goes for a faster but more risky attack. Claws are quickly extended and ideally seize the prey with a deadly embrace; this is usually enough to kill or sufficiently wound the victim. The talon legs can also be used as part of the attack, and are able to easily puncture skin and many armours with deeply penetrating wounds.

The Terrorax prefers to make lightning fast strikes designed to cripple the prey, but if needed can fight on the ground against a determined foe. If the victim puts up too much of a fight, the Terrorax often temporarily retreats back into the trees and makes ready for another attack.

Captured prey, either dead or still alive, is quickly taken back up the stalks to be safely consumed away from other possible predators. Few can withstand the power of its claws, and the grounds below Terrorax lairs are strewn with cracked carapace plates and ruined power armour. After the claws crack apart the victim, meat is serrated and fed into the maw, where powerful jaws and teeth devour the flesh. Once fed, a Terrorax often climbs into a secluded location in the trees to digest its meal, but stays on constant guard as most predators know this is the time when it would be most vulnerable. Even in this state, however, only the most desperate or foolhardy would dare attack a Terrorax. Burnscour is littered with the corpses of those, both animal and human, who thought themselves ready to face this monster.

Terrorax								
WS	BS	S	T	Ag	Int	Per	WP	Fel
43	—	(8) 47	(6) 38	49	18	38	23	--

Movement: 8/16/24/48   **Wounds:** 28
Armour: Chitin (Body 6, Legs 6, Head 3).   **Total TB:** 6
Skills: Acrobatics (Ag) +10, Awareness (Per) +10, Climb (S) +20, Dodge (Ag), Silent Move (Ag) +20, Tracking (Int).
Talents: Heightened Senses (Touch), Sprint, Swift Attack.
Traits: Arboreal†, Bestial, Brutal Charge, Fear (2), Multiple Arms, Natural Armour, Improved Natural Weapons, Quadruped, Size (Enormous), Sturdy, Unnatural Strength (x2), Unnatural Toughness (x2).
†Arboreal: The Creature is an expert at manoeuvring through foliage and climbing up and down tree trunks. It may use its normal Movement when making any Climb action and not suffer any penalties for movement through forest or jungle terrain. It can also utilise dense foliage rather than the ground for movement purchase.
Weapons: Crushing Claws (1d10+10 R; Pen 2 R; Tearing), Talon Legs (1d10+8 I; Pen 4).

THORNMAW

"We didn't notice anything until we saw the blood dripping around us, and looked up. That's where we found what was left of the missing Astropath, and the thing that was eating him."

—Deck Officer Severine Pyle, 24th Deck Command,
The Light of Calixis

We encountered *The Iron Wing*, an ancient but now derelict Imperial freighter, drifting on the far outer edges of Footfall. What records we could find of it indicated it had been lost for several centuries, after setting out from Port Wander with a shipment of supplies for some of the Expanse's far colony worlds. It now drifted empty, gutted, and ruined, with no sign of the thirty thousand souls that should have been aboard. There was only the evidence of hard fighting, with the scars of small arms fire and explosives on many of the decks. We assumed pirates, probably Eldar Corsairs given the lack of absolute carnage. It wasn't until my team entered one of the cargo bays that we discovered the reason for the ship's state.

Ensign Barlowe was the first to die. We heard his death scream over the vox followed by the tone of a flat-lining signal. Unterholz was next but he at least got a few shots off, letting us find what was left of him quickly. As we gathered over the blood that marked his corpse, the creature attacked us. It flew down from the girders overhead and lashed out with what seemed like dozens of long talons. The razor-sharp edges of its bony limbs slashed through void suits and skin with ease. Blood sprayed, men screamed, and we fired all we had into the thing's bulk. I dove over Alberse and got off a few shots, but to little effect that I could see.

It lashed out at our people, moving quickly about the cavernous hold and striking out with those awful limbs. I then saw something far worse, when one of the men was lifted up to the maw at the bottom of its body. We could make out the terrible crunching sound above our shooting, and the blood spilled even more heavily.

It was only by the grace of the Emperor that we lost as few as we did, most to the talons and mercifully few to that hideous maw. When it was all over, the beast lay broken across the deck, shattered by weapons fire, its limbs finally stilled. Its strange body was ruptured and torn and foul ichor leaked across the floor plates. I saw Alberse stare fixedly at the thing's arcing horns, ready to break some off for his trophy wall, when Seneschal Darvos quickly cautioned him away with a loud shout as the thing twitched once more, before we reduced it to a messy pulp.

There were more in the other holds, but now that we knew what was about, we were able to ready ourselves properly and killed off most we saw hiding in the darkness above us—massed heavy bolter shots seemed very effective. We found many more of them, long dead, indicating the Wing's crew gave a good account before perishing. Darvos believes the few we encountered were patiently waiting for more prey to arrive. I just hate to imagine what it must have been like to face them without the kind of weapons we had.

FLOATING HUNTER

A Thornmaw is a truly bizarre-looking entity. Its bulk is a rough teardrop shape and seems to lack an outer skin, formed instead of dense masses of exposed muscle and sinew. The upper half of the monster is heavily covered with projecting spikes and spines that get larger and thicker the further up the body they go. Atop the body is a crown-like arrangement of six to eight large curving horns upon which are often displayed assorted trophies, usually the remains of previous kills. On the bottom of the body is a dripping mouth filled with grinding teeth and surrounded by clusters of menacing armoured talons. The Thornmaw uses these grasping limbs to snatch up its prey and draw them into its mouth, where it rends them into easily devoured gobbets of flesh.

While the Expanse has only seen very isolated encounters with this being, reports indicate a Thornmaw seems to wait with unnerving stillness as it readies itself for attack. With the mouth is closed and the talons gone limp, while extremely distinctive its appearance is still not so unnatural that the true danger is apparent. Indeed, given the incredible nature of many of the other denizens of the Expanse, on two occasions it was taken for some sort of alien plant life whist it was resting on native foliage. While it can move with speed when pursuing prey, it seems to conserve this mobility until necessary.

Thus, a Thornmaw may simply float slowly in the air, and those seeing it for the first time may simply dismiss it as just another strange but non-aggressive alien life form unless they take extra care to scrutinise it closely or maintain the properly alert readiness necessary for survival in the Expanse. Once it is ready, though, the Thornmaw slowly descends, seeking to ambush its victims while they are unaware. However, other Thornmaws have been reported to hide themselves away, secreting themselves amidst the branches of tall trees, near the ceilings of shadowy rooms, or the upper gantries of a voidship's cargo bays. Once out of sight, it seems to prefer to wait and snatch up lone individuals in their tentacles and devour them. Given the few numbers of encounters, however, it is very possible the creature may exhibit other patterns of behaviour in other situations.

Seen up close, a Thornmaw reveals its true essence. The tiny but malevolent eyes spaced between the clusters of tentacles indicate its predatory nature, as well as the talons themselves, which when extended appear as segments of razor-sharp chitin and bone. The Thornmaw tends to use these to snatch up and entrap its victims, flensing away skin in preparation for feeding. Worse yet, the Thornmaw has enough limbs to engage several enemies at once; one encounter reports the creature was able to ensnare one individual while lashing out at anyone else brave enough to try and rescue him. It is also able to impale enemies on its collection of horns, and some incidents have noted past remains still affixed to the thing's body as grisly mementoes of past feedings.

The prey, once entangled by the powerful limbs and subdued by the attack, is then devoured in thin grinding bites, usually head first. Some Explorers related grisly tales of Thornmaws having even been known to dismember their victims slowly, snipping off limbs bit by bit before going in for the final kill. The sudden and unexpected way it attacks, along with the horrifically painful nature of its feeding manner, leads many to believe it also feeds on the prey's psychically released terror and agony, perhaps even more so than the actual flesh consumed.

There have only been isolated encounters with this creature in the Koronus Expanse, most prevalent along regions of calm warp tides. This, along with the widespread locations reported (including aboard ships travelling through the warp), lead some to believe it may indeed use hidden passages through what the xenos call web ways to travel throughout the void. The first and most infamous is from the freighter *Light of Calixis*, where it appears only a few score Thornmaws slowly moved through the ship, leaving bloody remnants of unlucky crew in their wake. Despite aggressive searches that managed to kill off a few of the beings, and even the venting of some compartments to the void, the foul things managed to devour everything in their path. The final communications reveal the extent of the terror, with search parties falling prey to the beasts as they sought out their missing compatriots. Only a few crewmen survived in a single saviour pod, luckily found on the outskirts of Lucin's Breath, with wild tales of dangling arms that ripped apart bodies and awful maws that bit through skulls with terrible ease.

Since then, there have only been a handful of incidents, for which many a Rogue Trader has given praise to the God-Emperor. Calixian spire nobles with a penchant for xenos collectibles and always eager for the latest and rarest of finds have already created a demand for huge thorns and bony tentacle lengths, and Cold Traders have made small fortunes crafting clever fakes to satisfy their endless desires.

Thornmaw

WS	BS	S	T	Ag	Int	Per	WP	Fel
33	—	43	53 (10)	46	24	38	33	—

Movement: 1/2/3/6 **Wounds:** 12
Armour: Tough hide and chitin (All 2). **Total TB:** 10
Skills: Awareness (Per), Climb (S), Concealment (Ag) +10, Dodge (Ag), Silent Move (Ag).
Talents: Ambidextrous, Combat Master, Heightened Senses (Sight), Swift Attack.
Traits: Dark Sight, Fear (2), Hoverer (4), From Beyond, Multiple Arms, Natural Armour, Improved Natural Weapons, Only Hovers†, Size (Average), Strange Physiology, Unnatural Senses (10m), Unnatural Toughness (x2).
†Only Hovers: If forced to the ground, a Thornmaw can barely crawl and has an effective Move of 1.
Weapons: Bone Talons (3m; 1d10+4 R; Pen 0; Flexible, Mono, Snare, Tearing), Grinding Teeth (1d10+4 R; Pen 2).

UNQUENCHED

"Beware the deserts of Vaporius, there is more than endless sand and cruel sun out there to kill a man. Things stalk those wastes, dark, cursed things cast out from the cities and shunned by even the Priest-Kings."

— Yrr Nirt, Scion of the Builders Temple

I have seen many inhabited worlds in my travels but few as desolate as Vaporius; a ball of baking rock, choked by deserts and blasted by its blazing yellow star. It was during my time on that cursed place that I was to encounter another of the horrors of the Expanse, and a cruel mistake made by the tyrannical Priest-Kings of that world. Alberse was leading a search for a remote crash site, somewhere in the azure deserts south of the city of Tyniss. Our party was made up of several crew and a few locals, whom I had hired as guides. We were days into our crossing of the desert when one of the men spied a figure on the horizon. At once the guides became unsettled, shouting at me in their local tongue.

As the figure approached, I could see it was a woman, though the wind, sand, and sun had baked her flesh almost black and her eyes were but sunken pits. Worse still, parts of her flesh had caved in upon themselves and bone gleamed whitely through—I realised then that she was no longer alive. Even as my crew went to investigate the figure she turned on them, reaching out and grabbing the closest of the poor fools. I have seen few sights as terrible as what I witnessed that day, when the thing drew all liquid from the man, his skin collapsing in on itself until his flesh became dust and was blown away by the wind. All this happened in the space of a few heartbeats, and while the remaining crew fired on the dead woman with their lasguns, I had to drag Alberse away to safety. The guides had already run, and seeing as there was now nothing left of our fallen, I hastened to follow them.

Later the guides told me about the Unquenched; men and women with the Psyker's gift, twisted by drinking from the wells of the Priest-Kings into monsters of endless thirst and doomed to wander the wastes. It is said that at first they retain their humanity, but then over days and months the psychic power of the waters mixes with their own latent spark and their soul is warped and twisted until they become a living embodiment of thirst. At first, their psychic power turns upon themselves and their bodily fluids are consumed, flesh and blood drained away, leaving only desiccated meat and sun baked bone. Then they seek out any source of moisture they can find, draining fluid from all who cross their path, drinking it up and turning it to dust.

They said the Unquenched can exist in this state for years or even decades, until their bodies eventually turn to dust and they become a psychic force drifting across the sands, seeking out the fluids of living things. Over many years, legends say, this force grows weaker until eventually it cannot move and becomes trapped in a place, such as a cave or ruin, giving credence to stories of cursed locales where to enter is death. I can think of few fates worse than becoming an Unquenched, though encountering one certainly comes close.

PSYCHIC ABOMINATIONS

Only the Priest-Kings know for sure what creates the Unquenched, or why they must be cast out rather than simply killed (if in fact they can be killed), but they seem to have existed for as long as the Priest-Kings have held power and for as long as the Waters of Vaporius have flowed. There are no formal reports concerning these beings, or at least none that have been shared with outsiders. From what those that have visited Vaporius have pieced together from rumour and legend, it seems that the Unquenched are humans possessed of psychic talent, but not of the bloodline of the Priest-Kings.

On the civilised worlds of the Imperium, such individuals would be killed or given over to the Black Ships as per the Will of the Emperor, but the Koronus Expanse is without such appropriate measures to protect mankind from itself. Vaporius lacks even the specialised control and trained adepts to detect those with the psyker's touch, which some worlds of the Expanse use to keep their own populations safe from the taint of the warp.

So, like most of the people of Vaporius, they drink from the waters and submit to the control of their rulers, though it is at this point the change begins, a violent taint which mixes in their soul as the psychic dominance which flows from the waters to the Priest-Kings is turned back upon them and their own gifts are mangled and twisted into the abomination known as the Unquenched.

At this point, the Priest-Kings are quick to take them, snatching them from their beds at even the hint of corruption. What transpires then is known only to those privy to the innermost secrets of the glass cities, but after a time the tainted citizen is cast out into the desert, taken far from the city and abandoned. Whether it is the water or the ritual that starts the process, the outcast is doomed to become an Unquenched and roam the wastes until their very soul fades upon the wind. However, they never stray too close to the glass cities, perhaps another result of whatever the Priest-Kings inflict upon them, preferring to remain lurking among the rocks and dust of the great wastes of their desert world.

UNENDING THIRST

The Unquenched are at their heart psychic creatures, warped by the foulness of the waters and transformed into something both more and less than human tied to their dead flesh until it turns to dust around them. Once the contagion takes them and the waters warp their innate psychic talents, they are for all intents and purposes dead, animating their bodies through sheer will rather than any semblance of true life. Their psychic power then becomes focused on the consumption of fluid and, with an unholy compulsion, they are attracted to any kind of moisture, be it the blood of a man or a canister of promethium. Even as the transformation into Unquenched consumes them they retain their intelligence and, in some cases, even their personalities if they are strong of will. Without the means to talk (their vocal cords and throat among the first things to fall prey to their psychic thirst), only those with telepathic abilities or similar means to communicate without words can reach them.

Cutting through the blinding desire of the Unquenched to feed on liquids is difficult at best. This is especially so if the Unquenched has been outcast for more than a year, as their humanity erodes just like their flesh and eventually they forget they were even men and women of the glass cities. Rumours do persist of Unquenched that aid travellers on Vaporius if they are well sated, their knowledge of the wastes being almost without parallel. Others claim that the Unquenched are always aware of each other, linked in some way by the taint which has taken their souls, and the "younger" of their kind can warn travellers away from the older and more monstrous Unquenched, or the places inhabited by the spirits of those which can no longer wander.

DESERT TREASURES

Unquenched are also said to inhabit the deep places and caves beneath the desert, where they burrow down into the sands in search of underground rivers and streams. Some say that this is also where they horde their vast accumulated treasures, the possessions of those they drain dry, safely stored away from desert raiders eager to quench their own thirsts.

Such deposits would certainly sate even the most rapacious of Rogue Traders should they exist and be uncovered, leading several expeditions into the vast depths of sand and dust, all returning parched and empty, or not at all. The lack of success has lead some Explorers to suppose the Unquenched

themselves are propagating these tales in a cunning effort to drive prey to themselves, which is perhaps more likely than surely fanciful stories of fabulous treasures in the desert.

Unquenched								
WS	BS	S	T	Ag	Int	Per	WP	Fel
40	10	20	30 (6)	45	22	30	50	13

Movement: 4/8/12/24   **Wounds**: 20
Armour: None.   **Total TB**: 6
Skills: Awareness (Per), Concealment (Ag), Silent Move (Ag).
Talents: None.
Traits: Burrower (4), Dark Sight, Fear (1), From Beyond, Strange Physiology, Unnatural Senses (50m), Unnatural Toughness (x2).
Weapons: Withering Touch (1d10+5 E; Pen 0).

Special Rules

Children of the Immaterium: An Unquenched that has its body destroyed (either by normal means or through age) gains the Incorporeal trait and is restored to full Wounds. Should the creature then be destroyed again in this form, it returns within 1d10 days unless it was killed by psychic attack or other warp-based means.

Unending Thirst: An Unquenched exists for the sole purpose of feeding on the fluids of all those it encounters, in a perverted parody of the Priest-Kings' own relationship and control over the Waters of Vaporius. Even the touch of the Unquenched can be deadly and, given time, the creature can drain all moisture from even the most resistant of substances, reducing them to dust. Due to their unnatural energies, attacks from an Unquenched ignore Armour unless it is warded in some way against psychic attack. In addition, when an Unquenched inflicts critical damage on a foe, do not roll on the Critical table—instead reduce the victim's Toughness by the amount of critical damage inflicted. If the Toughness reaches 0 or less, it is turned to dust and dies. Creatures which survive such an attack recover this lost Toughness at a rate of 10 per day provided they have access to sufficient fluids.

UR-GHUL

"Once those things have your scent, it is over."

—Savant Francis Evanent, 4th Mercantile Fleet of House Killian

Alberse had received an astropathic communiqué that an old friend of his, Captain Timmir of the *Labours Won*, was in trouble on Aubray's Folly, and of course he had to come to his aid. We were able to get to the planet's surface without incident and, amongst the multitudes of factories and other debris, we found a wrecked craft, one of the heavy cargo lifters from the *Labours Won*. When our vox calls went unanswered we decided to check the interior of the wreck.

We went from hold to hold searching for any clue, any hint of Timmir and his crew. We knew for several minutes that something was following us, but Alberse kept pressing the search. The click-click of hard claw to metal flooring, as well as a chuffing noise, alerted us to something's presence. We chose to set up an ambush in a hallway leading from the engines. The craft's emergency lumens, red and hazy with dust, were the only light we had when the thing made its appearance.

It was definitely human in shape, but only just, rail thin with skin that shone like a hard bruise in the bloody illumination. The face was simply a slit-like mouth full of needle teeth and a series of pits, through which the thing chuffed and puffed the stagnant air. The thing stopped for a moment, squatting with one clawed hand caressing the metal flooring. It lifted its head, opened its mouth, and took in a long whoosh of air, tongue lashing out as if to taste us from afar. It then howled a most disdainful sound, one full of melancholy and spite. I knew then that it was hunting us just as much as we were hunting it.

Before I could give the word to attack, a sudden scream came from behind. The body of a rating suddenly rose up and shook, his back and legs held by two creatures like the one we watched. Their claws and teeth quickly reduced his solid girth to ribbons of flesh and sinew. We were suddenly surrounded by several of the things. Our group circled together and began to fire.

In a matter of minutes, the ship's hall was crowded with bodies, both man and xenos. Blood and ichor coated the floor, making movement even more difficult, the stench of death and sweat permeated the thin air. The remaining few of us stood back to back as the filth circled us, looking for an opportunity to strike. Our guns were dangerously low on ammunition by this time, and we struck out with whatever we had at our side, be it blade, rod, or fist, trying to find an opening for us to take advantage of and get back to our ship. I was able to lash out and cut two of the things that circled us, dropping them to the floor. We saw our chance and as one we ran.

From then until we got back to our craft, all I remember is running and shooting and pushing Alberse along. They tracked us all the way, and we were barely able to ram the hull doors of our lander closed before they reached us. They were fast and relentless, and we were lucky to get out alive. Without our firepower and the lander so nearby, it might have gone badly.

BLIND TRACKERS

The Ur-Ghul is a lanky humanoid xenos that seems to mimic many aspects of a human. The musculature and basic physiognomy of the creature definitely points towards the blessed form of humanity, but that is where the similarities end. The xenos' skin is incredibly resistant to damage, almost as hard as iron. Its hands and feet carry wicked claws, which it uses to rapidly grab onto and incapacitate its prey. Reports indicate that it has an astounding dexterity, able to move with an almost unnatural grace and quickness. Several Calixian Beast House records even contain rumours that the Ur-Ghul has the ability to escape bonds and cells by twisting and contorting its body in unwholesome ways. These abilities, when added together, make the xenos a terrifying creature when it comes to combat. The beast's head, however, contains the secrets of what makes it such a superb predator.

The face of an Ur-Ghul is something that few could forget. The somewhat flat visage is deeply cut by a wide, thin mouth filled with needle-like teeth. The thick, muscular tongue is long, and can be extended far beyond the thin lips. It is also particularly sensitive, able to sense another creature many metres away simply by tasting the prey's sweat and breath in the air. Above the mouth sits a series of cavernous sense pits instead of a single nose or eyes. These pits extend far into the skull creating large sensory regions. Accordingly, the nostrils are extraordinarily acute and can pick up not only airborne scents, but also detect heat emanations, air vibrations, and some say even warp disturbances.

An Ur-Ghul is a very efficient hunter despite its lack of any discernible vision senses, able to track its quarry for kilometres using an easy looping gait that covers long distances with low effort. It can keep such pace for long durations, waiting for the right time to finish off its prey. Once it is ready, the Ur-Ghul's speed is unnatural. It rapidly becomes a fury of claws and teeth as it tears its prey into gobbets of flesh, and often begins to feed while its victim is still alive.

Once in this state of frenzied feeding, this viciousness makes it a very hard creature to stop. A few who have survived such encounters claim they had to pry the jaws of a dead Ur-Ghul off its still struggling victim, as the ferocious mandibles would not go slack even in death. Such is the terrible essence of the Ur-Ghul, for nothing can stay its unrelenting nature, not even death.

EVOLVED TO HUNT

The Ur-Ghul appears to be an omnivorous humanoid with pack tendencies, certainly suitable to fill an ecological niche on many a planet. It has been sighted multiple times throughout the Ragged Worlds, suggesting an origin somewhere amongst this isolated region. It has also been firmly documented to exist on no less than five other planets from other regions in the Expanse, however. While the theory of parallel evolution is somewhat accepted by most branches of the Magos Biologis, to have such a creature evolve on so many differing planets with different climes and ecologies seems to suggest transportation rather than evolution. Who or what is behind such transportation is basis for much speculation, especially as to what possible motivations could be directing such efforts.

A few radical xenos savants have even suggested that Eldar raiders have some powerfu and secret link to the Ur-Ghul now found on several worlds in the Expanse. One ancient dissertation found in the depths of Hive Sibellus in the Calixis Sector makes mention that the Ur-Ghul's original homeworld is called Shaa-dom, but does not mention what system or even sector of the galaxy this world occupies. Several more adventurous Explorators and xenographers have searched for this planet, but as of yet it has not been located. More disturbingly, few of these missions have returned at all. If this is due to erroneous data concerning the world's location or whatever was awaiting those questing after the Ur-Ghul is yet another mystery concerning this species.

HIDDEN MASTERS

Taproom tales at Port Wander tell that these things have been seen in close approximation to Eldar pirates and raiding parties, used as some kind of tracking hound. Those who have survived some of these xenos raids have even spoken of seeing creatures whose features resemble the Ur-Ghul taking part in the attack. They had been used to hunt down those who sought to escape the raiders, fleeing away in frantic attempts to reach safety or hiding places where they could wait until the xenos departed. The attempts were doomed to failure. The Ur-Ghuls were loosed to roam the area, and soon caught the exhilarating scents of desperation and fear left in the air. In each report, none escaped the beasts, and their prey were dragged weeping and screaming back to the xenos raiders to meet their terrible fates.

One unverified but popularly recounted account relates that a particularly high-ranking member of this enigmatic xenos race personally commanded one such beast, using it as part of vile blood-sport raids and other foul practices. The story says the xenos employed the beast to track down a human the Eldar believed had wronged him in some unfathomable way. It managed to track down the unfortunate prey across the varied surface of Janto III deep within the Unbeholden Reaches, a world known for its bleak rocky plains and pestilent marshland. The hunt went on for weeks, ranging far across broad swaths of a remote and scantly inhabited continent, but finally the Ur-Ghul caught up with its victim, who did not long survive the debt he had to pay. The cruel xenos directing the beast seemed to delight as much with the hunt as it did with the method of payment.

Such thoughts are likely just so much fancy, mere void travellers' stories to enliven spire parties or to put fear in their trading associates' dreams. Some xenos savants worry though that beings able to command such terrible beasts are perhaps even more puissant than previously believed. It is definite that, as mindless hunters, the Ur-Ghul are certainly dangerous enough; if actually under the direction of sentient xenos races their threat level can only increase.

Ur-Ghul								
WS	BS	S	T	Ag	Int	Per	WP	Fel
42	—	31	35	49	18	48	33	12

Movement: 4/8/12/24   **Wounds:** 16
Armour: Toughened Skin (All 2).   **Total TB:** 3
Skills: Acrobatics (Ag) +10, Awareness (Per) +20, Contortionist (Ag), Climb (S), Dodge (Ag), Silent Move (Ag) +10, Tracking (Int) +20.
Talents: Assassin's Strike, Berserk Charge, Catfall, Combat Sense, Die Hard, Fearless, Leap Up, Heightened Senses (Smell and Taste), Hard Target, Sprint, Step Aside, Swift Attack.
Traits: Blind, Natural Armour (All 2), Improved Natural Weapons (Claws), Sturdy, Talented (Tracking), Unnatural Senses (Smell, Taste) (20 metres).
Weapons: Claws (1d10+3 R; Pen 1; Tearing), Teeth (1d10+3 R; Pen 0).

VOID KRAKEN

"Twas twice the size of the biggest asteroid I ever did see, all stone and teeth and tentacles like some nightmare staring us right in the face. The cap't, he said it was just a moon at first and to think no more on it, but I's knew better. I told him I did, I says to him that there is no moon…"

–Deckmaster Cybin Lyttle, Chartist vessel *The Lone Pilgrim*

I have heard countless tales told of creatures of the dark void in my travels, fearsome beasts which dwell in the empty stretches of nothing between worlds and prey on ships. For the most part I pay such nonsense little mind, considering it the drunken talk of voidfarers, or mistaken encounters with xenos ships amid the trackless reaches of the Expanse. There is one tale, however, which I can attest to from experience; a creature so deadly that only a handful of crews have ever crossed its path and returned to tell the tale. They call it the Void Kraken, a fearsome creature of the black said to inhabit the deepest parts of the Expanse. I think it takes its name after an ancient Terran monster of the abyssal oceans, though I never found out for sure.

My encounter with the beast came while I was traversing the Accursed Demesne, travelling with the esteemed Rogue Trader Tallen Alberse, long before I agreed to enter his employ and on a mission that I will not go into here. Given the run of the bridge, I was passing the interminable days of travel between the equally tiresome warp jumps when a hue and cry was raised among the deck officers. Alberse himself came rushing from his chambers, though at first I could not discern the reason for the alarm. Then I saw it reflected in the vast vista-panes of the ship's viewing array, another ship, at first mistaken for debris drifting closer through shards of tumbling rock. Smaller than our own vessel, it was badly damaged, the result of battle, perhaps, or simply of long years in space. Stranger still, it seemed almost wrapped in coils of stone. While my own mind struggled to understand what I was looking at, Alberse was quick to act, having evidently encountered such a beast before. Bellowing orders, he commanded his crew to break hard away from the wreck and the curious stone thing feasting upon its hull.

Even as our ship began to turn, the thing reacted, uncoiling kilometre-long silicate tentacles to reach out across the void toward us. I could only look on in horror as this beast of stone and crystal, which must have been at least two or even three kilometres in length, tore itself away from the desiccated hulk and pushed itself toward us. Suddenly the night was illuminated by lance fire as Alberse gave the beast a broadside, beams and blasts powerful enough to punch through void shields merely washing over its hide. With a terrible shriek of metal, one of the tentacles tore down the side of our craft, but thank the God-Emperor it did not catch, and we were able to slip away. Only when the creature was far behind us did Alberse breathe easy and tell me just how close we had come to death. I've made it my business since to keep things from getting that close again.

HUNTERS OF THE DEEP

The physiology and nature of the Void Kraken are largely unknown, even to the most well-travelled Explorers of the Expanse. This is doubtless the result of their rarity and difficulty to hunt and detect, but could also be that they represent more than a single species of void behemoth, several variations on the beast mistakenly considered a single race of creatures. Whatever the truth of the Void Kraken's origins, a number of facts are largely agreed upon by those who have come into contact with them. They are almost certainly some form of silicon-based creature, without blood, true bone, or fluid to keep them alive. Instead, it is believed by those few adepts to consider the beasts that the Void Kraken draw their animus from the very space debris they often resemble.

Kraken appear to be solitary, asexual creatures that reproduce by dividing themselves, much in the same fashion as amoebas or single-celled organisms. A Kraken tears off a piece of itself and flings it at a world (ideally airless and devoid of life) to create a hatchling which then burrows into the surface of the planetoid, feeding off the rock for decades or even centuries before emerging as a fledgling Kraken and flinging itself into space to hunt (another reason for choosing small asteroids or rocks with little gravity to overcome for the young). There is speculation that Kraken might mate, and some process of fertilisation is required for these hatchlings, but so far there has been no proof, or conceivable way to tell a male Kraken from a female Kraken, if such things do indeed exist.

Void Kraken feed off minerals found in rock, which explains their interest in ships. The hulls of most void-worthy vessels present a Kraken with a concentrated collection of metals, ores, and silicates for it to feed on, a tempting and tasty morsel for the beast. Small ships have the most to fear from the Kraken, as the beast's size and strength, especially when striking from ambush in an asteroid field or close to a world, can quickly overpower a ship and render it helpless to fight back. Even larger vessels are not immune, however, and Void Kraken attack things many times their own size, latching onto them like a limpet mine. Only ship-borne weaponry is any defence against a Kraken, and only then if the vessel detects the Kraken early enough and manages to drive it off with broadsides or lance strikes.

Once a Kraken has entangled a ship, it only disengages when the ship has been consumed or (if the ship is much larger than the Kraken) once it has taken a substantial bite from its hull. This process of consumption is as ponderous as the Kraken itself, however, and it is possible for a particularly brave crew to venture out onto the hide of the beast while it is feeding and lay mines on it or try and cut away its tentacles. Such a task is fraught with danger and the Kraken often reacts quickly to such "parasites" on its hide by throwing up small fanged tentacles to rake back and forth, scouring its stony flesh clean. Sometimes a Kraken declines to consume a ship straight away, or, if it has fed enough on its hull, it may leave the wreck alone. In these cases, Kraken have been known to drag lifeless ships from one system to another, gathering the hulks around remote worlds or in deep space, possibly to feed on at a later time.

VOID KRAKEN

Hull: Unknown (Void Beast).
Class: Unknown (Void Beast).
Dimensions: 1.8 km long (+1 km with tentacles extended), 500m abeam approx.
Mass: 7 megatons approx.
Crew: Not Applicable
Accel: 1.3 gravities max acceleration

Speed: 3   **Manoeuvrability**: +40
Detection: +40   **Hull Integrity**: 50
Armour: 17   **Turret Rating**: 2 (Tentacles)
Void Shields: 0

Weapons: Tentacles (Strength 6; Damage 1d5+2; Crit Rating 4; Range 0, Entangle†), Maw (Strength 2; Damage 1d10+2; Crit Rating 4; Range 0).

†Entangle: If a Kraken hits a vessel with its Tentacles, it can immediately make an attack with its Maw. If this Maw attack also hits, the Kraken has wrapped itself around the ship and begins to feed, automatically hitting with its Maw attack each future round until dislodged or destroyed. The ship may fire upon the Kraken, but then itself takes half the damage inflicted on the creature due to the close proximity. The crew may also attempt to break free by making a **Very Hard (–30) Pilot (Space Craft)+Manoeuvrability Test**; the Kraken, however, automatically hits with one final Tentacle attack as the ship disengages. A feeding Kraken cannot be targeted by another ship's weapons as it is too close to the vessel (unless this is not a concern!).

Special Rules

Neither Beast Nor Ship: Void Kraken are monsters of truly gargantuan proportions, some growing to the size of small escorts with tentacles that can stretch for kilometres trailing through the void. As such a Void Kraken is more akin to a space ship than it is to a more mundane planetary creature, and is largely immune to all but the most potent of weapons. To reflect this, the Void Kraken is treated as a vessel using the rules from page 212 of the ROGUE TRADER Core Rulebook with the following exceptions:

- Void Kraken have no crew and when called upon to perform an action that requires a Characteristic Test, use a base value of 35.
- Void Kraken are largely made of rocky material and have few components that can be damaged by ship weaponry or ordnance, as even their tentacles can be re-spawned as needed. Void Kraken do not suffer Critical Hits, but are instead destroyed when reduced to Hull Integrity 0.
- Void Kraken weapons use the Macrobattery rules.
- Void Kraken cannot be the subject of boarding actions.
- Void Kraken have no Morale rating like normal ships and are effectively fearless. Whenever a Void Kraken suffers damage to its Morale, this damage is ignored.
- Void Kraken are fiendishly difficult to detect, as they are, in essence, living asteroids and only the most sophisticated sensors can reliably pinpoint them. When scanning for Void Kraken, vessels suffer a –30 penalty to all Detection Tests (–50 if they are not aware what they are looking for). Void Kraken more than 8VU away are completely undetectable. At the GM's discretion, bonuses may be applied if it is obvious where the Kraken is (i.e. there are no asteroids or other debris in the area), though Kraken do not usually stray into zones where they have no cover.

USING XENOS CREATURES IN ADVENTURES

"The foolish view them as dangers to be eradicated. The wise view them as profits waiting to be grasped."

–Rogue Trader Gal Maximoff

The Koronus Expanse offers an endless variety of beasts and plants to be used in **ROGUE TRADER** games, ranging from ones the Explorers might already find familiar to others they may never fully understand. The region should always be full of hidden dangers and threatening mysteries, and every planet should offer life forms to challenge both the players' combat and business skills alike. Even familiar and usually non-hazardous beings might become aggressive in the worst circumstances or when left to settle on worlds not properly suited for them. Some threats might even remain an enigma, with the Explorers never certain what exactly they faced, leaving it a threat hanging over them for future adventures. The Expanse is vast and unknowable, and should not give up its secrets easily.

The encounter ideas below represent some ways the xenos creatures presented in this book can be used in **ROGUE TRADER** adventures. They can form the nuclei of entire campaigns, or be inserted into existing adventures to add additional dangers. Such beings can serve as the target for acquisition, where the Explorers are actively seeking out the beasts or plants as part of a mission or quest, and may have information pertinent to their goal (or perhaps, as is more often in the Expanse, they are woefully mistaken as to the accuracy of their data). In other settings, the xenos life forms are an unexpected intervention, and likely menaces for the Explorers. In these situations, it is much more likely the Explorers are unprepared for such attacks, and may have little or no knowledge of their bestial foes. Like much in the Expanse, the knowledge they gain in these encounters should prove invaluable in later adventures, should they survive the experience.

Becoming Prey: The simplest way to introduce xenos creatures into games is to offer them as a mini-adventure to Explorers travelling across a planet (or even the void), especially to an area they have not visited before. This can turn a routine (and possibly boring) transit into one fraught with peril and danger. Explorers travelling on foot or in primitive vehicles make for easy targets, and every corner or nightfall can become an opportunity for an unwelcome surprise. Even Explorers that assume they are in perfect safety within armoured transport or flying craft might find themselves attacked by sufficiently powerful (or sufficiently sneaky) beings that can rupture armour, insinuate themselves inside sealed berths, or bring down a vessel due to sheer numbers.

Much of the time the Explorers are unprepared for such assaults; soon they may find themselves stalked by either the beasts that initially struck them or some new being, thus turning a single attack into a longer adventure. For Explorers more used to larger-scale conflicts or massed naval battles, such tense encounters where they must defend themselves from persistent hunters can force the Explorers to improve their teamwork skills lest they fall one by one. They may even find the beasts hunting them can become profitable new sources of income, should they discover the creatures suitable for the Beast Houses or other xenos collectors.

Breakout: A Rogue Trader is, at his core, precisely that—a trader. As such, he is almost always carrying cargo from planet to planet, and it is very possible his cargo may become a hazard. The most common scenario is that the cargo itself is a danger, such as cages of deadly creatures destined for the Beast Houses of the Calixis Sector or private xenos-pens in the crystalline towers of a hive spire. While it is likely these containers are carefully watched and thoroughly secured, the very nature of the life forms within guarantees that they are very likely to escape captivity, especially if the buyer insists they not be harmed or sedated on the journey. For animals or plants evolved to survive on Death Worlds, breaking out from such enclosures is all too often an easy task. In other situations, the beasts might be stowaways, unknowingly gathered up in other goods or even hatching in transit.

When xenos creatures escape whilst on board a vessel, especially one already in the warp, all manner of things may occur, few of them good for the Explorers. Reports may issue from the lower levels of crewmen gone missing, or even found ripped to shreds far beyond the norm of deck-fighting. Ancient components might succumb to onslaughts of ravenous insects or entire compartments become uninhabitable from wildly reproducing spores. For some creatures, the unpleasant environs in the depths of a vessel may be welcome respites from their normal homeworlds, allowing them to thrive in ways that would be impossible elsewhere. The Explorers may find themselves being hunted as they seek to eradicate such threats to their ship.

Bring Them Back Alive: The Koronus Expanse offers vast resources ripe for plunder, with the easiest involving acquisition and transport of megatonnes of mineral wealth or agri-world foodstuffs. Other resources are more limited in scope but offer much greater degrees of profit, as with the Beast Trade, one of the foremost ways to accumulate wealth without overflowing cargo bays. In terms of profit to weight ratios, this is perhaps second only to the Cold Trade, but without the associated dangers of dealing in xenos artefacts. Capturing creatures for resale, though, presents many difficulties even beyond the obvious hazards of working in close proximity to such beasts. Highly-trained and experienced trackers and hunters are perhaps the greatest necessity, for without them the beasts usually cannot be found (or found in a manner that allows their capture). Non-lethal weaponry is also needed, such as specially formulated needle rifles or sedation grenades that can subdue a creature without harm. Each animal or planet may also require unique containment bays, dietary supplies, and carriage from the scene of capture to the landed cargo shuttle.

These and other essentials usually mean only the rarest and most unique creatures are worth such efforts and, depending on the creature, mass quantities may be desired in order to

ONE NIGHT ON JANX IV

Janx IV is a small, temperate world located on the edges of the Egarian Dominion, covered with huge marshes and thin forests separated by deep lakes filled with stagnant water. Few animals roam its surface. Rogue Trader Abram Valmaux claimed the world on discovery, desperately eager to fully plunder the world as his coffers were running low. Initial scans had indicated the planet hosted large promethium deposits buried deep under the swamp waters, and pre-fabricated drilling stations and refinery plants were quickly dropped from orbit along with attendant populations of indentured labourers and servitors. Soon regular shipments of weapons-grade promethium were making their way to Port Wander for transport into the Calixis Sector, but after only a few months these ceased without explanation. Valmaux journeyed back to the planet, only to find his installations in ruins.

None of his work force could be found. He assumed it was an attack from a rival Rogue Trader, until routine surveillance pic-captures revealed untold multitudes of creatures emerging from the surrounding waters one night. Millions of pale, worm-like forms had fully overrun the terrified defenders, chewing through anything in their way, be it metal or plasteel, flesh or bone. Masses of the things surged over men in moments, dragging them to the decks in struggling forms that grew still as they were pushed along by the remorseless, fleshy tides. In less than an hour, the complex was devoid of life; even the endless pools of blood were cleansed as the invading waves of creatures scoured the manufactorums bare before disappearing back into the waters.

This attack did not occur again, and Valmaux was soon able to repair and re-establish his operation. Magos Biologis investigators have not been able to recover samples of the creatures, and theorise one of the many drilling probes tapped into a pocket where the beasts resided. Additional defences have been added, but all know that should the creatures emerge again there is little that can be done to stop them. It is not known if any of the worms have been transported off-world in any of the promethium shipments; it may be many years before a population grows to sufficient size to become as dangerous as that found on Janx IV.

establish a stronger profit level. Exceptionally dangerous and unique creatures may be transported as single deliveries, both to ensure the buyer a greater degree of rarity and also to make capture and transport as smooth as possible. These may include creatures utterly illegal to possess in the Calixis Sector due to their lethality, speed of reproduction, or other factors, and may necessitate further specialised equipment to avoid detection. Despite all of these factors, establishing regular Beast Trade routes and connections can develop into highly profitable sideline travel to accompany other Endeavours.

The Great Hunt: The wilds of the Expanse lure many of the wealthiest and most daring from the Calixis Sector to venture forth in search of new adventures. Such individuals might be jaded by the ease of their regular lives, and look to such expeditions as singular opportunities to once again prove their mettle away from the many luxuries their normal routines provide. Here they may remember the men they once were, the ruthless individual that clawed his way up to become ruler, a man as dangerous as any beast.

In other grand hunts, the outings are major events involving many nobles and requiring huge entourages of retainers and sycophants to ensure proper splendour and ceremony throughout. The goal on such cavalcades might be less what beasts are killed than what garments are worn or refreshments are correctly served. Explorers commissioned to provide the nobility of Calixis with such sport may find dangers more from politics than mere beast attack. They may even be secured to act as bodyguards for nobles as part of the excursion or as part of expeditions already assembled, to ensure no untoward "accidents" occur with all the firepower loosened on the hunt. Where simply surviving against the lethal beasts of the Expanse is one effort, keeping others alive against both those creatures and their equally deadly peers is certainly another.

Knowledge is Power: The Tech-Priests of the Magos Biologis have endless fascination with the variety of species living in the Koronus Expanse. Studies of these creatures offer new revelations into the ways of the flesh, the better to replace it with holy machine. They also offer new possibilities for toxins and other alchaemical processes, or perhaps something as mundane as a new foodstuff to feed the teeming masses of the Calixis Sector. Xenologists also crave the alien, desiring such creatures to enhance their knowledge of the xenos races across the Expanse. These personalities and others pay handsomely for transport across this untamed region to specific planets, where they can conduct research.

Here the Explorers provide safe passage for these individuals, perhaps to worlds they are familiar with but more likely to new locations never before seen. This should be especially true if the researchers are intent on seeking out creatures that heretofore only exist in rumour or legend. Once they have landed, the Explorers are expected to defend against any threats the planet might pose, including other creatures, native races that might not appreciate such a visitation, rival researchers, hostile organisations, and anything else that might interfere with successful investigations. They are expected to keep the researchers themselves alive, both to ensure proper payment in many cases but also to establish a good reputation for future missions of this type.

Obsession: The Expanse is dominated by strong-willed individuals, larger than legend and beyond any morality or laws other than what they deign to observe. Such personages are also not always fully rational, and may be consumed by goals others would not consider sane or prudent. Such considerations are of no concern for the truly obsessed though, and the exotic creatures of the Expanse have fully captured the mania of more than one void traveller. The megafauna located

on many worlds are a prime example, each capable of tearing apart entire manufactorum complexes or flattening a Baneblade super-heavy tank with ease. Other targets of obsession may be smaller but no less lethal, those singular predators that have become legend. Here, some may seek out the beast that injured them before, to pay it back for the damage it had done earlier. This damage may also be purely financial in nature; many a Rogue Trader has lost what was left of his fortunes attempting to destroy the beast that almost ruined him years ago. Locating the specific creature that tore off an arm, or scarred their body horribly, might entail killing hundreds of similar creatures until he finds the correct beast, assuming he ever does.

Other individuals may quest to find the thing that killed a beloved relative or bonded friend, perhaps journeying from the Calixis Sector for the first time to conduct this affair of honour. Here they soon find that the Expanse does not show mercy, even to those on such noble pursuits. Those who showed cowardice against a species may seek redemption through killing another of them. An agent of the Adeptus Ministorum might seek out holy combat against the creature that desecrated a shrine or obliterated a mission. In all cases, the individual is guided not by profit or survival, the two guiding traits of most Explorers, but by reasons that do not allow for any argument or appeal. They often pay extremely well for the services of those who can aid them on their quest, something Explorers can appreciate far more than their obsession.

Purge the Deviants: To the horror of the Adeptus Ministorum and others correctly faithful to the God-Emperor, the Expanse hosts many beasts that dare steal the Holy Form of Man. Some may be true xenos creatures which approximate human morphology due to parallel evolution or other natural development, while others may be debased humans brought low through sin or other corrupting elements. The reasons matter not to the truly devout, who only see quasi-human abominations that should be put to the torch. For those who perfectly follow His Ways, even for such fallen humans the only real solution is to wipe the planet clean of their taint, as such things have dwelt too long in darkness and are surely beyond even His Sight. The Ecclesiarchy has no express remit in the Expanse, but this should hardly dissuade them from action.

The Explorers might be hired to offer assistance to such missions, where the goal might be to eradicate populations of such creatures, or even scour the planet entirely. It is also possible the nature of their group and leadership may lead them to take such actions on their own, for even if it might not profit them directly, surely such actions are of their own reward for the God-Emperor and His Glory. Those attempting such feats may find themselves facing creatures more dangerous than first appearances would suggest or, worse yet, strains of humanity that have developed powerful abilities and become dangerous beings that would have been culled on more civilised planets.

Rescue: A common mission for Explorers is to conduct rescue operations, where they travel to a new planet to investigate a downed vessel or damaged ground complex. They may also come across a crippled voidship and attempt to affect repairs, conduct salvage, or aid any who still live. In many of these cases, xenos creatures can be added into the mix to add tension and complexity to what could seem a routine mission, and turn it into a struggle to defend themselves, any survivors, and any valuables left intact from a wide variety of possible attacking creatures. These might not be immediate threats, and could appear only later in the mission when all seems to be going well. Late night visitations from stealthy predators, hordes of rapacious vermin leaping out in the heat of the day, and many other hazards can cause the Explorers to quickly consider how profitable the mission might really be, should their lives be in constant danger far beyond what was expected.

It is also possible the creatures themselves are the cause of the incident. Stowaway beasts and flora might come to aggressive life once in a newer environment, such as that of an oxygen-rich and humid vessel. Violent life forms, having escaped their insufficient holding cells or containment bays, could cause havoc throughout a ship or complex, killing off vital crew or destroying essential power systems. Other predators may have also come across the existing wreckage, and the survivors may already be fighting for their lives when the Explorers arrive on the scene. When combined with earlier beast attacks, this offers a situation where multiple sets of creatures may be threatening the Explorers at the same time. If some of the escaped beasts are considered valuable commodities, the mission could turn into rescuing one set of creatures whilst destroying another.

Aliens of the Expanse

Eldar
•
Orks
•
Rak'Gol
•
Sslyth
•
Strixis
•
Yu'Vath

CHAPTER II: ALIENS OF THE EXPANSE

"Of course I don't trust anyone I deal with. If they were human I'd be fine with knowing they can't be trusted, as I still know why they are in the deal. A xenos though... who knows what's really motivating a xenos?"

—Rogue Trader Sven Larpenteur

Mankind faces many dangers in the Koronus Expanse; navigation alone presents many hazards, especially in simply reaching the area. The clearest threats, though, are those posed by other sentient races, especially those also capable of void travel, as they may threaten humans on worlds other than their own. The true faithful of the Adeptus Ministorum offer a simple solution to this concern: exterminate all forms of alien life and any traces of their existence, all for the glory of the God-Emperor. This is, however, rarely practical or even possible, as the Expanse exists outside the boundaries of Imperial dominion. Even within Imperial space, many xenos races pose constant threats to Mankind, and in the lawless Expanse they are even more dangerous. Here, the xenos roam at whim, spreading their unholy influence across the stars.

Most Rogue Traders find this situation quite to their liking. Where there are no laws or Imperial jurisdictions, there is great opportunity for profit. Despite the official proscriptions against such things, there is a huge appetite for xenos knowledge and technology in the Calixis Sector, and plenty who pay handsomely to quench such desires. Within the dangerous reaches of the Koronus Expanse few things are more prized, for good or for ill, despite the huge risks involved.

Such xenotech is highly sought after in the Sector by heretical xenographers, jaded spire-nobles, Ordo Xenos agents, radical factions of the Adeptus Mechanicus such as the Disciples of Thule, and many others for a variety of reasons. The purposes they are desired for can only be speculated upon; however, no loyal servant of the God-Emperor would dare traffic in such innately corrupt and unholy merchandise. Possession of xenotech is heavily proscribed (often to a lethal degree), so most trading occurs through the channels of the Cold Trade. Many a respectable tavern or trading post on Port Wander is merely the front for this highly lucrative business, serving as the middle ground for Rogue Traders bringing these illicit goods into the Sector and smugglers who then transport the items to buyers.

Some xenos races of the Expanse frequently deal with humans, either willingly or unwillingly, and despite some tales of combative misunderstandings are known more for their commercial dealings rather than their military conflicts. Many Rogue Traders commission the Kroot as mercenaries, whilst others cautiously hold the Stryxis as trading partners and sources of esoteric information. Such dealings have lead to the rise of some very successful dynasties, but have been the ruination of many more. Those who forget that the alien always remains alien, and that xenos are at their core a threat to mankind, rarely live to regret the error.

Those Rogue Traders who do maintain frequent contact with xenos cultures run the risk of unwanted attention from the Inquisition. Other, more devout Rogue Traders are apt to only deal with xenos races through the torpedo ports of their warship. These militants prowl the warp routes of the Koronus Expanse, preying on those xenos they can overwhelm and collecting information on others for future assaults. The latter are sometimes joint ventures with a house's warfleet and segments of the Imperial Navy brought specially into the Expanse for the battle. To these Rogue Traders, for every xenos destroyed the Expanse moves one step closer to becoming a truly civilised region.

Not all xenos go so quietly into the void's cold embrace, however. Numerous conflicts between different races and Mankind have been fought within the Expanse. These engagements are often bloody and brutal beyond measure, with neither side asking or giving quarter. Typical of these is one of the Expanse's first recorded conflicts between man and xenos, said to have occurred in 152.M41 near the dead world of Foulstone. Imperial histories state that there the treacherous Eldar ambushed a small fleet led by Rogue Trader Synbar Lockhart; these "Crow Spirits," as they call themselves, managed to destroy nearly a dozen of House Lockhart's vessels. His house was crippled, and from that day forward Lockhart became obsessed with eradicating the Eldar from the Expanse.

The Eldar are just one of many hostile races within the Koronus Expanse. Some of these xenos civilisations have been encountered in other areas of the galaxy, though their behaviour elsewhere cannot be taken as typical for those dwelling in the Expanse. Several of the races in the Expanse are thought to be unique to the region, such as the mindlessly savage Rak'Gol, though this is still pure conjecture from Calixian xenobiologists who are, for the most part, simply thankful that these menaces are on the other side of the Maw. Those who regularly truck with xenos believe they comprehend the dangers they face in each encounter; the wisest know this full knowledge is forever beyond them. It is these unknown dangers that are perhaps the greatest threats. Some whisper that even dead races such as the fallen Yu'vath still haunt uncharted areas of the Expanse, awaiting their time to reclaim their dominions. None can gainsay this, for the Expanse is full of such dark areas that are forever bereft of the Emperor's Light as long as xenos roam its stars.

NEW TALENT: TOUCHED BY THE FATES

Some of the adversaries presented here are extremely dangerous individuals, meant to be rivals or even nemeses to Explorers. Such NPCs have a number of Fate Points equal to half his Willpower Bonus (rounding up). He may use these Fate Points in the exact same way as an Explorer, and may even "burn" a Fate Point to survive death and destruction. In addition, the rules for Righteous Fury apply to this character.

THE ELDAR

"The humans think they conquered the stars and brought order and civilisation to the chaos of the void, when all they have is what we left for them; the bitter scraps of the most powerful empire this galaxy has even known."

–Ghost Captain Tyniss of the Crow Spirits

In my time with Lord-Captain Alberse I have travelled much of the Expanse and encountered numerous and terrible xenos species which inhabit that dark and lawless place. Some we have even made deals with, traded goods and even found common cause, at least for a time. Few, however, match the cunning and duplicitous nature of the Eldar. Don't be fooled by their soft words and musical speech or by the frailness of their ships; they are treacherous in a way humans can only hope to aspire to.

The most notable encounter I recall with these aliens was during the exploration of the Ork pirate base known as the Frozen Talon, a planetary fragment on the edge of the Accursed Demesne. Charts and rumours uncovered in Footfall had indicated the presence of ruins on the Talon and Alberse believed there might be artefacts of worth there, left over from some forgotten civilisation and unnoticed by the simpleminded Orks. No sooner had we entered the Talon's system than we were approached by a lone Eldar vessel of the Twilight Swords clan under banner of parley.

The ship's Captain was named Kolyr Glimmer as best we could understand, and was also interested in the Talon. He offered to aid us in navigating the asteroid fields surrounding the fragment as well as hold off the Orks for a small cut of bounty the ruins might offer.

Looking back, Alberse should have known better, as should have I, as the Eldar never offer assistance without a significant interest, and Eldar seldom share when it comes to artefacts and relics—and never if they are taken from the ruins of their long lost empire. Greed clouded our judgement, along with the chance to tackle the Orks with reduced risk to our own ship, and so we agreed and a deal was struck.

As per the plan we had devised, our own vessel and the Eldar ship made a hit-and-run attack on the Ork base, drawing away their own ships into the asteroid field while landing a boarding party on the Talon to plunder the ruins. We would then swing back and pick them up before exiting the system and leaving the Orks in our wake. For the most part, the plan went well, and with the aid of the swift Eldar vessel we drew the bulk of the Orks away from the Talon while a party of Eldar and humans secretly infiltrated the base and made for the ruins. No sooner had we broken for the asteroids, however, than the Eldar vessel vanished among the debris, leaving us alone against the Orks. Only through skill and courage were we able to fight our way back to the Talon to try and pick up the boarding party, still at that point believing the Eldar had not truly abandoned us. When our party made no reply to vox hails, we entered the base, fighting our way through scores of Ork warriors. It was then we discovered the extent of the treachery; our own party had been murdered by the Eldar, which had then taken the artefacts from the ruins (which we only then discovered to be Eldar), and made their escape.

Eventually, we fought our way out of the system and through the Orks, but only after losing many good men and sustaining damage to the *Aureus*. We should have remembered one simple rule when first we encountered those deceitful xenos: never trust an Eldar.

THE DYING RACE

The Eldar are an ancient and enigmatic species which dominated the galaxy millions of years before the rise of the Imperium. Hugely technologically advanced and knowledgeable in the secrets of the universe, the Eldar once controlled or traversed much of the domain humans now claim. These times are past, however, and even by the time humanity's star was rising the Eldar had already begun to fade into the darkness of history, their civilisation crippled and decaying from a doom now millennia old. Today the Eldar are few in number, hidden away in distant, secret parts of the galaxy, sailing the void in their great world-ships or reduced to raiders and pirates. Their civilisation has fragmented and has largely become nomadic, its once-great clans and peoples travelling in vast armadas of ships and aboard mighty Craftworlds, gargantuan vessels the size of cities or larger in space. The Eldar race has also fragmented over the centuries, with some choosing to wander far from their kin or turn their backs on their past while others cling to the teachings of their ancestors and try vainly to keep their civilisation alive. Whatever teachings they follow, all Eldar retain the technologically sophisticated weapons and ships of their forebearers and, even though their numbers are but a tiny fraction of mankind's, they remain a significant force within the galaxy and a constant threat to the Imperium and its worlds.

Within the Koronus Expanse, like many of the fringes of Imperial space, the presence of the Eldar is a very real threat to the Imperium, and though they do not often openly make war upon mankind, woe to the Rogue Trader who chooses to oppose them or meddle in their alien designs. Legends and rumours have it that many of the worlds in the Expanse were once controlled by the Eldar, and still hide ruins and secrets which the ancient race guards jealously from outside interference. Thus an Explorer may not know he has angered the Eldar by simply setting foot on a remote world until an Eldar vessel emerges from the darkness to destroy him. More likely, though, Explorers face the Eldar in the void, where they make for deadly raiders and pirates. Clans such as the Crow Spirits and the Twilight Swords are a plague upon Imperial shipping, their vessels practically impossible to track and difficult to detect before they strike. Occasionally, Explorers may even be able to make deals with the Eldar, in those rare instances where humans have something the Eldar require, or where the combined might of humans and Eldar are the only hope of facing a greater threat. Quite apart from rousing the interest (and subsequent bloody retribution) of the Inquisition, such pacts are almost always short lived, ending either in violence and betrayal, or the abrupt and mysterious disappearance of the Eldar, gone as swiftly as they arrived.

AN ANCIENT HISTORY

Once the worlds and peoples of the Eldar were numerous, their fleets vast and swift, and their warriors feared by all those who opposed them. For countless centuries the galaxy belonged to the Eldar, all other races pale shadows next to their might and power. Graceful cities of slender towers and glittering white colonnades could be found from one end of the galaxy to the other, and Eldar worlds epitomised culture, knowledge, and the peak of civilisation. The Eldar themselves were an enlightened people, who pursued art, language, and learning as much as they mastered the ways of war and conquest. For millions of years their people prospered, and they were the greatest of the galaxy's races; unopposed and unchallenged in their supremacy.

Like so many great societies their fall was slow in its coming, but all the worse for the heights they had achieved. The Eldar mind is a complex and tangled labyrinth of emotion and thought, and Eldar are far more susceptible to the highs and lows of extreme emotions. Such was the case with the great Eldar civilisation, and as their power grew so too did their hunger for new experiences and new sensations. Over long centuries, this began a slow rot in the heart of the Eldar empire, as more and more Eldar turned to a path of decadence and emotional excess, indulging in their every whim and giving themselves over their basest desires. Cults sprang up devoted to hedonistic pleasures and debased rituals, the

ELDAR LANGUAGE

The language of the Eldar is an ancient and complex dialect built upon and refined over millions of years. Compared to the crude blunt sounds of High or Low Gothic, its words flow from one to the next, each sentence a complete idea as much as a collection of letters or numbers. Humans can imitate Eldar speech to a certain degree, with sufficient training, but compared to a native speaker they are slow and halting at best. This is largely because the Eldar language is not words alone, but also accompanied by a detailed set of poses and gestures. The way an Eldar stands, the cast of his features or how he moves his hands can all change the meaning of words, sometimes dramatically. Further complicating matters is that each Eldar word or symbol is as much a concept as it is a name for something. Thus while the Eldar word for rock might mean rock, it might also be used to convey permanence or stability, or in a different context lack of life or thought. To a human, words gain meaning from their context and the words around them, while to an Eldar the words themselves already possess infinite meaning, manipulated by a crooked finger or slight inflection when speaking.

side effect of a culture that no longer needed to concern itself with common labour or the need for personal wealth. Even as the alien empire prospered, its success fuelled this dark heart of indulgence and depravity, the pastimes of the idle populace becoming increasingly at odds with the ancient ideals of their ancestors upon which their civilisation was built; and so the cults gained greater power and began to overtake Eldar society altogether.

It was at some point during this long unrecorded slide into decadence that a dark power deep within the warp took notice of the Eldar, a psychic echo of their own excessive culture and the depths to which it had sunk in the pursuit of increasingly powerful emotions and sensations. Though it had no name at first, it was given life by the Eldar themselves and their increasingly depraved actions. As it grew in power so did the Eldar's madness; each a vile reflection of the other, each feeding off the other's twisted heart. For long years the Eldar turned upon themselves, sinking to sickening depths; torturing and killing their own kind, eating their own dead, and mutilating their once-great civilisation, until finally the warp god they had created emerged into full consciousness and power. The Chaos God Slaanesh was born.

In its moment of birth, Slaanesh, the embodiment of all the Eldar's darkest whims and wanton cruelty, let out a howl across the void, a psychic scream heard by every living Eldar, tearing a hole in the fabric of reality itself. In the blink of an eye the heart of the Eldar civilisation was ripped out, its worlds plunged into the warp and all but a handful of its people killed instantly as the new-born god tore their souls from their flesh. Only those far from the epicentre survived, those who had fled to the edges of the galaxy and cut themselves off from their decadent kin. The Eldar were not alone in the damage dealt by Slaanesh, and countless humans, Orks, and other races also suffered, though it was the end of the Eldar as a galactic power and the beginning of their decline; never again would their civilisation command the stars, nor would they be more than scattered nomads, the remains of a broken peoples, brought down by their own pride and hubris.

ELDAR PHYSIOLOGY

Physiologically, Eldar appear much like humans, though they are usually taller, more slender of limb, and always more graceful in the way they move. Their faces are also longer, with sharp, pointed features, tapered ears, and almond-shaped eyes that give them an ethereal, otherworldly cast. Their dark liquid eyes are also markedly different from human eyes, deep and full of ancient secrets, assuring any man who looks too long into them just how alien the Eldar really are, and that, despite some passing physical resemblance, they are nothing like humanity. Part of these differences lie within the physical nature of the Eldar and their long natural life span, which far exceeds that of even the most long-lived human, even taking into account the many ways in which man might try and prolong his existence and cheat death. Paradoxically, though the Eldar have exceptional longevity, their metabolism is far faster than that of a human, their hearts beat more quickly, pumping their blood around their body in a rapid crimson torrent. It is speculated that this increased blood flow improves their reaction speed and brain function, allowing them to act and react far more quickly than humans can.

ELDAR CLANS AND CRAFTWORLDS

Within the Koronus Expanse there are several different Eldar clans and at least one documented Craftworld. Among the corsairs are counted the Crow Spirits and the Twilight Swords, large roving fleets of Eldar vessels which have been known to plunder the void from Winterscale's Realm all the way to the Accursed Demesne. There are also many minor corsairs, some consisting of but a single wraithbone ship or single extended Eldar family—like the *Dark Lament*, an ancient cruiser captained by the mysterious Sydra Voidwalker, which has haunted the Heathen Worlds for countless years. Only the most learned Explorers can discern the difference between clans, or the relationships between them—and just like the fluid nature of Eldar emotions, the web of alliances between corsairs can change more quickly than humans can follow.

Corsairs are also the most likely of the Eldar groupings to make deals with human traders and void-farers, given their familiarity with the Expanse and their limited resources. It is not unknown for clans to make use of humans (and other races) to complete their goals, whether it is a simple act of piracy or something more complex involving the worlds once controlled by their race. In either case, an Explorer would do well not to trust the clans too far, as deals with the Eldar have a way of turning and a greedy captain may well get more than he bargained for.

DEAD GODS

Once the Eldar had many gods; each was an aspect of their rich and diverse civilisation, and an expression of the differing aspects of the Eldar themselves. Among their numbers were counted Asuryan, the Phoenix King and lord of the Eldar gods; Vaul, the Smith and Creator; Isha of the Harvest; Lileath, the Maiden of Dreams and Fortune; and Morai-Heg, the Wise Crone. All of these were lost when the Eldar civilisation was destroyed, lost to the warp and to the memory and minds of countless Eldar. Only two have survived into the present day: The Laughing God Cegorach, worshiped by the enigmatic Harlequins, and Kaela Mensha Khaine, the Eldar god of war. It is said that when Slaanesh arose, Khaine was strong enough to survive the battle, but in the process was rent into a thousand pieces and scattered across the void, where he eventually came to rest in the heart of each of the Craftworlds. These fragments are what give the Avatars their life and in this way the god lives on.

Of more concern to the Imperium, and with a greater presence than the clans, are the Craftworlds. These cities of the void have the resources and power to conquer worlds should they see fit, and arguably have the most effect on the galaxy as their Farseers work quietly behind the scenes to manipulate the course of galactic events. Within the Expanse, the Eldar of Craftworld Kaelor sometimes make their presence known, protecting the ruins of their civilisation and furthering the unknowable goals of their race. An Explorer plundering the lost worlds of the Expanse is likely to cross paths with the Craftworld sooner or later should he lay claim to worlds where Eldar ruins can be found.

These Eldar are quite different to the corsairs and even to their dark kin, and function more like the Eldar of old, protecting their interests much as the Imperium jealously guards its worlds. In contrast to the heavy-handed tactics of the Imperium, the Eldar do not crush their foes in a vulgar display of might, at least not right away. Instead, the Eldar often manipulate others to do their fighting, or tempt, trick, and fool Explorers into avoiding worlds they wish to protect. Should a captain and his crew persist in countering the Eldar's agenda, they often find themselves targeted by the Guardians and Aspect Warriors of the Craftworld itself. More than one Rogue Trader has discovered too late that he has become the target of a Craftworld's wrath when he mistakenly thought he was dealing only with scattered tribes and cowardly pirates.

Eldar within the Expanse are seldom encountered near the Maw or Footfall, and it is almost unheard of for their ships to actually traverse the unstable passage between the Calixis Sector and the Koronus Expanse. This is doubtless because of their access and understanding of the Webway, which allows them to travel great distances without risking transition into the warp. Travellers that delve deeper into the Expanse are far more likely to encounter Eldar, and rumours place the location of Craftworld Kaelor somewhere out beyond the Heathen Worlds, following a vast circuit which takes it along the edges of the halo zones and into places few Explorers are brave enough to tread. Like most Craftworlds, though, it remains secluded from the Eldar's dealings with other races and far from risk of direct attack, its inhabitants instead using the Webway to reach any region they desire and protect those worlds of interest to its Farseers.

Clans like the Crow Spirits and the Twilight Swords are believed to have bases throughout the Expanse, pirate havens where the Eldar can repair their vessels and horde their wealth. Though they are considered a fantasy by many, there are those who swear they have seen such places, sometimes built around the hidden remains of Webway portals in the deep asteroid fields of the Accused Demise or even under the noses of other aliens like the Orks of the Undred-Undred Teef. More than once, Imperial forces have launched endeavours with the aid of Rogue Traders to find these bases and destroy them, though to date no one has found definite proof of their existence, and even their general location remains largely a mystery.

PATHS OF THE ELDAR

The Eldar mind can be a fractious thing, given to extremes and excessive indulgences. In part, this was the root of the Eldar's doom and the seed that gave birth to the cults and the destruction of their empire. To harness this part of Eldar nature and use it for more productive means, the inhabitants of Craftworlds choose to focus their attentions and energies into specific areas, mastering a craft or vocation rather than let themselves be seduced by new sensations or distractions. These areas are known to the Eldar as Paths, each a specialised role which an Eldar devotes his abilities to and masters over the course of decades or even centuries of training and practise. These Paths can vary greatly within the society of the Craftworld, and encompasses all manner of trades and skills as well as all the arts of war. The Eldar Aspect Warriors are built around the Paths, and an Eldar that chooses to become an Aspect Warrior, such as a Howling Banshee or Striking Scorpion, does so at the expense of everything else, until they have complete understanding of their chosen means of combat.

SPIRIT STONES

The Paths are not the only practise born out of the death of the Eldar empire, and not the only means the Eldar have of protecting themselves—from both their own natures and the hunger of the Chaos god they unleashed. When an Eldar dies, his soul, like that of a human's, is cast off into the warp. While a human soul retains nothing of its living consciousness, an Eldar's mind is stronger both in will and psychic power and remains aware of its terrible fate. Thus death, and being lost to the warp and the inevitable attentions of Slaanesh, is the most terrible end an Eldar can imagine. To avert this fate all Eldar wear a polished gemstone on their breast known as a waystone, which has been psychically attuned to them in particular. When an Eldar dies, his or her spirit is then trapped in the waystone and carried back to its Craftworld where it becomes part of the wraithbone structure itself.

GHOSTS OF THE EXPANSE

Eldar endeavour to see every waystone taken from a fallen member of their race returned to their Craftworld and interred in the wraithbone vaults beneath its surface. In reality many are lost, either because there are no living Eldar to collect them or because they are stolen by greedy aliens or foes looking for trophies or profit. In the Expanse there is a shadowy facet of the Cold Trade which deals in such artefacts, and certain traders in Footfall pay high prices for a waystone with the spirit of an Eldar inside. These curios are usually smuggled back into the Imperium to adorn the mantle of some decadent noble lord or lady, but the power a waystone holds can be used for darker purposes. For a Rogue Trader, dealing in spirit stones is a dangerous game, and can draw the violent attention of both the Inquisition and the Eldar (who take a very dim view of those who would defile their dead), not to mention the inherent risks of dealing with the kinds of twisted individuals who would use the stones for dark magic and warp sorcery. Just a few stones can bring immense profit, though, and the lure of easy Thrones is often too much to ignore.

The suspended souls of a Craftworld are known as the Infinity Circuit and are one of the most closely guarded secrets of the race. Together the souls of the Infinity Circuit merge and mix over centuries as they exist in an eternal limbo accessible only by the most skilled and high-ranking of the Craftworld's Warlocks and Farseers. Though it is far from an ideal existence, it is still preferable to the fate which awaits them in the warp—an eternity as playthings in the hands of hungry daemons and vengeful gods. The Craftworld Eldar are not the only Eldar to use waystones, and both Corsairs and Exodites also use them as a means of protection from the warp after death.

As can be imagined, the Eldar go to great lengths to recover a waystone lost to them, so that the soul within can be properly saved from extinction or worse. Many a Rogue Trader unknowingly transporting "harmless xenos gems" has found his ship left as ruined metal as Eldar raiders seek out any rumours of such items with unrelenting prosecution.

THE WEBWAY

Eldar Craftworlds can only travel slowly through the void and are incapable of the warp travel used by the Imperium, and while Eldar vessels can and do make use of warp voyages they prefer not to, as it is dangerous, unpredictable, and still relatively slow. Instead, the Eldar use a far more sophisticated and mysterious method of travel across the stars and between worlds known as the Webway. Created long ago based on the teachings of the fabled Old Ones, it is a network of gates which link worlds, sectors, and stars from one end of the galaxy to another. Each Craftworld has its own gate, and therefore access to the network, which it uses to send men, materials, and even ships to far-flung destinations. The Webway also allows the Eldar incredible strategic freedom when fighting

their battles, and more than one Imperial or alien commander has been surprised by the sudden appearance or disappearance of Eldar troops on worlds or in systems considered secure.

It is said that the Webway can take a man or a ship to places no ordinary warp voyage can reach, secret and forbidden places known only to the ancient aliens. Since the Fall which claimed so many of their race, the Webway has become damaged, the psychic birth of Slaanesh tearing at its seams and cracking its gateways. Now the Webway has become a dark labyrinth of tunnels and portals where a wrong turn or pathway can lead a traveller to his doom, and only the most skilled Eldar can navigate it with something resembling safety.

ELDAR TECHNOLOGY

Unlike the crude and primitive mechanisms of the Imperium or the brutish and basic artefacts of lesser alien races, the Eldar have refined their technology to an almost perfect level. Using psychotropic engineering, nearly all Eldar weapons, armour, ships, and even cities are crafted from living plastics that respond to the user and are psychically attuned to the Eldar themselves. Crafted largely from a substance known as wraithbone, Eldar technology is usually as beautiful as it is deadly, with smooth lines, ergonomic grips and sights, and lightweight design which puts the bulky and crude tech of humanity to shame. Eldar weapons and armour are more grown than manufactured, often at the hands of skilled Bonesingers, the architects of the Eldar cities and masters of shaping the wraithbone. Each one is crafted for a specific owner and made with his or her body in mind. An Eldar's weapons or an Eldar's suit of armour are never as effective in the hands of a human as the Eldar it was created for, the imprinted psychic purpose lost to the blunt mind of mankind.

Ostensibly, the weapons of the Eldar mirror many of the effects of Imperial weapons, casting bolts of plasma or sending out rays of burning concentrated light. These are but cosmetic similarities, however—Eldar weapons are considerably more advanced in nature, and considerably more deadly.

CLOSE-COMBAT WEAPONS

Eldar make use of many kinds of close-combat weapons, from mono-edged chain blades to flickering, energy-wreathed swords and spears. Far more advanced than their human counterparts, each of these weapons is perfectly balanced and keen edged, reducing the user's reliance on raw strength and allowing unparalleled displays of finesse and skill at arms.

LAUNCHERS AND PROJECTILES

Eldar missile launchers use the same ancient principles as human weapons, though they differ in both size and design, and are almost universally lighter and easier to wield. They also use far more advanced projectiles, missiles with massive destructive force at a fraction the size of anything humanity can produce. Such is the difference in scale that Elder missile launchers rarely need to reload in battle, since their pods bristle with scores of ordnance.

LASER WEAPONRY

As with missile and plasma technology, Eldar long ago mastered the use of light as a weapon and created some of the most advanced and effective laser weapons known to the galaxy. From simple pistols and guns to rapid repeating cannons, laser weapons make up a significant proportion of the Eldar arsenal. One of the things which makes these weapons so effective is the perfection with which the Eldar craft their laser-focusing crystals, each one masterfully grown and polished to a flawless finish.

MONOFILAMENT WEBS

Many Eldar weapons, like the Shadow Weaver cannon, fire clouds of monofilament fibres. These terrible weapons enmesh the target in a tangle of almost-invisible wires which literally cut them to pieces, either where they stand or as they try to escape. Smaller weapons like the Harlequin's Kiss use similar principles, relying on coils of monofilament wire to cut their foes to bloody ruin.

PLASMA WEAPONRY

Unlike the extremely hazardous plasma weapons used by Imperial troops, the plasma weapons of the Eldar are both sophisticated and safe to use. Long ago the Eldar mastered the use of plasma technology, and this is no more evident than in their Star Cannons and similar weapons, which capture the fury of burning plasma in complex containment fields while never risking overheating or explosion.

SHURIKEN WEAPONRY

Ranging in size from pistols and rifles up to vehicle-mounted cannons and support weapons, shuriken catapults and casters work using the same basic principle. Each has a clip of solid core ammunition. When activated, the weapon then uses high-energy pulses to shave off a mono-molecular "shuriken" from the solid ammunition core and fling it down the barrel at hyper velocities, cutting down all in its path.

WARP-BASED WEAPONRY

Perhaps the most feared of all Eldar weaponry, these weapons manipulate reality itself, tearing holes in the materium and flinging foes into the madness and horror of the warp. Known as distort cannons, commonly called D-Cannons, and used primarily as support weapons (and by the silent and terrible Wraithguard), these devices represent some of the most advanced weapons used by the Eldar, and are the most horrifying to behold in action.

ELDAR ARMOUR

Wraithbone is also used to craft the armour of the Eldar, from the light psycho-plastic suits worn by the Guardians to the heavier yet still flexible plate version the Aspect Warriors wear in combat. Like their weapons, each suit of armour is fitted for its user, and responds to their psychic signature. Lightweight and allowing unrivalled freedom of movement, it reacts to attacks by hardening before a blow lands, then becoming flexible once more. Eldar do not just make use of personal armour; they also use a variety of sophisticated fields and cloaking devices on their persons, vehicles, and even their starships, ranging from energy barriers and repulsion auras to holographic mirages and distortion effects.

DARK REAPER

The warriors of the Dark Reaper temple are among the most feared and mysterious known to the Imperium. Personifying the aspects of their alien god as destroyer and harvester of souls, they are the long arm of death incarnate, reaching forth from any distance to claim its victims. The Dark Reapers specialise in delivering a shower of precisely-targeted death across the battlefields of the galaxy, often before their enemy knows it is under attack.

When the Eldar march to war, the Dark Reapers hold back behind the advancing lines, ready to lend fire support across a wide front. Any concentration of enemy infantry or light vehicles can then be broken up and pummelled into submission from afar and prepared for the inevitable assault of the Eldar advance. The power of the Dark Reapers is such that only the most heavily-armoured foes are even remotely safe. Many a Rogue Trader has been brought to ruin when a trusted retinue or expensive mercenary unit has descended into an alien landscape seeking xenos artefacts and treasures, only to be battered to pieces under the torrent of fire unleashed by a team of Dark Reapers. Often when Eldar dignitaries appear to conduct negotiations, an unseen Dark Reaper is watching over the proceedings to ensure the safety of their charges.

The Dark Reapers are ensconced in the heaviest armour available to Eldar warriors. The thick plates and reinforced strapping of their psycho-sensitive armour is adorned with weapon stabilisers and graceful limb supports. Those warriors in the Expanse wear gleaming black armour with bone accents; their helmets bear a signature skull motif, adorned with wide sensor wings to either side that house an array of targeting and tracking equipment.

Warriors of this temple carry the large Reaper Launcher into battle. It fires a fusillade of armour-piercing missiles with such a withering number of shells that an entire area can be saturated with a single salvo. Though smaller than the bulky Imperial shells, each Reaper missile round can pierce all but the strongest armour.

It is not entirely implausible that any number of spectacular attacks occurring across the Expanse may have been the work of Dark Reapers. Lord Veldire of House DeFrane, a Rogue Trader of dark reputation, was in the process of completing admittedly hostile negotiations with trapped Eldar dignitaries when his entire force was devastated by long-range cascading fire from a nearby tower. There were few survivors, and the attacking marksmen disappeared without a trace.

Dark Reaper								
WS	BS	S	T	Ag	Int	Per	WP	Fel
34	49	36	35	(10) 50	35	47	45	32

Movement: 5/10/15/30 **Wounds**: 18
Armour: Aspect Armour (All 7). **Total TB**: 3
Skills: Acrobatics (Ag) +10, Awareness (Per) +10, Climb (S) +10, Concealment (Ag) , Dodge (Ag) +10, Forbidden Lore (The Black Library, Xenos, The Warp) (Int), Intimidate (S) +20, Scrutiny (Per) +20, Silent Move (Ag), Speak Language (Eldar, Low Gothic).
Talents: Blind Fighting, Crack Shot, Hard Target, Heightened Senses (Sight and Sound), Jaded, Marksman, Mighty Shot, Nerves of Steel, Rapid Reaction, Rapid Reload, Sharpshooter, Sprint.
Traits: Auto-stabilised, Dark Sight, Unnatural Agility (x2).
Weapons: Reaper Launcher (275m; -/-/6; 2d10+2X; Pen 7; Clip 60; Reload 2 Full; Accurate, Reliable), Shuriken Pistol (30m; S/3/5; 1d10+2R; Pen 4; Clip 40; Reload 2 Full), xenos fighting knife (1d5+4R; Pen 2).
Gear: 2 cartridges of Reaper Launcher ammunition, 2 clips of shuriken pistol ammunition, xenos-crafted medikit, waystone gem, scanner, and helm (incorporating an Omni-Scope, re-breather, photo-visor, and micro-bead).

FIRE DRAGON

No Eldar Aspect Warriors revel more in destruction than those who serve the temple of the Fire Dragons. Taking as their totem the fierce, fire-breathing creatures of Eldar legend, they epitomise the brutal, wanton destruction of war. When called to arms their goal is the total annihilation of their foes to the exclusion of all else.

In battle, the Fire Dragons are tasked primarily with targeting enemy tanks and heavy installations. Wielding their terribly effective fusion guns, these elite warriors make a mockery of the heaviest vehicle armour and the most well-prepared fortifications. When these weapons are turned upon regular infantry, the results are even more horrific.

While these warriors excel as demolition experts, they may also be called in should a transaction or negotiation turn bitter; few protective armours, including the mighty Tactical Dreadnought Armour of the Adeptus Astartes, can withstand the concerted attention of the Fire Dragons.

Those Fire Dragons operating in the Expanse wear medium-weight armour, made from the same psycho-sensitive material used by other Aspect Warriors. It is usually coloured in fiery hues of muted reds and golds, then studded with rubies and carnelians. Their dreaded fusion gun allows them to bring this fire to their enemies, fuelled by the heat of the very stars themselves. These weapons are capable of reducing flesh and armour to molten slag in moments, and only its relatively short range mitigates its lethality in combat.

Fire Dragons are so skilled with their chosen weapons that they are capable of using the Eldar version of a melta-bomb at a distance. They are able to throw these explosives in such a way that the shaped charge is still effective, visiting focused devastation upon the target from a relatively safe distance.

Rumours abound of Rogue Traders who run afoul of Eldar dignitaries finding themselves stranded after the sudden and brilliant destruction of their transportation. Baron Torvald Binder, a Rogue Trader late of Faldon Kise in the Calixis Sector, found out firsthand how treacherous the Eldar can be when he arranged a meeting with a particularly elusive Autarch on the desiccated ruins of Jerazol. Binder left his Aquila lander in a sheltered vale for the meeting, only to have his negotiating position severely weakened with its fiery destruction moments later.

Fire Dragon

WS	BS	S	T	Ag	Int	Per	WP	Fel
36	49	36	35	(10) 50	35	47	45	32

Movement: 5/10/15/30   **Wounds:** 16
Armour: Aspect Armour (All 6).   **Total TB:** 3
Skills: Acrobatics (Ag) +10, Awareness (Per) +10, Climb (S) +10, Demolition (Int) +20, Dodge (Ag) +10, Forbidden Lore (The Black Library, Xenos, The Warp) (Int), Speak Language (Eldar, Low Gothic).
Talents: Crack Shot, Deadeye Shot, Hard Target, Heightened Senses (Sight and Sound), Hip Shooting, Jaded, Mighty Shot, Nerves of Steel, Quick Draw, Rapid Reaction, Sharpshooter, Sprint, Technical Knock.
Traits: Unnatural Agility (x2).
Weapons: Fusion Gun (20m; S/-/-; 2d10+9E; Pen 13; Clip 6; Reload Full; Reliable), Shuriken Pistol (30m; S/3/5; 1d10+2R; Pen 4; Clip 40; Reload 2 Full), xenos fighting knife (1d5+4R; Pen 2).
Gear: 2 clips of fusion gun ammunition, 2 clips of shuriken pistol ammunition, 2 melta-bombs (SBx2; S/-/-; 5d10E; Pen 10; Blast 2; can be thrown or placed in the standard fashion), 5 demolition charges, xenos-crafted medikit, waystone gem, scanner, and helm (incorporating re-breather, photo-visor, and micro-bead).

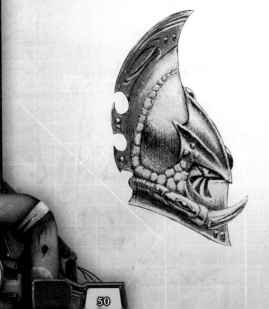

HOWLING BANSHEE

The alluring and mysterious Eldar warriors of the Howling Banshee temples style themselves after a fearful figure in Eldar legend, a terrifying harbinger of woe and death whose horrific shriek can separate body from soul. In battle, they embody the very essence of the swift and artistic fatal strike. To witness a Howling Banshee in melee is to see the personification of precision and efficiency in deadly combat.

The Howling Banshees fight like a choreographed team, gliding across contested terrain and striking the opponent's strongest infantry, sowing confusion and disruption. With their terrifying shrieks echoing across the devastated landscape, often their mere appearance is enough to cause an enemy commander to quit the battlefield.

The characteristic bodysuit armour of the Howling Banshee temple is lighter than other Aspect Warriors, allowing for more freedom of movement but retaining the characteristic flexibility and rigid defence when struck. Within the Expanse these warriors are almost always clad in dull ivories and subdued reds, reminiscent of bones and blood. Unlike other temples, they are exclusively female.

The Howling Banshees carry a shuriken pistol and the graceful Banshee power sword into battle, but their emblematic wargear is the Banshee Mask built into their helmets. This mask contains an array of psycho-sonic amplifiers that intensifies their distinctive battlecry into a devastating weapon. Crushing waves of sound and psychic force hammer the target, stunning and even causing horrifying neural damage to their foes. The xenos then step in for the kill; tavern tales in Port Wander speak of the Howling Banshees dancing about downed opponents, awaiting the perfect moment for the elegant final blow.

In the Koronus Expanse, the only verified sightings of the Howling Banshees have been in the retinues of Eldar commanders. They are used primarily as bodyguards in sensitive situations and in circumstances where the beauty of these primarily female warriors can pose a useful tactical distraction. Most traders dismiss tales of the Howling Banshees acting as assassins to eliminate key personnel or security assets as pure speculation and unsubstantiated gossip, designed to thwart profitable business ventures. Recently, rumours have intensified though of tall, lithe figures half-glimpsed escaping from fresh atrocities across the Accursed Demesne. Strange shrieks have been reported echoing down the halls of understaffed research and observations stations across the region, and entire lines of investigation have been halted as specialists scattered throughout the Expanse have died mysterious and often bloody deaths.

Howling Banshee

WS	BS	S	T	Ag	Int	Per	WP	Fel
52	41	34	31	(10) 58	38	47	45	38

Movement: 5/10/15/30 **Wounds:** 15
Armour: Aspect Armour (All 5). **Total TB:** 3
Skills: Acrobatics (Ag) +20, Awareness (Per) +10, Charm (Fel) +10, Climb (S) +30, Concealment (Ag) +10, Dodge (Ag), Forbidden Lore (The Black Library, Xenos, The Warp) (Int), Security (Ag) +20, Shadowing (Ag) +20, Silent Move (Ag) +10, Speak Language (Eldar, Low Gothic), Tracking (Int) +10.
Talents: Ambidextrous, Assassin Strike, Berserk Charge, Blademaster, Catfall, Combat Master, Counter Attack, Furious Assault, Hard Target, Heightened Senses (Sight and Sound), Jaded, Leap Up, Lightning Attack, Nerves of Steel, Quick Draw, Rapid Reaction, Sprint, Step Aside, Swift Attack, Two Weapon Wielder, Wall of Steel.
Traits: Unnatural Agility (x2).
Weapons: Banshee Power Sword (1d10+9E; Pen 6; Power Field, Balanced), Shuriken Pistol (30m; S/3/5; 1d10+2R; Pen 4; Clip 40; Reload 2 Full).
Gear: 2 clips of shuriken pistol ammunition, xenos-crafted medikit, waystone gem, scanner, and helm (incorporating re-breather, photo-visor, micro-bead, Banshee Mask†).
†Banshee Mask: When a Howling Banshee makes a Charge Action, she may choose to activate her mask as part of that action. The object of the Howling Banshee's charge must pass a **Difficult (–10) Willpower Test** or count as Surprised (even if possessing the Rapid Reaction Talent) and suffer 1 wound for every two Degrees of Failure; targets with Resistance (Psychic Techniques) may use this talent against the attack. Wounds received in this way ignore all armour except fully-enclosed helms with auto-senses. In addition, while the Howling Banshee wears her helmet, she gains the Disturbing Voice Talent.

SHADOW SPECTRE

"Honestly! Being spooked by a few unknown xenos skulking around near the dig site! That hill is hundreds of metres away, and at that range, a few infantry can hardly pose a threat to -"

-Final words of Alek Lir, Excavator Engine Driver

In recent decades in the Expanse, tales have spread of spectral forces that bring destruction down upon even the most well-prepared party, especially along the Rifts of Hecaton. Accounts have circulated of established Rogue Traders and their retinues destroyed by half-seen, floating figures garbed in pale robes. Imperial xenographers have now begun to connect these reports with the whispered tales of the Shadow Spectres, perhaps the least well-documented of the Eldar Aspect Warriors.

There are no substantiated sighting of these xenos warriors in the Expanse, and all reports seem more the result of poor quality amasec than reputable accounts. They tell of ethereal figures, floating gently in midair, that appear out of nowhere to unleash devastating firepower and then disappear again, leaving only burning wreckage behind. All tales agree that the more xenos present, the more deadly their impact, and few armours are proof against their wrath.

Scholars can only speculate regarding these warriors' armour and weapons, but much can be guessed from what the Imperium knows of Eldar capabilities in general. It can be assumed that the Shadow Spectres don light psycho-sensitive armour for battle, given the reports of their manoeuvrability and airborne movements. Most tales in the Expanse have them in soft grey or faded white armour, with pale streamers and tattered robes that trail behind them as they drift upon the wind.

Their weapon appears to be a laser rifle variant of the crystalline cannons found on their heavy grav-tanks, called a Prism Rifle. These smaller weapons share many traits with the Eldar Lasblaster, with the additional ability to somehow link together for more power and range; this may explain the wildly varying reports of the weapon's efficacy in combat reports. Shadow Spectres also appear to employ a form of mobility via xenos jet packs, given the reports of sustained flight.

Many xenos scholars hold that these aspect warriors represent the righteous vengeance of the unquiet dead. It is possible these warriors are used in other roles than battlefield terror weapons, but as of yet there are none who have lived to speak of them.

Shadow Spectre								
WS	BS	S	T	Ag	Int	Per	WP	Fel
40	49	31	36	(10) 59	38	46	48	32

Movement: 5/10/15/30   **Wounds**: 18

Armour: Aspect Armour (All 5).   **Total TB**: 3

Skills: Acrobatics (Ag) +20, Awareness (Per) +10, Climb (S) +10, Concealment (Ag) +10, Dodge (Ag) +20, Forbidden Lore (The Black Library, Xenos, The Warp) (Int), Pilot (Spectre Jet Pack) (Ag) +20, Scrutiny (Per) +20, Search (Per), Silent Move (Ag), Speak Language (Eldar, Low Gothic).

Talents: Catfall, Crack Shot, Disturbing Voice, Fearless, Hard Target, Heightened Senses (Sight and Sound), Jaded, Leap up, Marksman, Mighty Shot, Nerves of Steel, Rapid Reaction, Sharpshooter, Sprint, Step Aside.

Traits: Unnatural Agility (x2), Auto-stabilized, Dark Sight.

Weapons: Prism Rifle† (30m; S/-/-; 2d10+4E; Pen 12; Clip 60; Reload Full, Reliable), Shuriken Pistol (30m; S/3/5; 1d10+2R; Pen 4; Clip 40; Reload 2 Full), xenos fighting knife (1d5+4R; Pen 2).

Gear: Spectre Jet Pack (confers the Flyer 12 Trait), Personal Holo-field††, 2 extra prism rifle clips, 2 clips of shuriken pistol ammunition, xenos-crafted medikit, waystone gem, scanner, and helm (incorporating re-breather, photo-visor, and micro-bead).

†Prism Rifle Ghostlight: Multiple Shadow Spectres may use the sophisticated targeting matrices in their Prism Rifles, called Ghostlights, to combine their weapons for one devastating attack. All Shadow Spectres must spend their turn joining their weapons into this unified mode; when the final Shadow Spectre's initiative turn arrives, it fires the Ghostlight-aimed merged shot as it would make a normal shooting attack. Each prism rifle involved in the attack increases the Range of the attack by 30m and the Damage by 1d5+3.

††Personal Holo-field: These exotic devices break up the image of the wearer as he moves, making him difficult to target with any accuracy. Enemies suffer a –20 to all Weapon Skill and Ballistic Skill Tests when attacking the wearer. Additionally, when stationary the holo-suit user gains +30 bonus to any Concealment Tests.

STRIKING SCORPION

The Eldar of the Striking Scorpion Temple epitomise stealth and force in warfare. Exemplifying the strategies of clandestine activity and overpowering strength in battle, these highly trained close combat troops wield the dual weapons of force and surprise in service to their mysterious homeworlds.

On the battlefield, Striking Scorpions often infiltrate the enemy's rear and strike targets essential to strategic operations. Attacking from the shadows, they also target well-armoured enemy infantry, bringing them down in a welter of blood, spinning monomolecular disks, and roar of chainswords.

An Aspect Warrior is never seen without its distinctive gear, always in colours and designs that indicate the warrior's temple, craftworld, and rank. Striking Scorpions wear a heavy, plated suit of psycho-sensitive armour that conforms to their bodies' fluid motions but turns rigid when struck. Examples sighted in the Expanse have typically been a muted green and gold, perhaps to aid with stealth.

This uniformity extends to their weaponry as well. Striking Scorpions almost exclusively wield an Eldar Shuriken Pistol and Scorpion Chainsword, the latter a deceptively fragile appearing blade that issues a soft and menacing roar as it slices foes apart. The signature weapon of every Striking Scorpion, however, is the Mandiblaster. Located on either side of the warrior's helmet, these weapons fire in tandem to launch a fusillade of needle-like crystals in a rain of accelerating lasers, erupting in a devastating plasma discharge. Activated through a neural link within the armour, these weapons can bring a foeman to his knees before combat is even joined.

Most Aspect Warriors witnessed so far have been in service to high-ranking Eldar officials working for the Eldar Craftworlds rather than in full scale combat. These officials, both the mysterious Farseers and the more straightforward Autarchs, are often accompanied by retinues of Eldar warriors to serve them in their quests and dealings. There have been whispers, however, of these warriors being put to more direct uses.

Rumours have circulated for the last several years of Striking Scorpions infiltrating various installations, neutralising guards or outright destroying colonies that have unknowingly incurred the Eldar's wrath. On the fringes of the Expanse there are tales of mysterious armoured figures guarding seemingly innocuous ruins or ancient battle sites. Those who venture too close to learn more are rarely heard from again. Further rumours even accuse Striking Scorpions of eliminating various members of the Adeptus Mechanicus and other Imperial organisations during their travels through the Expanse.

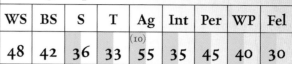

Striking Scorpion								
WS	BS	S	T	Ag	Int	Per	WP	Fel
48	42	36	33	55 (10)	35	45	40	30

Movement: 5/10/15/30 **Wounds**: 18
Armour: Aspect Armour (All 6). **Total TB**: 3
Skills: Acrobatics (Ag) +10, Awareness (Per) +10, Climb (S) +20, Concealment (Ag) +20, Dodge (Ag), Forbidden Lore (The Black Library, Xenos, The Warp) (Int), Interrogation (WP) +10, Intimidate (S) +10, Shadowing (Ag) +20, Silent Move (Ag) +20, Tracking (Int) +10.

Talents: Ambidextrous, Catfall, Combat Master, Crippling Strike, Double Team, Hard Target, Heightened Senses (Sight and Sound), Jaded, Leap Up, Lightning Attack, Nerves of Steel, Quick Draw, Rapid Reaction, Speak Language (Eldar, Low Gothic), Sprint, Two Weapon Wielder, Wall of Steel.

Traits: Unnatural Agility (x2).

Weapons: Scorpion Chainsword (1d10+6; Pen 3; Tearing, Balanced), Mandiblasters† (3m; S/-/-; 1d10+3 E; Pen 2; Clip 30; Reload Full, Reliable), Shuriken Pistol (30m; S/3/5; 1d10+2R; Pen 4; Clip 40; Reload 2 Full), 2 Plasma Grenades, 2 demolition charges.

†**Mandiblasters**: These may be used once per round as a Free Action and count as a single attack. They may also be used in Melee combat in the same manner as a Pistol weapon.

Gear: 4 clips of shuriken pistol ammunition, xenos-crafted medikit, waystone gem, scanner, and helm (incorporating re-breather, photo-visor, and micro-bead).

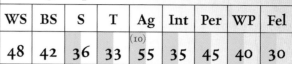

SWOOPING HAWK

Vengeance and retribution are constant themes within Eldar legends, and the root philosophy behind many Aspect Warrior temples. The temple of the Swooping Hawks takes as its totem a creature of great beauty and grace whose purpose within the mythology is to swoop down upon oath-breakers and traitors, and destroy them in a whirling display of retaliatory justice.

Across countless battlefields, the Swooping Hawks use their agility and speed to reconnoitre ahead of the main Eldar advance, often striking at the enemy's weakest points far behind the battlefront. Using their dreaded grenade packs and the saturating fire of their lasblasters, these warriors can threaten any enemy asset anywhere on the field. The Swooping Hawk's flight also allows him to access areas other, less mobile, searchers would find hard to reach. Oftentimes these xenos are seen soaring around the cyclopean ruins of ancient xenos civilisations, or delving deep into enormous craters and fissures in the crusts of dead, desiccated worlds. It is not known what these warriors are seeking, but only the most intrepid explorers would dare to investigate.

Aside from the impressive wings that sweep up from their shoulders, each made up of thousands of feather-like gravitic plates, the Swooping Hawks of the Expanse are often identified by their usual light armour of lacquered blues and turquoise, polished to a rich lustre with accents of white or bone, though other colours have appeared. Their primary weapon is the Lasblaster, a refined and elegant energy rifle far more efficient and powerful than the standard Imperial lasgun. In addition, the Swooping Hawks also carry small micro-grenade packs that can drop devastating explosives down upon their targets in mid-flight.

Though they lack the sheer power of some other temples, the Swooping Hawks' use of harassing attack from above makes them terrible foes. Explorers operating around the Accursed Demesne whisper tales of the fate of archaeologist Haddracke Cain. Cain and his band of servitors and debt-labourers landed on the dead world of Melbethe in search of xenos artefacts, but were ambushed while deep within the Abyssal Maze. Their path to safety became strewn with the bodies of their fallen, riddled with las-burns one by one as they fled. Cain's body was never found.

Talents: Catfall, Crack Shot, Hard Target, Heightened Senses (Sight and Sound), Jaded, Marksman, Mighty Shot, Nerves of Steel, Rapid Reaction, Sharpshooter, Sprint, Talented (Pilot) (Swooping Hawk Wings).

Traits: Unnatural Agility (x2).

Weapons: Lasblaster (100m; S/2/4; 1d10+3E; Pen 4; Clip 60; Reload Full, Reliable), Swooping Hawk Grenade Pack† (Range: special; S/-/-; 1d10+5X; Pen 4; Blast (3); Clip 10; Reload 2 Full, Reliable), Shuriken Pistol (30m; S/3/5; 1d10+2R; Pen 4; Clip 40; Reload 2 Full), xenos fighting knife (1d5+4R; Pen 2).

Gear: Swooping Hawk Wings††, 2 extra Lasblaster clips, 2 clips of shuriken pistol ammunition, xenos-crafted medikit, waystone gem, scanner, and helm (incorporating re-breather, photo-visor, and micro-bead).

†**Swooping Hawk Grenade Pack**: This small pack can be used to make one free attack per turn on any target flown over as part of the user's regular move, counting as being at Long Range.

††**Swooping Hawk Wings**: These allow the Swooping Hawk to glide safely down from any height and make an unlimited number of short jumps, doubling his Base Movement in any direction and ignoring all intervening terrain and obstacles. The Swooping Hawk must normally land at the end of his turn, but may use maximum power to gain the Flyer (12) Trait for up to five minutes before the wings require a minute to recharge.

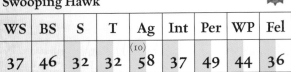

Swooping Hawk

WS	BS	S	T	Ag	Int	Per	WP	Fel
37	46	32	32	(10) 58	37	49	44	36

Movement: 5/10/15/30   **Wounds**: 15

Armour: Aspect Armour (All 5).   **Total TB**: 3

Skills: Acrobatics (Ag) +20, Awareness (Per) +10, Climb (S) +10, , Dodge (Ag) +20, Forbidden Lore (The Black Library, Xenos, The Warp) (Int), Pilot (Swooping Hawk Wings) (Ag) +20, Scrutiny (Per) +20, Search (Per), Silent Move (Ag), Speak Language (Eldar, Low Gothic).

WARP SPIDER

One of the strangest tales of the Eldar Craftworlds is of creatures living in the fabric of each vessel's infinity circuit, defending against warp incursions as they travel through the Empyrean. Referred to as Warp Spiders, these creatures are said to melt into the infinity circuit, travelling throughout the ships and appearing wherever they are needed.

The Warp Spider Aspect Warriors epitomise the doctrine of swift and aggressive defence personified by their totem creature. Much like the Warp Spiders of their itinerant homes, these xenos exemplify sudden and terrible attacks from unanticipated or unknown quarters, counterattacking with silent, vicious effectiveness.

In battle, the Warp Spiders use arcane technology to circumvent enemy defences or frontline formations to make precise, targeted attacks at the most significant threats. With their terrible weapons and silent materializations inside the most secure areas, they cause confusion and terror across a broad front of enemy advance, attacking where the foe is most vulnerable and disappearing before a counter strike can be mounted.

Warp Spiders operating in the Expanse are easily identified by their large suits of armour. Wide shoulders house the specialised Warp Jump Generator that allows them to make a mockery of any readied defence. Their primary weapon is the Death Spinner, which spools a ball of monofilament wire into a temporary suspension field at the muzzle of the weapon, then hurls the deadly snarl at its target. Although relatively short-ranged, the effect of these whispers of xenos razor-sharp wire is horrifying as it slices through entangled flesh and bone. The more the victim struggles to get free, the more the filaments cut deeper until there is little to recognise as the original target.

Their most unique wargear is their Warp Jump Generator. This arcane technology allows the warrior to make short, controlled warp jumps in a much more precise and predictable manner than any fielded by Imperial forces. There is still a deadly element of risk involved in each jump, however; there are reports of these warriors sometimes teleporting into solid objects or even other soldiers with spectacularly fatal results.

Warp Spiders in the Koronus Expanse have typically been sighted amidst Eldar enclaves that have recently appeared on unsettled planets, perhaps as part of exploration expeditions. As with many Aspect Warriors, while tales of increasing activity have multiplied, there are few concrete reports. Rumours of Rogue Traders isolated by the sudden and messy deaths of their entourages before negotiations with the xenos, or of personnel in various securely-locked observation stations across the Expanse brutally murdered at their work stations, are typical.

Warp Spider								
WS	BS	S	T	Ag	Int	Per	WP	Fel
45	48	35	37	(10) 52	35	48	48	30

Movement: 5/10/15/30   **Wounds**: 16
Armour: Aspect Armour (All 7).   **Total TB**: 3
Skills: Acrobatics (Ag) +10, Awareness (Per) +10, Climb (S), Dodge (Ag), Forbidden Lore (The Black Library, Xenos, The Warp) (Int), Pilot (Warp Jump Generator) (Ag), Search (Per), Security (Ag) +20, Silent Move (Ag) +10, Speak Language (Eldar, Low Gothic), Tracking (Int).
Talents: Catfall, Crack Shot, Deadeye Shot, Foresight, Hard Target, Heightened Senses (Sight and Sound), Jaded, Mighty Shot, Nerves of Steel, Quick Draw, Rapid Reaction, Sprint, Step Aside.
Traits: Unnatural Agility (x2).
Weapons: Death Spinner (30m; S/3/-; 2d10+8 R; Pen 0; Clip 20; Reload Full, Blast (1), Reliable), Shuriken Pistol (30m; S/3/5; 1d10+2R; Pen 4; Clip 40; Reload 2 Full), xenos fighting knife (1d5+4R; Pen 2).
Gear: Warp Jump Generator†, 2 cartridges of Death Spinner ammunition, 2 clips of shuriken pistol ammunition, xenos-crafted medikit, waystone gem, scanner, and helm (incorporating re-breather, photo-visor, and micro-bead).
†**Warp Jump Generator**: This wargear allows the Warp Spider to make small, controlled jumps through the warp, disappearing with a soft clap and reappearing many metres away with a rush of displaced air. The Warp Spider may double its Base Movement and ignore intervening obstacles. In addition, he may choose to push the mechanisms of the generator to move a further 2d10 metres with no penalty, but should the Warp Spider roll double ones, he must pass a **Hard (–20) Willpower Test** or disappear forever, claimed by the warp. Should he pass the Test, he may only take a Half Action next turn as he staggers back into the material universe.

WRAITHGUARD

Rarely seen by humans, the Wraithguard are thought to be very uncommon to the Expanse. Tales from distant battlefields, though, talk of these animated hulking constructs forming implacable waves, moving inexorably across blasted landscapes, ignoring all but the most potent attacks and bearing terrifying weapons capable of obliterating any man-made substance.

Xenographers believe the Wraithguard are almost never utilised except in times of desperate war. It is known that the Eldar look upon their deployment with sadness and regret. However, the most rapacious Rogue Trader would have to think twice about crossing any Eldar who is guarded by these tireless sentinels and their gruesome weapons.

Constructed from the same psychoplastic, bone-like material as the larger Wraithlords, Wraithguard share the same basic design, down to the beautiful gems scattered across the armour. Although not as powerful or implacable as a Wraithlord, the fear inspired by these lesser cousins is no less severe due to their unique weapon, the Wraithcannon.

The Wraithcannon uses unknown xenos technology to fire unstable matter, opening a small warp rift at the target in a wide variety of effects. These can range from messy implosions to a sudden and complete disappearance as the foe is dragged into the warp forever. No armour has ever been found to be effective against this weapon, and only its relatively short range and long recycle time offer any hope at all to forces arrayed against the Wraithguard. Its power source is unknown; all that can be determined is that once removed from its bearer, the weapon becomes nothing more than interesting but useless xenos sculpture.

In the Koronus Expanse, Wraithguard have been sighted acting as silent bodyguards for the most important Eldar psykers. When these dignitaries deign to meet with humans, they are often flanked by two Wraithguard standing eerily in the background. Few confirmed records exist of Wraithguard being used in actual combat, though this could be due to a lack of survivors in the case of such encounters. Despite this, enough rumours abound of the efficacy of their weaponry and their fearsome abilities to firmly establish their reputation.

†**Wraithcannon**: When a target is hit by a Wraithcannon, roll 2d10. This is the amount of Damage the Wraithcannon inflicts, ignoring Armour and Toughness. In addition, if the Damage result is 19-20, the target is destroyed outright, regardless of the number of wounds it possesses (Fate Points may be burned as normal). If the Damage result is 2-10, the target takes Damage and is teleported a number of metres equal to the result in a random direction (see page 248 of the ROGUE TRADER Core Rulebook).

If the target is teleported into the same space as another object, move the target into the closest available space; the target then takes 1d5 additional Damage, ignoring Armour or Toughness. As long as the Wraithguard is active, the weapon never runs out of power. If removed from the user, it falls silent forever.

NEW TRAIT: WRAITHSIGHT

Wraithguard and Wraithlords are vessels animated by the soulstones of long-dead Eldar warriors and can sometimes lose their focus in the mortal realm if left unattended. If there is a friendly Eldar psyker such as a Farseer or Warlock within line of sight of the vessel, then it may act normally. If the vessel is alone, however, then it must make a **Challenging (+0) Perception Test**. If successful it may act normally. Otherwise, it moves off in a random direction (see page 248 of the ROGUE TRADER Core Rulebook) at its normal Move (i.e., not running), and takes no other actions until the next Round when it may attempt another Perception Test.

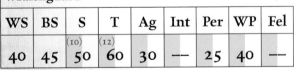

Wraithguard

WS	BS	S	T	Ag	Int	Per	WP	Fel
40	45	(10) 50	(12) 60	30	—	25	40	—

Movement: 4/8/12/24
Wounds: 20
Armour: Wraithbone (All 5).
Total TB: 12
Skills: None.
Talents: None.
Traits: Auto-Stabilised, From Beyond, Machine (5), Improved Natural Weapons, Size (Hulking), Strange Physiology, Unnatural Strength (x2), Unnatural Toughness (x2), Unnatural Senses (Sight, Sound), Wraithsight.
Weapons: Wraithcannon† (50m; S/-/-; Damage Special; Pen Special; Clip Special; Reload Special, Reliable), Fist (1d10+10 I; Pen 3).

WRAITHLORD

History abounds with tales of enormous statues magically coming to life in defence of primeval crypts or to avenge ancient wrongs. The image of these towering constructs shuddering into animation is ingrained in the human psyche, and explains the visceral reaction most Explorers have when first encountering the Wraithlords.

A graceful statue of Eldar manufacture, each Wraithlord is encrusted in glittering gemstones and scrolling alien glyphs. With a smooth, featureless head sweeping back from broad, fragile-seeming shoulders, the inhumanity of the gigantic statue is immediately evident. Their armour is decorated by arrays of gleaming precious stones, which Imperial scholars believe both power and guide these daunting constructs. A Wraithlord's seemingly delicate armour is nearly impossible to breach without the heaviest of military-grade weapons, and in battle they form mobile strong points, spearheading assaults as they lead elite Eldar warriors against their foes.

Sightings of Eldar Wraithlords in the Koronus Expanse are exceedingly rare. In skirmishes with security forces or indigenous feral enclaves, a Wraithlord dominates the encounter, presenting an almost unstoppable threat. Often local authorities have assumed these towering figures were mere statuary, only to be proven horribly wrong as they awakened with a fearsome array of weaponry and deadly purpose.

Wraithlords are entirely constructed of a psychoplastic, bone-like material. Those few specimens that have been seen in the Expanse are a uniform bone colour, with ribbons or streamers of light blue hanging from various points. They do not appear to be armed uniformly; various sightings have reported shuriken weaponry, flamers, an array of heavy weapons, and even massive swords wielded with alarming grace and skill.

The vast majority of humans in the Expanse have heard only the vaguest whispers about these towering devices. Most information comes from disabled Imperial Guard personnel who have left the Imperium behind for a life beyond Port Wander. These veterans tell soul-shivering tales of massive figures visiting destruction all around them with blasts of vile xenos power and sweeps of their huge blades. It is said that even the mightiest warriors of the Expanse should rethink their battleplans should they find themselves facing such a foe.

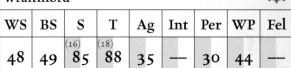

Wraithlord								
WS	BS	S	T	Ag	Int	Per	WP	Fel
48	49	(16) 85	(18) 88	35	––	30	44	––

Movement: 6/12/18/36   **Wounds:** 70
Armour: Wraithbone (All 13).   **Total TB:** 16
Skills: None.
Talents: Crushing Blow
Traits: Auto-Stabilised, From Beyond, Machine (13), Natural Weapons, Size (Massive), Strange Physiology, Unnatural Strength (x2), Unnatural Toughness (x3), Unnatural Senses (Sight, Sound), Wraithsight.
Weapons: Shuriken Catapult (60m; S/3/10; 1d10+4R; Pen 6; Clip 100; Reload 2 Full), Flamer (25m; S/-/-; 1d10+4E; Clip 10; Reload 2 Full), two Wraithlord Fists (each 2d10+18 I; Pen 10) or one Wraithlord Fist and one Wraithsword (2d10+22 E; Pen 10; Power Field, Balanced).
The Wraithlord can also choose a single weapon from the following options: Bright Lance (120m; S/-/-; 4d10+10E; Pen 13; Clip 35; Reload 2 Full), Eldar Missile Launcher (280m; S/-/-; 1d10+6E; Blast (3); Pen 6; Clip 5; Reload 2 Full), Scatter Laser (100m; -/-/12; 1d10+7E; Pen 2; Clip 120; Reload 2 Full), Shuriken Cannon (120m; S/-/10; 1D10+7R; Pen 6; Clip 60; Reload 2 Full), Starcannon (120m; S/3/-; 1d10+6E; Pen 12; Reload 2 Full).

AUTARCH

Compared to humans, the Eldar are incredibly long-lived. In the ancient past, this xenos race learned the dangers of unfettered indulgence, much to their loss, and so their society is now rigidly structured around the concept of the Paths of Life. Over the course of their long lives, Eldar choose many different Paths, not moving onto another until they have mastered their current choice. The Paths most familiar to Imperial scholars are the Paths of the Warrior and the Paths of the Seer.

Following the Paths of the Warrior, an Eldar choose one Warrior Aspect of their war god, Kaela Mensha Khaine, and pursue it to total mastery. Most of these warriors then put aside their armour and weapons and pursue a new Path, completely unrelated to warfare and violence. Rarely, an Aspect Warrior becomes lost on the Path, forever trapped within the pursuit of martial superiority; these warriors become the dreaded Exarchs, the leaders and high priests of the Warrior Temples.

Even rarer, however, are those Eldar that do not become lost along the Warrior Path, but rather develop a deep fascination with all elements of warfare and conflict. Often these Eldar master one Warrior Path only to leap to a different Warrior Path, mastering that as well. Frequently they master many different Paths, becoming utter experts in the Eldar arts of war. They develop a passion for wider tactical studies and elaborate strategic planning. Specialists and scholars in all forms of warfare and conflict, these Eldar attain the highest military rank for any of the Craftworld warriors: the Autarch.

On the battlefield these beings are the supreme commanders of the Eldar warhosts. An Autarch oversees every battle from its initial planning stages to the final, killing blow. Despite maintaining a wider view of events, the Autarch is still a fearsome warrior in his own right. Because of their background on the Path of the Warrior across many different temples, the Autarch is familiar with a dizzying array of weapons and wargear, and can easily adapt to whatever roles the current battle requires.

In recent experience within the Koronus Expanse, Autarchs have often served as the lead negotiators when Eldar consent to address humans directly. In larger parties led by the vaunted Eldar psychic leadership, these consummate warriors have been seen acting as military advisors to a Farseer on the rare occasions when these highest of Eldar leaders appear among humans. When Eldar parties venture off on their own, often seeming to pursue knowledge or artefacts of ancient providence, an Autarch often leads these small teams on particularly important missions. Sometimes an Autarch ventures forth on his own in search of information or historical data to further their military studies.

The armour and weapons of the Autarchs are second to none among xenos warriors already famous for wielding some of the most lethal equipment known to the Imperium. Protected from head to toe in intricately-decorated psycho-sensitive bone plate glittering with multi-coloured gems of dazzling quality, the Autarch is also warded by the most advanced personal forceshields to be found in the Expanse. The colour of this elaborate armour varies from one individual to the next, perhaps to denote rank, personal history, or

various possible allegiances. The training and status of the individual so armed and armoured is among the best and highest, as they are masters of almost every Eldar weapon or piece of wargear available.

Autarchs are thought to be rare in the Koronus Expanse, with confirmed sightings only within the last few decades. They seem to be guiding some sort of concerted effort, often investigating events or phenomenon or exploring various regions. Other times they attempt to negotiate or forcibly acquire the return or access to various artefacts of ancient xenos origin. Xenographers agree the Autarchs appear to have become more aggressive, acting openly to dissuade human exploration in certain systems even as they delve deeper themselves.

LEGENDARY AUTARCHS OF THE KORONUS EXPANSE

Among the most infamous Autarchs operating in the Expanse is Athanwe Illunivar, Scourge of Serator Prime. Terrible in his defence of the Eldar, their ancient sites, and their artefacts, Illunivar has brought many an inquisitive Rogue Trader to ruin. In recent history, Illunivar appears to have become a major guardian of sites and locations sacred to the Eldar, in particular throughout Winterscale's Realm.

Illunivar's complete destruction of the Rogue Trader Pietro Ironarm's flotilla in orbit around Valcetti's Salvation marked the intensifying of Eldar aggression in the region. Ironarm's flotilla had followed years of research that indicated the hidden location of an ancient xenos crash site on Salvation.

Soon after the first survey craft had landed, however, a wave of Eldar assault ships attacked, destroying all of the ships in orbit. The Rogue Trader's forces still on the ground were annihilated by an overwhelming force of Aspect Warriors, led by Illunivar himself, his Swooping Hawk Wings allowing him to descend upon Ironarm as he fled into the desert.

More insidiously dangerous is Autarch Nyathuren Kith-menras, the Wandering Scholar. Most often alone, she travels from planet to planet compiling a collection of all knowledge concerning ancient battles. All of her research revolves around mankind's earliest wars within the region, and she has amassed vast amounts of knowledge from that period, but she does not part with her wisdom lightly. To beg for her assistance is often more dangerous than to meet her in open combat. A Rogue Trader desperate enough to brave the Scholar's wrath, however, may seek out Kith-menras when all other options have been exhausted, but most come to regret the decision.

After years of fruitless searching for any news regarding his father's lost fleet, Rogue Trader Josef Sendaarin sought the guidance of Kith-menras. Though she proved almost as elusive as the information he originally hunted, Sendaarin finally tracked down the Eldar war-sage on the battlefield world of Zayth. None know the price she exacted from this desperate scion of a once-noble family, but he returned to Port Wander a broken man and has not spoken of his father since.

Most elusive and mysterious of all Autarchs, however, is Surinthiel Mihrendelas, the Collector. From Port Wander to the Rifts of Hecaton, from the Frozen Sisters to Aubray's Anvil, Mihrendelas can be found, tracking down rumours and legends of ancient xenos artefacts. Ruthless in the extreme, no price is too high and no sacrifice too great in the pursuit of these artefacts.

Several Rogue Traders have been utterly ruined through the acts of Mihrendelas, their only crime being in his way. Renowned Rogue Trader Bradfreid Craven was rendered all but destitute when he was stranded on Solace Encarmine, his ship destroyed in orbit when Mihrendelas created a new asteroid field from the planet's third moon in search of a legendary artefact. No one knows if the xenos was successful or not.

Autarch

WS	BS	S	T	Ag	Int	Per	WP	Fel
65	65	38	39	62 (12)	55	50	51	40

Movement: 6/12/18/36 **Wounds**: 38
Armour: Aspect Armour (All 9). **Total TB**: 3
Skills: Acrobatics (Ag) +20, Awareness (Per) +10, Charm (Fel) +20, Climb (S) +10, Command (Fel) +20, Deceive (Fel) +20, Dodge (Ag) +20, Forbidden Lore (The Black Library, Xenos, The Warp) (Int), +20, Inquiry (Fel) +10, Interrogation (WP) +20, Intimidate (S) +10, Logic (Int) +20, Pilot (Swooping Hawk Wings, Warp Jump Pack, Spectre Jump Pack) (Ag) +20, Scholastic Lore (Military) (Koronus Expanse) (Int) +20, Scrutiny (Per) +10, Silent Move (Ag) +10, Slight of Hand (Ag) +10, Tech-Use (Int).

Talents: Air of Authority, Ambidextrous, Assassin Strike, Berserk Charge, Blademaster, Catfall, Combat Master, Counter Attack, Crack Shot, Crippling Strike, Deadeye Shot, Disarm, Double Team, Dual Strike, Foresight, Furious Assault, Hard Target, Heightened Senses (Sight and Sound), Infused Knowledge, Into the Jaws of Hell, Jaded, Leap Up, Lightning Attack, Marksman, Master and Commander, Master Orator, Mighty Shot, Nerves of Steel, Precise Blow, Quick Draw, Rapid Reaction, Sharp Shooter, Sprint, Step Aside, Sure Strike, Total Recall, Talented (Pilot), Touched by the Fates, Two Weapon Wielder (Ballistic, Melee), Void Tactician, Wall of Steel.

Traits: Auto-stabalised, Dark Sight, Unnatural Agility (x2)

Weapons: Shuriken Pistol (30m; S/3/5; 1d10+2R; Pen 4; Clip 40; Reload 2 Full), xenos fighting knife (1d5+4R; Pen 2), 2 Plasma Grenades.

The Autarch may choose one of the following melee weapons: Banshee Power Sword (1d10+9 E; Pen 6; Power Field, Balanced), Diresword (1d10+3 E; Pen 6; Best Quality, Balanced, target must pass a **Challenging (+0) Willpower Test** or suffer additional 2d10 wounds ignoring Toughness or Armour, ignores the effects of enemy power fields), or Scorpion Chainsword (1d10+6 R; Pen 2; Tearing, Balanced).

He may also take one of the following ranged weapons: Avenger Shuriken Catapult (80m; S/3/10; 1d10+4 R; Pen 4; Clip 30; Reload Full; Reliable, Tearing), Death Spinner (30m; S/3/-; 1d10+6R; Pen 0; Clip 20; Reload Full, Reliable), Fusion Gun (20m; S/-/-; 2d10+9E; Pen 13; Clip 6; Reload Full, Reliable), Lasblaster (100m; S/2/4; 1d10+3E; Pen 4; Clip 60; Reload Full, Reliable), Reaper Launcher (275m; -/-/6; 2d10+2X; Pen 7; Clip 60; Reload 2 Full, Reliable), or Prism Rifle (30m; S/-/-; 2d10+4E; Pen 12; Clip 60; Reload Full, Reliable).

Gear: Personal Forceshield†, 2 clips of shuriken pistol ammunition, 2 extra clips of ammunition for his other chosen weapon, xenos-crafted medikit, waystone gem, scanner, and helm (incorporating re-breather, photo-visor, and micro-bead). He may also choose two additional items: a Banshee Mask or Mandiblasters, and either Swooping Hawk Wings, a Warp Jump Generator, or a Spectre Jet Pack.

†Personal Forceshield: In addition to their intricate armour, Autarchs rely upon personal forceshields for protection. An Eldar Personal Forceshield has a Protection Rating of 55. Each time the Autarch is attacked roll a d100. If the result is lower than or equal to 55 the attack is nullified and has no effect on the Autarch (although the attack may have an impact on the Autarch's surroundings or other nearby characters, such as weapons with the Blast quality). If the roll is a 02 or lower, the field has overloaded and ceases to function until it is recharged or repaired (requiring a successful **Very Hard (–30) Tech-Use Test**).

ELDAR WARRIORS

"Pitiless aliens all. Don't be fooled by their graceful movements or soft voices; they might look a bit like us but they are every bit as dangerous as an Ork and will kill you just as quick should it suit their purposes."

–Void Master Jaden Hoyt, *Winterscale's Lament*

At heart, every Eldar is a warrior. Throughout their long lives an Eldar treads many paths, most devoting themselves to one of the Aspects for a time and learning the arts of war much as they study their ancient lore or master the crafts and skills of their ancestors. In this manner all Eldar are warriors, each one gifted with a knack for battle learnt through long years of practice and the benefits of a lifespan far greater than that of a human. In fact, where a human only masters a single vocation, be it soldier, farmer, or scribe, an Eldar masters many and often to a degree which far exceeds a human's crude ability. Combined with advanced technology and the support of specialised troops in the form of the Aspect Warriors, Eldar warriors are an able and resilient foe with a methodical approach to war focused on cunning and guile as much as brute strength.

While Eldar appear similar to humans in their physiology, they are superior in many ways, not counting their extended life spans and the additional experience it affords them. Eldar are typically quicker and more coordinated than humans, and though they are not especially more resilient to injury, their speed coupled with their skill means they often avoid harm by giving their foes only a fraction of a second to react before they make their own attack, be it a well-aimed shot from a Shuriken Catapult or a swift stroke from a mono-bladed chainsword.

An Eldar's mind also works faster than that of a human's and this, in conjunction with their natural speed and grace, also allows them to work flawlessly when in combat groups, keeping avenues of fire open for their companions and providing interlocking arcs of covering fire while at the same time out-flanking and surrounding their foes before they are aware of the danger. Many Imperial Guard squads have been overcome by Eldar warriors in this way, the agile aliens taking the initative from the more sluggish human troops, sometimes even before the humans are aware they have been engaged. This manner of warfare is also central to the Eldar's mentality, for they shun the kind of attrition attacks, and blunt, bloody assaults so common to humanity and many of the aggressive xenos of the Expanse. For the Eldar, each warrior is a valued individual, precious to their Craftworld or clan and not simply a tally on a regimental roster to be expended like ammunition against the foe.

CRAFTWORLD KAELOR GUARDIANS

Eldar Guardians make up the bulk of the armies of Craftworld Kaelor and consist of citizens from every strata of its society. At some time or another almost all Eldar serve as a Guardian and don armour and take up arms for their people. For some, this may be a brief time in their lives (of course, brief for an Eldar may still cover many decades) before they move on to other Paths, either equally martial (such as in the service of one of the Aspect Warrior Paths) or more focused on the crafts and culture of their race. Unlike the

and usually seen as indistinguishable from other kinds of Eldar, Corsairs, while not common by any stretch, are the most frequently encountered Eldar within the Expanse. Any who travel beyond Footfall or systems clustered around the mouth of the Maw run the risk of encountering either Crow Spirits or Twilight Swords, clans known to ply the void throughout the Koronus Expanse. While they are often tarred with the same brush as human pirates or their own sadistic dark kin the Dark Eldar (a detail lost on most void-farers), the Eldar Corsairs of the Expanse do seem to possess a greater degree of honour and purpose than would seem necessary for simple piracy. Though this is a distinction mostly irrelevant to the crews of the ships which fall prey to them, it is one that certain captains and Rogue Traders especially have taken advantage of, making deals with Corsairs or even enlisting their aid against greater foes.

It is also a mistake to think of Eldar Corsairs as outcasts or pariahs from the Craftworld kin; they seem equally as invested in their race's survival, and just as interested in the pillaging of Eldar ruins or events which would adversely affect any of their people, whether they are part of their Corsair clan or not. This all contributes to make the motives of Eldar Corsairs mysterious at best, and while they might seem to be simple pirates, plundering alien and Imperial shipping alike, there are usually deeper motives at work. For all the seeming randomness of Corsair raids, they are usually following a well-laid plan with far-reaching consequences.

Eldar Guardian/Corsair

WS	BS	S	T	Ag	Int	Per	WP	Fel
41	43	30	30	(8) 47	35	40	40	30

Move: 5/10/15/30   **Wounds**: 12

Armour: Xeno Mesh (Head 3, Body 4, Arms 4, Legs 4).

Total TB: 3

Skills: Acrobatics (Ag), Awareness (Per) +10, Barter (Fel), Deceive (Fel) +10, Dodge (Ag), Evaluate (Int) +10, Forbidden Lore (The Black Library, Xenos, The Warp) (Int), Gamble (Int), Navigation (Stellar) (Int), Pilot (Jump Pack) (Ag), Medicae (Int), Silent Move (Ag) +10, Speak Language (Eldar, Low Gothic, Void Cant (Corsairs only)) +10.

Talents: Catfall, Leap Up, Quick Draw, Resistance (Fear, Psychic Techniques), Sprint.

Traits: Unnatural Agility (x2).

Weapons: Shuriken Catapult (60m; S/3/10; 1d10+4 R; Pen 6; Clip 100; Reload 2 Full; Reliable) or Shuriken Pistol (30m; S/3/5; 1d10+2 R; Pen 4; Clip 40; Reload 2 Full; Reliable) and Xeno–crafted Chainsword (1d10+5 R; Pen 2; Tearing) or (Corsair only) Lasblaster (100m; S/2/4; 1d10+3E; Pen 4; Clip 60; Reload Full; Reliable), 2 Plasma Grenades, 2 Blind Grenades, xenos fighting knife (1d5+4R; Pen 2).

Gear: 3 spare ammunition clips, Waystone gem, Jump Pack (Corsairs only), Void Gear† (Corsairs only).

†Void Gear: Corsairs wear specialised void gear as part of their armour, providing full life support as well as long-ranged vox and auspex. This also grants the user Flyer (12) in zero gravity.

common conscripts of humanity, Eldar Guardians come to their calling already armed with a wealth of knowledge of war and combat, which they then hone for many more years, focusing on the task as only the mind of an Eldar can. This means that every Guardian is an expert at his or her role within their squad and capable of taking on other tasks should the need arise. Eldar also possess more independence and initiative than human warriors, and while a human soldier has his individuality beaten out of him, the Eldar embrace their uniqueness and accept that the false ranks so loved by humanity are but titles which do not especially empower or elevate the man or woman who bears them.

The Eldar of Kaelor choose to become Guardians for their Craftworld because of a desire to protect their people, not because a far-off monarch or unseen authority has commanded it so. Where the forces of Craftworld Kaelor are found, their Guardians are never far off, and for an Explorer the presence of these Guardians is often the first sign of the Craftworld's involvement, representing a mobilisation of its populace to war. In this way, the Eldar Guardians are much the same across the galaxy as they are within the Expanse and represent the few remaining people of a dying race defending their species by turning to the ways of war.

CROW SPIRITS AND TWILIGHT SWORD CORSAIRS

The corsairs of the Expanse are Eldar which have chosen to turn away from the Paths embraced by their Craftworld kin and ply the void in tight-knit clans aboard graceful ships of solar sail and wraithbone. Considered pirates by the Imperium

AVATAR OF KHAINE

The Avatar of Khaine is the living embodiment of war and awakens in times of conflict to aid the armies of the Eldar against their foes. Filled with the spirit of the Bloody-Handed God, the Eldar's fearsome god of battle, the Avatar towers over the battlefield; a fiery juggernaut of death standing three times the height of a man and clad in molten armour of baroque and eldritch design. In one hand it clutches a flaming blade inlaid with potent runes of death while the other constantly drips blood from a clawed fist, a grim reminder of Khaine's own unquenchable thirst for carnage and bloodshed. The most terrible aspect of the Avatar are its eyes, burning pits of rage which embody the very soul of destruction and fill all those which gaze upon them with an inescapable terror and despair. To see the Avatar striding across the battlefield leaving a trail of flaming footsteps in its wake is to look upon the face of death and feel the ancient alien anger of the Eldar made manifest.

In battle, the Avatar of Khaine is usually only encountered at the head of a large host, leading scores of warrior Eldar and Aspect Warriors into the foe, using its size and strength to punch holes in the enemies' lines or smash their fortifications to pieces. Such is the power of the Avatar that its blade can cleave battle tanks in two or hack apart even fortress gates, leaving only scraps of molten metal in its path. Its flaming aura is equally deadly and those that stray too close to the Avatar feel the heat rolling off its ancient armour, hot enough to burn flesh and set hair and cloth aflame if its passes too near. Between the plates of armour, the skin of the Avatar appears as magma, deep reds and glowing blacks which move with the ponderous motion of lava as they ebb and flow across its body. Understandably, the Avatar suffers little from fiery weapons; their heat and destructive power wash across it like water might slide off human skin. Those who witness it and live have seen a true god of war

The Avatar only awakens in times of need, and dwells for most of its existence as little more than a hollow shell, devoid of life or purpose in the heart of an Eldar Craftworld. Each Craftworld has its own Avatar, cold and lifeless, seeming merely a charred suit of ancient armour kept within a sacred chamber deep beneath the wraithbone spires and domes. It is a tradition as old as the Eldar themselves that awakens the Avatar and brings vengeful life into its form so that it might march to war against the Eldar's foes. When war approaches, the Eldar choose a bold warrior from among their Exarchs, a member of their race with the will and courage to embody the Eldar's own skill at arms and thirst for victory. Known as the Young King, this chosen warrior is taken to the deep chambers where the Avatar's shell resides and in a secretive and complex ritual is given over, mind, body, and soul to Khaine, so that his essence might fill the Avatar with life and give it the rage and power to go to war. At the completion of the ritual, the Young King is completely consumed by the Avatar and ceases to exist as he once was, his essence instead mingled with that of the Bloody-Handed God and funnelled into the Avatar, giving it the strength and will to move and fight. Almost at once, the Avatar's armour begins to smoke and heat while the runes on its flesh and weapons begin to glow. Finally, the Avatar's eyes burst into flame and it rises from its tomb to answer the Eldar's summons and lead their

warriors against the enemies of the Craftworld. Once its task is complete, the Avatar returns to the Craftworld, its armour cooling and the fire fading from its eyes to sleep once more. Of the Young King there is no sign, his spirit extinguished by the ordeal, perhaps to sit at the side of Khaine himself like so many Young Kings before him or perhaps lost forever on the tides of the Immaterium, another soul spent in the Eldar's slow and inevitable decline toward extinction.

It is rare for Explorers to encounter the Avatar of Khaine, unless they go to war against the Eldar or accompany those who do. To its lament, the Imperium of Man has faced the Eldar many times during the long and bloody history of the two races, and records of the Avatar and the carnage it has wrought against humanity can be found by canny Rogue Traders among the accounts of the Administratum and the holy writings of the Ministorum. There are as many interpretations of the Avatar as there are accounts, however. Explorers are likely to find that many conflict, some likening it to a mechanical engine of war while others claim it is a daemon of battle given the form a giant Eldar warrior. What they all can more or less agree upon is the effect the Avatar has upon those Eldar which march beside it, boosting their courage and filling the normally fragile aliens with a deep and violent lust for war. It is also agreed that the creature seems to be the very essence of fire itself, its blood like magma and its flesh hewn of burning rock. While there are rare instances where it has been felled in battle, the flame vanishing from its flesh and the light going out of its blade, it always seems to return, rising again like the anger of the Eldar themselves to once more stride into battle.

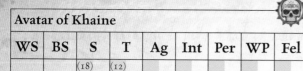

Avatar of Khaine

WS	BS	S	T	Ag	Int	Per	WP	Fel
86	47	(18) 60	(12) 60	55	35	40	65	30

Movement: 8/16/24/48   **Wounds**: 145

Armour: Molten Armour (All 11).   **Total TB**: 12

Skills: Awareness (Ag), Dodge (Ag), Intimidate (S).

Talents: Blade Master, Combat Master, Crushing Blow, Furious Assault, Lightning Attack, Swift Attack.

Traits: Daemonic, Fear (4), From Beyond, Size (Massive), Stuff of Nightmares, Unnatural Strength (x3).

Weapons: The Wailing Doom† (3d10+20 R; Pen 9; Power Field or 20m; S/—/—; 5d10+8 R; Pen 13; Clip unlimited).

Gear: None.

†The Wailing Doom: When the Avatar awakens, it takes up a fearsome and terrible weapon known as the Wailing Doom. This weapon can take many forms, but most often takes the shape a towering blade or multi-spiked spear, the surface glowing with potent psychic energies. In addition to being able to punch through most armours with ease and kill multiple foes with broad sweeps or powerful thrusts, the Avatar can use the Wailing Doom to focus its terrible rage into a bolt of searing energy, literally melting enemies where they stand and turning vehicles into piles of smouldering slag metal.

Special Rules

God of War: The Bloody-Handed God is the very essence of war for the Eldar and the spirit of one of their gods made flesh. For an Eldar warrior, the mere sight of the Avatar is enough to fill his heart with courage and a steely determination to defeat his foes. Any Eldar in the presence of the Avatar of Khaine which can draw line of sight to at least a part of it gains the Fearless talent. This talent remains in effect as long as they remain in the presence of the Avatar.

Molten Armour: Fire and heat surround the Avatar and pour off its ancient armour like lava from a rent in the earth. Those that stray too close to the creature are burnt and weapons which rely on fire themselves are largely ineffective against it, their beams, sprays, and blasts washing off it like smoke striking water. Creatures striking the Avatar in melee or standing within 2 metres of it must make a **Challenging (+0) Agility Test** or suffer 1d10+3 E Damage and catch Fire (see page 260 of the Rogue Trader Core Rulebook). In addition, weapons which cause Energy Damage have no effect on the Avatar unless exotic and unusual in nature (as determined by the GM).

Immortal Essence: The Avatar of Khaine cannot be truly killed; even should its form be broken and destroyed, as long as its Craftworld endures, it can be awakened to return again and again. When the Avatar is destroyed, its body burns to nothing as its essence is returned to its Craftworld; therefore its body, armour, or weapons cannot be taken by its foes.

ELDAR ADVENTURE SEEDS

Eldar have never been a common sight in the Koronus Expanse, aside from the various well-known Corsair Fleets. Recently, however, Craftworld Eldar began to take a more active interest in the region. There are reports of new enclaves on uninhabited worlds, and more disturbing still is their association with tales of the sudden destruction of several human colonies. Eldar luminaries seem to be combing the Expanse for information and ancient relics.

The Eldar now entering the Koronus Expanse seem to be pursuing a wide-ranging list of topics from the recent recovery of the *Gaunt Triumph* to collections of ancient mythical stories and legends from across the region. Many are thought to hail from Craftworld Kaelor, and the violent and capricious nature of these newcomers are the cause of growing concern among the human leaders of the Expanse, not leastwise because human agencies can only guess as to what they truly seek.

Despite the fact that full-sized Eldar armies have not yet been unleashed upon the Expanse (or at least none have survived to report such instances), large parties of these xenos warriors have started to take a more aggressive stance against humans in a variety of situations. Many research and observation stations have been targeted, as well as libraria and other repositories of knowledge. There have been reports of their involvement in kidnappings, artefact thefts, and outright assassinations. Though none of these accusations have been verified, tensions continue to rise.

Many representatives of various Rogue Trader cartels and other Imperial organisations have had violent run-ins with parties of Eldar, most commonly when investigating phenomena and rumours of ancient relics, particularly along the edges of the Rifts of Hecaton. Eldar forces are suddenly limiting access to regions that had been relatively safe for human exploration for centuries. These disputed zones range from the systems of dead worlds such as Illisk to verdant planets like Choir.

Given the rapidly-evolving situation with the Eldar, Rogue Traders and their representatives are far more likely to encounter them than in the past. Commonly, the Eldar may try to stop Rogue Traders from accessing ancient ruins or lost xenos technologies. In other rare circumstances, the Eldar might alternatively attempt to elicit their assistance in recovering an artefact or gaining information. A Rogue Trader may also inadvertently stumble upon an Eldar mission to secure an artefact, person, or location, and risk attack as the xenos strive to keep their actions a secret. In all circumstances there is only one certainty, and that is none may ever assume to fully know the true motivations of the Eldar.

The following are some adventure ideas featuring the Eldar operating in the Expanse, and how these ancient and powerful xenos can interact with Explorers.

ASSISTANCE

While daring the Processional of the Damned in pursuit of a legendary lost ship, the Explorers encounter a small Eldar vessel that demands they turn around and leave the area. The Eldar vessel is on the edge of the system and seems to be mounting a recovery operation in the general area of the lost ship. The Explorers may desire to confront the xenos, perhaps discovering first hand the firepower even the smallest of their ships possesses. They may instead bargain with the xenos, perhaps to offer assistance for a price or promise of safe passage. Covertly discovering what the Eldar are seeking would be most profitable.

XENOS VS XENOS

Searching a sprawling xenos ruin on Naduesh for a fabled artefact, the Explorers are ambushed by the Children of Thorns as they attempt to leave the cyclopean labyrinth. Just as things look bleakest, another war party of Eldar descends to confront both parties. Hopes of escape seem to rest with winning the newcomers over to the Explorers' side, but history is rife with tales of the price for Eldar aid.

ARTEFACTS

Deep within the treasure hold of a derelict ship, the Explorers find the remains of a large xenos statue of unknown origin. Amidst the shattered bone-like stone lie several striking gemstones of ethereal beauty and warmth. These could be the remains of a Wraithlord and its controlling waystones. An Eldar vessel has recently entered the system, known to be seeking out xenos artefacts. The opportunity for profit could be immense in their return, or the wrath of the Eldar could be even greater should the xenos doubt how they were obtained.

PERSON OF INTEREST

The Explorers are approached by a mysterious woman willing to pay a vast amount for passage to Port Wander. Before departure, though, they are intercepted by an Eldar representative demanding the surrender of the woman, accused of assassinating a prominent Eldar leader. The xenos is willing to pay handsomely for her return, if he can be convinced that the Explorers were not involved. If they refuse he swears they shall regret their action. Surrendering a human over to the xenos may harm their reputation, but the Explorers may be able to work both sides of the deal and come out doubly ahead, should they live through it.

THE ORKS

"Of all the races I have battled throughout the galaxy, the Ork is the hardest to comprehend. They wage war with machines that should not work, care little for strategic gains, and are just as likely to slaughter each other as the enemy. How does one battle an enemy that defies all logic?"

–Rogue Trader Varnael Larik

I first saw the amazing fighting prowess of an Ork some years ago in the fighting pits of Rexxis VII. Alberse had conducted another of his deals deep in the catacombs of the arena, and after its completion we headed topside for some "light entertainment." The crowds were in a frenzy as combatants slaughtered one another. A massive Ambull had fought through three other opponents and the betting was furious that it would kill its next victim just as quickly. When the gates opened, a hulking Ork stepped into the arena and let out a mighty roar at his enemy. Cries of joy erupted from the masses as the challenger took his place in the pit. The Ork had very little armour and carried a huge axe at his side. I had heard that these weapons were called "Choppas" and were a favourite of the greenskin warriors.

The Ambull dove at the Ork with its claws open, but the Ork leapt to the side and avoided the hasty attack. He (or it, as I have no idea if the Orks have genders) lashed out with his axe and delivered a crushing blow to the beast's side. It was not daunted by the hit and quickly turned to continue its assault. The Ork simply bellowed another challenge and moved to intercept the creature.

It was the next exchange of blows that showed me the terrible might of the Ork menace. The Ambull lashed out and caught the Ork squarely, nearly severing the thick right arm. Such a blow would surely bring anyone (save maybe a mighty Space Marine) to their knees. The Ork was seemingly undaunted and brought the axe down in an overheard swipe. He split the skull of the Ambull in two, then swung again, cleaving the dripping head clean away.

As it stood there in the pit with his arm hanging only by a thin cord of muscle, the Ork bellowed out bestial cries, presumably demanding new combatants to fight. The crowd's cheering was even louder, revelling in the brutality he displayed. It was then I knew that fighting these beings would be quite a challenge, something I unfortunately soon found to be very true...

GREENSKINS IN THE EXPANSE

Ancient myths say that Orks were amongst the first xenos race that mankind encountered in the stars. Whether this is true or not, the Orks of the Koronus Expanse have inhabited that vast region of space since time immemorial. Many throughout the millennia have debated their origins in the Expanse, but all agree on one thing: the Ork menace is growing and can pose a serious threat to humanity's rightful presence in the Expanse.

One myth relates the arrival of a massive space hulk known as *The Price of Vengeance*, containing an early colony ship lost from a group of human worlds eons ago. The hulk was host to all manner of xenos, including thousands of Ork raiders. Veterans of many scores of previous assaults in other sectors, these greenskins spread across the Expanse and made it their new realm. Most xenologists hold this myth as more wishful thinking than fact, allowing for the possibility that the Expanse was once more of a paradise before the green tide washed over it, and that perhaps it might one day return to that state.

Another ancient legend recounted by some Ork Freebooterz says that the Brain Boyz, the mythical diminutive progenitors of the Ork race, populated parts of the Expanse with their kind before vanishing from the galaxy. This tale claims that the Brain Boyz of in the Expanse vanished into the Rifts of Hecaton, there to pursue an ancient agenda that would bring great glory to the Orks. Imperial Scholars place little faith into this legend, but it continues to worry many Ordo Xenos agents.

Whatever their origins, the Orks in the Expanse have been a constant source of conflict and strife to the Imperial agents who explore this wealthy region of space.

UNDRED-UNDRED TEEF

The main Ork Empire in the Expanse is known as Undred-Undred Teef, a collection of roughly a dozen systems located within the Accursed Demense. In addition to the four worlds commonly known to explorers, two others areas have recently gained notoriety in that region due to the efforts of especially daring Rogue Traders.

Vorgrat

The world of Vorgrat is a rogue moon that long ago lost its planet. The massive asteroid and debris field surrounding Vorgrat is believed to be the remnants of this world that was destroyed long ago in some epic cataclysm. This moon contains great stores of metals as well as a rare mineral compound known as Kellistraal. This compound is usually found only in the Calixis Sector and has been adapted for use in plasma drives, weapon cores, and a variety of other devices. The Orks have set up massive mines to harvest the metals and minerals from the world for their ships and weapons. The chief Mek Boy of Warlord Morgaash, Brackslik Metalhands, has been put in charge of this operation. Through his experiments with Kellistraal he has determined that it can boost the range of Kustom Force Fields a great deal, and he is working to refine this technology even further for use in Ork ships.

Madrok's Rok

In the asteroid field surrounding Stompgit, there is a massive Ork vessel known as *Madrok's Rok*. Finding this installation is not easy, as the outer shell of the Rok does not show any of the structures contained deep within. This huge free-floating space station is home to the Ork Freebooter Kaptin Madrok. He maintains this hidden presence near the stable warp routes of Stompgit to launch his raids elsewhere in the Expanse, and also likes to keep his eyes on "da kompitishun" in the area. Madrok has a rather sophisticated (for an Ork) system of navigating the asteroid field and keeping his Rok hidden from the other Ork ships in the area.

ORK PHYSIOLOGY

The standard Ork stands approximately six to seven feet tall, with a heavily-muscled but hunched posture, and its weight is over twice that of a man. These xenos have green skin that is extremely thick and tough. Most are covered in old battle scars and they wear these with a great deal of pride. They are also very smelly and unkempt; the only cleaning an Ork is likely to receive is from a shower of flamer blasts.

Studies of Orkoid cells reveal that they contain fungal and algal strains, which in turn makes them very resilient. Many Orks have been hacked to pieces only to have their Mad Doks stitch them back together again. As an Ork ages, he also slowly becomes larger and stronger. This process seems to be accelerated in some Orks, leading to mighty Warbosses and Kaptins arising who can defeat all challengers.

It is believed that Orks reproduce by spores and do not have a standard reproductive cycle. This is also believed to be why infestations are so hard to eradicate; spores left behind after the menace is defeated can result in new creatures emerging years after the original Orks were killed.

ORK "KULTUR"

Ork culture is based on the simple principle that the strongest rule. Those who would rise to the top must battle their way over their challengers if they hope to keep the masses in line. Orks live to make war throughout the galaxy and most of their societal norms and customs revolve around this principle. When a particularly strong Ork rises to power, other Orks from all over the planet (and surrounding worlds) are drawn to this leader by the promise of battle.

Orks seem to care little for material gain (with the exception of bigger guns and implements of battle) and simply live to wage war. However, Orks do have a system of currency and a primitive economy. Ork wealth is determined by "teef." The entire Ork economy revolves around teeth as currency. The teeth must be the large, tusk like teeth of Orks; human teeth are considered too puny to be of any value. The fact that Orks shed and regrow their teeth every few years means that there is a constant stream of wealth inside an Ork settlement. Even the lowliest Ork always has some wealth as he can simply pluck money straight from his own mouth if needed—assuming that a bigger Ork has not already done so.

CLANS, TRIBES, AND FREEBOOTERZ

Orks are broken down into clans and from there they are further subdivided into Boyz and Oddboyz, based on their role in the clan. The clans often come together for battle and it is not uncommon to see Orks of many different clans side by side on the battlefield. Clans are different from tribes in that a tribe is simply a group of Orks who live in the same geographical area, while clans embody a collective mindset and series of beliefs.

There are six major Ork clans found all across the galaxy. Imperial researchers remain puzzled how these clans have each spread so far and wide and yet maintained a sense of identity. Many hypothesise Orks possess a form of genetic "racial memory" containing their knowledge of technology, beliefs, and customs. The six clans commonly found in Ork "Kulture" are the Bad Moons, Goffs, Snakebites, Evil Suns, Deathskulls, and Blood Axes. The Orks of the Expanse have ties to these common clans, but due to the relative isolation that the Expanse provides, they adapted to this region differently.

A final group of Orks are the Freebooterz, wandering pirates and raiders who have adopted a different life than many of their terrestrial brethren and live out amongst the stars. They are skilled in ship-based combat and tend to adopt garish outfits mimicking naval garb seen on many other races. Freebooterz can sometimes be found in the employ of less scrupulous Rogue Traders who do not have the usual Imperial intolerance for xenos races.

ORK TECHNOLOGY

Adepts of the Machine God have long been fascinated and horrified by the arms and equipment of the Ork race. Simply put, Ork technology should not work. Studies of various captured weapons have killed many Tech-Priests as they tried to unlock their secrets. These deaths did not result from some insidious trap or safeguard, but from the weapon blowing up when in the hands of a non-Ork.

The crude nature of these assemblies of weapons and vehicles show that the Orks possess an uncanny ability to make things work no matter the technological base, using only what they refer to as "Orky No-Wots." They could never explain why they know how to make a shoota work, it just does. Mechanisms created by Ork Mek Boyz defy all logic on power sources, proper containment and shielding, and even means of locomotion.

No matter their location, Orks almost everywhere seem to possess similar vehicles, weapons, and armour. They may take on a variety of forms and appearances, but the basic functions and abilities of the technology are the same. Xenos Biologis savants relate tales of Mek Boys deep in the Expanse fabricating Kustom Force Fields that are functionally identical to ones found far away in the Segmentum Pacificus. This continues to further the theories of racial memory and genetic knowledge in the Orks.

CROSSING THE VOID

Orks utilise a large variety of ships to cross the great interstellar distances of the Expanse. Most Ork vessels such as the sport some kind of totem or decoration on the front to give it the appearance of a massive Ork head. Kill Kroozers, a common ramshackle Ork voidship, has this manner of prow. These vessels can be massive, and are classified as Battle Kroozers when they have reached a size in excess of thirty megatonnes or more.

Other Ork vessels found alongside the Kroozers include gunships and other escorts. The Orks utilise a small boarding ship known as a Brute Ramship to breach the hulls of their enemies, though most Orks are happy to ram any type of ship into their foes. Orks also use asteroids as warships, hollowing them out and adding in engines and weaponry so that they are capable of warp travel. These "Roks" make for extremely durable vessels, and can easily be created in each new system the greenskins attack to replace any losses they suffer.

Another method of travel favoured by the Ork race is via space hulks. These titanic amalgamations of numerous ships, asteroids, and other debris become mobile colonies for Ork raiders. When a space hulk is found by a tribe of Orks, they quickly board the vessel and begin scavenging all they can from the ship to fuel their war efforts. Mek Boyz begin fabricating weapons, armour, and vehicles almost immediately as metals and other valuable assets are salvaged and stockpiled in areas of the hulk. Often completely new ships can even be built inside the huge holds or caverns inside of massive space hulks.

A space hulk usually has no means of propulsion of its own. It simply travels on the flows and eddies of the warp, on a journey across the void. Industrious Meks and Weirdboyz can sometimes assist in moving a space hulk into a warp rift or other passage, but this is by no means an exact form of travel. This suits the Orks just fine, as it appeals to their sense of adventure and conquest—they feel that a space hulk is a gift from their gods Gork and Mork, taking them to new and exciting battles. A space hulk is often accompanied by fleets of Kroozers and other escort vessels as it moves through the Expanse taking it to its destination. When an Imperial world detects the arrival of a space hulk, it often sends waves of panic throughout the sector. There are many well known legends and rumours of the destruction such a vessel can bring, and many are based in horrific fact.

RED ONES GO FASTA

When it comes to transportation, Orks expect three things from their vehicles—speed, noise, and big guns. Orks often travel into battle hanging from the side of crude vehicles known as Trukks. These transports belch thick smoke as they cross the landscape, their raucous engines revving loudly as they go. An Ork Trukk can take on many different appearances, but all usually sport an open crew compartment in the back where Ork Boyz can quickly disembark for battle. The faster the Boyz can get into the action, the better the Trukk, in their opinion.

In addition to the common Trukk Boyz, an entire Clan of Orks dedicates themselves to battle from atop vehicles: The Evil Sunz Kult of Speed. This Clan specializes in warfare astride mighty warbikes, atop battle-scarred Wartrakks, or inside Warbuggies ready to explode across the battlefield (or sometimes just explode). These vehicles continue the Ork custom of defying logic in their construction; they look like they might fly apart at any second under the forces exerted upon them. This trait is also true of Ork starships and flyers, and many Speed Freaks find that piloting voidships is the ultimate expression of their way of life; many have secured themselves the coveted role of voidship pilot for Freebooter Kaptins across the Expanse.

The Orks of the Kult of Speed are able to achieve amazing speeds with their equipment due to what the Orks consider a must for most of their vehicles—a Red Paint Job. In their culture, Ork Boyz simply believe the red ones "go fasta."

There is no rationale as to why this should be true, but far too many Imperial Commanders have seen it first hand on the battlefield for it to be ignored. Many theorise it is simply that the better-constructed vehicles get this special paint, but then why would they slow down when the paint is scorched away? Common myth in the Expanse has it that it is the manifest will of the massed Ork consciousness. Orks are insistent that it be true, and thus it becomes so, despite any mechanism for it to happen other than their sheer determination. Despite ongoing investigation by the Adeptus Mechanicus, no definitive conclusion has been reached.

ORK WEAPONS AND EQUIPMENT

In a race dedicated to war above all other things, it is not surprising that Ork weapons are especially effective, and like their users, they are brutal in the extreme. Massive axes, huge guns, and insane technology are all a part of an Ork Warband on the field of battle, where Mek Boyz utilize their knowledge to create a large variety of weapons for the Boyz. The one thing they all have in common is a propensity for massive amounts of death and destruction.

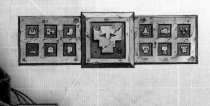

ORK RANGED WEAPONS

Despite their reputation for personal combat Orks also use a variety of ranged weapons, not only for their destructive power but also the sheer volume of noise they can generate.

Big Shoota

A larger version of the basic Shoota, this weapon is clearly superior in the Ork mind as it is bigger and thus better. The longer range and heavier firepower make it a popular weapon for Da Boyz.

Deffgun

Deffguns are cobbled-together shoulder-mounted weapons favoured by Ork Lootas, who pillage battlefields for as many different guns, ammo sources, and other weaponry as they can find, mashing them together indiscriminately to create these dangerous long-range guns.

Grot Blasta

Gretchin (or Grots) try to impress their larger Ork brethren with loud and noisy weaponry. A Grot Blasta is similar to a blunderbuss or other primitive slug thrower and is usually filled with nails, scraps, and other debris to fire a lethal burst of shrapnel at a foe.

Rokkit Launcha

An Ork Rokkit Launcha is a crude stick with a simple trigger on it to fire off the missile attached to the end. The stick is usually (but not always) long enough for the rokkit to blast free without setting the Ork on fire.

Scorcha

The pyromaniac Orks known as Burnas have created a very dangerous weapon that is both a flamethrower and powerful close-combat weapon. The Scorcha's long handle contains a nozzle at the end to distribute the highly combustible material in great gouts of flame. Conversely, it can be used as a short-range cutting instrument in the Ork scrapyards by focusing the flame into a tight, torch-like end. Burnas often use this setting in close combat to slice apart their opponents.

Shokk Attack Gun

Perhaps the most insane weapon that a Mek has ever created, in spite of the strength of this claim, is the Shokk Attack Gun, which opens a small tunnel through warp space. The Mek must have a supply of Snotlings to use as "ammunition," as well as a Runtherd to keep them lined up. He then sends a band of Snotlings through the force-field-protected tunnel and out the other end. One end of this tunnel is in front of the gun, while the other end is wherever the operator aims. When the Snotlings emerge from their journey through the warp, after being assailed all along the way by daemons and other horrors, they are crazed and in a state of mad frenzy. They immediately begin attacking anything they see with their teeth and claws, and can deliver amazing amounts of damage to enemy vehicles and troops. A crazed Snotling suddenly appearing inside a suit of power armour is not something to relish, as the famous Rogue Trader Cornelius Harrool could attest—if one could get him to ever admit it happened.

If triples are rolled for Damage with the Shokk Attack Gun, it has misfired in a catastrophic and possibly comical fashion! Roll once on **Table 3-1 Shokk Attack Gun Misfires** and resolve that result instead of the normal damage.

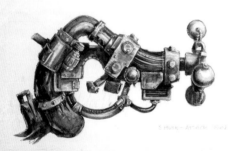

TABLE 3-1: SHOKK ATTACK GUN MISFIRES

D10 Roll	Misfire Result
1	Boom! The gun has exploded in a blast of energy, and the Mek is instantly killed.
2-5	The weapon spins out of control, and most of the Snotlings emerge far from target. The shot uses up 3 extra "rounds" of Snotlings.
6-7	The luckless Snotlings emerge as a messy and violent spray of blood and gore. Reduce the Damage to 1d5 and Pen to 0.
8-9	The gun's exit field spreads too wide. Increase the Blast value to 5, but reduce the Damage to 1d10.
10	The ammunition has gone out of control! A Snotling Mob attacks the Mek instead of entering the funnel for that shot.

MAD GENIUS: THE TECHNOLOGY OF THE ORKS

Ork Technology (or Tek) takes on a variety of forms and appearances, though there are many common similarities throughout their race. A Shoota, for example, is a common weapon amongst the greenskins all throughout the galaxy, though the actual appearance of a Shoota can vary greatly. The same standards apply to vehicles such as Warbikes, Trukks and Wartrakks—all have a common function and basic design while the actual look and workings can be very different. Why this is so is a matter of great debate amongst the Adeptus Mechanicus and Imperial Scholars, and the most widely accepted belief is that there is a form of genetic memory common to all Orks in which these technological ideas and advances are passed along. This hypothesis continues to be heavily debated across the Expanse.

Snazzgun

The Orks known as Flash Gitz love to spend as many teeth as possible on upgrading their Shootas into new and more dangerous versions known as Snazzguns. These weapons can be highly individualized, but all share one characteristic—they are extremely lethal. Flash Gitz are also known to hardwire their Snazzguns into their crude bionics to increase their accuracy. This does not often result in making them better shots, but it makes them feel bigger and more important around the other Boyz.

Snazzguns can shoot either solid projectiles or energy bolts and have a random penetration value listed because the velocity can vary with each shot fired. A Snazzgun that has been combined with targeting equipment or bionics loses its Inaccurate quality instead of gaining any bonuses to hit.

ORK MELEE WEAPONS

Like Orks themselves, Ork Melee Weapons are large, extremely durable, and very dangerous. They can range from simple lengths of bare metal or sections of deck plating, to highly complex but highly unpredictable mechanisms that only an Ork would dare use. No matter their form, each can multiply an Ork's already high degree of lethality to even greater levels.

Big Choppa

"Choppa" is the term applied to a multitude of basic Ork close-combat weapons, and Big Choppas are the huge two-handed variant of this staple device. These can be whirring chainaxes, massive meat cleavers, oversized weighted pipes, or many other large kinds of crude but effective implements of death.

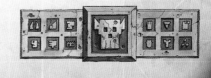

TABLE 3-2: ORK WEAPONS

Ranged Weapons

Name	Class	Range	RoF	Damage	Pen	Clip	Rld	Special	kg	Availability
Big Shoota	Basic	80m	S/3/10	1d10+6 I	1	40	1 Full	Inaccurate, Unreliable	6	Rare
Deffgun	Heavy	90m	S/4/8	1d10+10 I	2	50	2 Full	Inaccurate, Unreliable, Unwieldy, Storm	45	Extremely Rare
Grot Blasta	Basic	30m	S/-/-	1d10+3 I	0	5	2 Full	Inaccurate, Unreliable	7	Common
Rokkit Launcha	Basic	120m	S/-/-	3d10+5 X	6	1	Half	Inaccurate, Unreliable	15	Very Rare
Scorcha†	Basic	20m	S/-/-	1d10+4 E	2	6	Full	Flame, Unreliable	8	Rare
Shokk Attack Gun	Heavy	200m	S/-/-	3d10†† X	1d10	8	2 Full	Blast (3), Inaccurate, Overheat, Unreliable, Unstable	40	Near Unique
Snazzgun	Basic	100m	S/2/-	2d10 I or E	1d10	20	2 Full	Inaccurate, Overheats, Unreliable	7	Rare

Melee Weapons

Name	Class	Range	Damage	Pen	Special	kg	Availability
Big Choppa	Melee	—	2d10 R	2	Tearing, Unbalanced	10	Rare
Grot Prod	Melee	—	1d5+3 I	0	Shocking	2	Rare
Power Klaw	Melee	—	2d10††† E	10	Power Field, Tearing, Unwieldy	17	Near Unique
Tankhammer	Melee	—	2d10+3 X	7	Unbalanced, Blast (1d5-3)	10	Rare

†Scorchas can also be used as a Melee weapon (1d10+5 E; Pen 5, Unwieldy).

††If triples are rolled for Damage, the Shokk Attack Gun has misfired! See weapon entry for results.

†††Power Klaws add the users SBx2 to the Damage roll.

Grot Prod

Gretchin and Snotlings can be notoriously hard to keep under control. To make this task a bit easier, the Runtherds have developed a Grot Prod to keep the smaller greenskins in line. This shock stick delivers a jolt to the offending runt without permanently damaging it.

Power Klaw

Nothing makes an Ork happier than crushing a foe in his own hands. If one of those hands happens to be a lethal power field encased metal claw, all the better. A Power Klaw functions much like a Power Fist does for other races, and with it an Ork can tear the side from an armoured vehicle with ease.

Tankhammer

When a Tankbusta needs to pop open an armoured vehicle, his preferred weapon is known as a Tankhammer. This mighty maul is nothing more than a sledgehammer with explosives wired to it. The shockwave produced from the contact of the hammer and discharge of the explosives often sends the wielder flying backwards a few metres. When he has regained his senses, a flaming wreck is usually waiting to greet him. A Tankhammer is a one-use only weapon as the charge is expended upon detonation.

COMMON ORK TRAITS

Make It Work: Unreliable Ork weapons are not Unreliable in an Ork's hands.

Might Makes Right: Amongst Orks, a Kaptin can use Intimidate whenever he must make a Command Test.

Mob Rule: All Orks are latently psychic, an ability that increases in strength the more of them there are in one place, bolstering their confidence and courage to near fearless levels when they gather en masse. For every additional Ork within 10m, the Ork's Willpower is increased by +10 to resist the effects of Fear and Pinning.

ORK NOB

The largest, toughest, and baddest Orks who haven't yet risen to command their own warbands are known as Nobz. They form the retinues of the Kaptin and help keep the Boyz in line on the battlefield. It is from the ranks of the Nobz Mobz in the warband that leaders tend to emerge to challenge a Kaptin for the right to rule. Some like to make the Kaptin think they are perfectly content being the biggest and best fighters in a Kaptin's crew and the respect that comes with that place of honour. In truth, this is just the use of Ork "kunnin" as the Nob is really biding his time to slip that Choppa into the Kaptin's back and take his place in charge of the warband.

While they have the title of Nob, there is no actual hierarchy or caste that gives these Orks the right to rule. This is simply achieved through sheer brute force, and Nobz have no problem bashing in a few heads to get the outcome they are after from the Boyz in their crew.

Nob								
WS	BS	S	T	Ag	Int	Per	WP	Fel
46	19	(8) 49	(8) 47	39	29	34	32	34

Movement: 3/6/9/18   **Wounds**: 21

Armour: Flak armour (Body 2).   **Total TB**: 8

Skills: Command (Fel) +10, Intimidate (S) +10.

Talents: Air of Authority, Bulging Biceps, Crushing Blow, Furious Assault, Hardy, Iron Discipline, Iron Jaw, Lightning Reflexes, True Grit.

Traits: Brutal Charge, Fear 1, Size (Hulking), Make it Work, Mob Rule, Sturdy, Unnatural Strength (x2), Unnatural Toughness (x2).

Weapons: Snazzgun (100m; S/2/–; 2d10 I or E; Pen 1d10; Inaccurate, Overheats, Unreliable), or Slugga (20m; S/3/-; 1d10+4 I; Pen 0; Clip 18; Reload Full; Inaccurate, Unreliable), or Shoota (60m; S/3/10; 1d10+4I; Pen 0; Clip 30; Reload Full; Inaccurate, Unreliable); Choppa (1d10+11R; Pen 2; Unbalanced).

Gear: 2 Ammo clips, 2d10 Ork teeth ("teef"), shiny bitz, pet attack squig.

FREEBOOTERZ NOBZ

The Nobz that are found on the voidships of the Freebooterz are a different breed than the average Ork Nobz. They must oversee many different activities throughout the ships and serve as the Kaptin's Bridge Crew. On particularly well-run ships (something of an oxymoron in Ork vessels), the Nobz gravitate to areas they specialize in and give themselves titles such as Gun Nobz (overseeing the ship's weapons), Dek Masta (in charge of security and overall

Boyz behaviour on the ship), Ship Breaka (head of boarding actions), and any other titles they can think of. Many Freebooterz Nobz adopt a Brute Ramship or other small fighter from the voidship's bays to become their personal landing craft. This ship is decorated and adorned with all manner of totems and icons to show the Nob's prowess in battle. GMs should always attempt to equip Freebooter Nobz with the wildest and most ostentatious of gear and weapons.

KRUSHAS

After untold years of battle throughout the Expanse, especially on the outskirts of the Rifts of Hecaton, some Freebooter Nobz found themselves affected by the nearby warp rifts in strange ways. The powerful and unusual energies began to alter their brains, bringing on madness and overwhelming battle lust even beyond that normally found in Orks. Cunning Kaptins restrain these crazed Nobz below decks, bound in chains where they scream their war cries and chants to Gork and Mork to sate their thirst for battle. These Krushas fight without tiring when unleashed into battle. Many Kaptins in the Expanse fill a Ramship with these insane killers and launch into an enemy vessel. Once the hull has been breached, the Krushas do not stop until they have slaughtered everyone in their path or they meet their own end in battle.

Krusha Attack!: A Krusha loses himself in his battle frenzy, to the delight of many Kaptins (and detriment of any nearby Boyz). In this battle-crazed state, a Krusha lashes out mindlessly, his attacks clouded by his bloodlust and directed against friend and foe alike. If a Krusha Nob successfully hits his target when using the Charge Action, he immediately makes an additional attack against each target in range using the same bonuses and penalties as the original attack.

KAPTIN

"An' den 'e jumped on da big shiny git in da arma and smashed 'im right frough da deck, 'ed did. We'z fot dey'd bot' gotz krumped by da fall, see, but when we'z gots to da room with da rest of da shiny gits, da Kaptin was dere, killin' em an' waitin' fer us. That's why 'e's da Kaptin."

–Gorebusta, Ork Nob

Ork Warbosses lead their Warband against anything they find or that dares to get in their way, and are amongst the most prominent bringers of destruction across the Expanse. There is another type of Ork leader, though, one who not only leads a Warband but also commands his own ship to carry them. This is an Ork Kaptin, a terror of the void, and there are few things Imperial merchant vessels fear more.

To reach the rank of Kaptin, an Ork must prove himself to his fellow Boyz and Nobz on the ship. If a Kaptin doesn't command respect, he doesn't remain a Kaptin for very long. Many Warbosses and Kaptins in the Expanse have been in command of their tribes for decades and can strike fear into their lesser ranking Orks with a glance (though most prefer a mighty bellow or smack across the gob).

Ork Kaptins tend to tower over their subordinates and stand nearly eight feet tall. They are pure muscle from head to toe and proudly sport the scars of hundreds of battles. Most Ork Kaptins have acquired customised weapons and armour through their travels. At times this specialised gear takes on a life and reputation of its own, giving Orks and Humans throughout the Koronus Expanse reason to hunt down a Kaptin.

INFAMOUS KAPTINS OF THE EXPANSE

Across the Koronus Expanse, there are many different Kaptins who have made names for themselves as they leave a trail of devastated planets and ships across the void. From the infamous Warlord Morgash of the Undred-Undred Teef to the dreaded Freebooter Kaptin Borgum Backstabba, Imperial captains and Rogue Traders are always on the lookout for these mighty foes in hope that killing them adds to their own reputations and coffers.

Borgum Backstabba, Freebooter Kaptin

As a lowly Ork soldier on a Kill Kroozer in the Expanse, the Ork known as Borgrum loved the thrill of boarding enemy ships with his Freebooter crew, the Boneskulls. He earned a reputation for particular brutality in those boarding actions against Imperial ships. Blasting "umies," as Orks refer to humans, was a skill that he excelled at and he was chosen to personally accompany his Kaptin on a raid against the frigate *Hammer of Heresy*.

When the Orks boarded the ship, the fighting was fierce and Borgrum and his Freebooter Kaptin became separated from the other raiders below decks. Unbeknownst to the Kaptin, Borgrum had his sights on bigger things for himself, and used the chaos of the combat to plunge his Choppa deep into the back of his leader. Then, after dispatching the defenders, Borgrum made his way back to the raiding party wearing the Kaptin's oversized hat on his head and Shoota at his side. The other Boyz didn't seem to care much about the change in

command as the plunder was good and they didn't have to do the thinking on the next part of the attack. Borgrum easily assumed control of the Kill Kroozer *Gork's Gibletgrinda* and set off to make a name for himself in the Expanse.

Since taking control of the Boneskullz Freebooterz, Borgrum has launched numerous successful raids against merchant and Naval targets ready for plunder. He is currently planning a large-scale assault on the shipping lanes near the Maw, confident this should draw many new recruits to his cause.

Kaptin Krod, the Terror of Tyrex IV

The world of Tyrex IV hosted a small mining colony near the northern borders of the Expanse. A group of Imperial settlers established the outpost to take advantage of the rich promethium veins located deep within the planet. When the miners detected an unknown ship entering the outskirts of the system, they attempted to hail it. This only served to alert the Kill Kroozer *Krod's Krusha* to their location.

The next month would become what one colonist's distress call referred to as "Hell unleashed," as Krod's Boyz took great delight in slaughtering the miners while the Kaptin's Mek Boyz performed all manner of experiments to discover the various uses of promethium. Krod became increasingly more and more demanding for vast stores of promethium to be mined, and he worked his crews round the clock to harvest all he could. His trusted Weirdboyz continually asserted that a terrible danger was rapidly approaching, counsel that Krod took more and more seriously over time. Finally, Krod gathered his Boyz and left the world a shattered, broken shell. The excessive mining had destabilized the veins of promethium running deep in the core of the world, and as his ships left orbit Tyrex IV exploded. The massive explosion rained debris throughout the system and crippled three of the xenos ships as they made their escape. Krod has not been seen or heard from in the decade since the world's destruction, and many wonder if he fell victim to his own greed on Tyrex IV.

Rekka, the Mek Kaptin

It is not often that Kaptins of Freebooter crews are also skilled in one of the various Odd Boyz disciplines. Most Kaptins concentrate their time on plundering and fighting, which leaves them little room for other pursuits. Rekka is one of those rare exceptions. He is a Mek that rose to command his own crew and ship. From the bridge of his Battle Kroozer, *Gorkicus Meks*, this cunning greenskin has carved a path of plunder throughout the southwestern segment of the Expanse all while continuing to create new Ork technology for his Boyz to use.

One of his most notable claims to fame (among the other Freebooterz) is the development of a massive ship-mounted Shokk Attack Gun. Like its smaller, shoulder-mounted counterpart, this massive weapon opens a tunnel between two points through the warp. Rekka uses this weapon to send hordes of Boyz into enemy ships; the sudden appearance of scores of greenskins inside the secured areas of a ship catches the defenders off guard and gives the Freebooterz a decisive advantage. Rekka has also created special helmets for his warriors

to wear that help shield them from the horrors of the warp tunnel, though often sending helmetless, crazed, warp-terrified Boyz into battle works just as well for him. This whirling doom has crippled at least three human warships, making Rekka one of the most wanted Freebooterz in the Expanse.

Kaptin								
WS	BS	S	T	Ag	Int	Per	WP	Fel
50	50	(12) 60	(10) 55	36	35	35	40	30

Movement: 4/8/12/24   **Wounds:** 50
Armour: 'Eavy Armour (Body 5, Head 3, Arms 3, Legs 3).
Total TB: 10
Skills: Awareness (Per) +10, Barter (Fel), Carouse (T) +10, Climb (S), Command +20 (Fel), Common Lore (Ork) (Int) +20, Common Lore (War) (Int) +20, Common Lore (Koronus Expanse) (Int), Dodge (Ag), Intimidate +20 (S), Navigation (Stellar) (Int), Pilot (Flyers, Space Craft), Speak Language (Low Gothic, Ork) (Int).
Talents: Air of Authority, Bulging Biceps, Common Lore (Ork, The Expanse), Crushing Blow, Fearless, Furious Assault, Hardy, Into the Jaws of Hell, Iron Discipline, Iron Jaw, Touched by the Fates, True Grit.
Traits: Too 'Ard Ta Care†, Brutal Charge, Enormous, Fear (1), Make It Work, Might Makes Right, Mob Rule, Resistance (Heat, Cold, Radiation), Size (Hulking), Sturdy, Swift Attack, Two Weapon Wielder (Ballistic, Melee), Unnatural Strength (x2), Unnatural Toughness (x2).
†Too 'Ard Ta Care: The Ork is simply unconcerned with trivial matters like extreme temperatures, hard vacuum, poison, disease or breathing. The character gains a +20 bonus on all Toughness Tests to resist the effects of heat, cold, vacuum, suffocation, disease, poison and any other adverse environmental conditions which require a Toughness Test to resist.
Weapons: Shoota (60m; S/3/10; 1d10+4I; Pen 0; Clip 30; Reload Full; Inaccurate, Unreliable); Power Klaw (2d10+12 E, Pen 9, Power Field, Unwieldy), or Choppa (1d10+15R; Pen 2; Unbalanced), or Big Choppa (2d10+15 R; Pen 2; Tearing, Unbalanced). Many Kaptins have Kustom Weapons and GMs should feel free to create modified versions of Ork weapons befitting the biggest and toughest Ork aboard.
Gear: 2 Ammo clips, 4d10 Ork teeth ("teef"), scavenged metal and components, two ammo clips his weapons, wildly ostentatious (for an Ork) clothing.

KOMMANDOS

As a race, Orks are not known for their stealth, as they tend to barrel headfirst into battle with a loud Waaagh! Kommandos break this mould and excel at infiltration, ambushes, and other decidedly "un-Orky" ways. Why these Orks have chosen to go against form in such a drastic way is another of the many mysteries of Ork culture that is heavily debated by Magos Biologis throughout the Imperium.

Ork Kommandos are often sent ahead of an invading force to scout out defences and sow discord and terror amongst the enemy troops. The nightly raids and lightning attacks from the cover of darkness keep the defenders on edge and wear down their stamina in advance of the main attack force. Under the guidance of Kommando Nobz, the greenskins work tirelessly to destroy emplacements and other structures to make it easier for the rest of the warband to overrun the defences.

When Kommandos engage in open warfare, they often enter battle astride massive Warkoptas that have been assembled from a variety of looted vehicles. These twin-bladed vehicles drop their passengers directly into battle behind enemy lines through the use of repelling lines (though many Kommandos ignore the lines and just dive straight into battle from above). They also make use of individual Deff Koptas as support vehicles and fast attack flyers. The speed at which they can disrupt enemy lines is staggering and the unmistakable whirl of a Kopta's blades can send shivers down even a hardened veteran's spine.

THE BATTLE OF FELDARRA PRIME

The planet of Feldarra, deep in the Ragged Worlds, came under attack by an unknown enemy nearly a century ago. It began with a series of grisly murders in the capital that targeted local PDF forces. These brave men and women were found dead in back alleys, outside their residences, and even at their duty posts. After nearly a month of nightly killings, the overall morale of the PDF was shattered. The terrified soldiers invented all manner of tales for what was striking at them; tales of horrid Tyranid monsters or daemonic beasts ran rampant.

Finally, on the 43rd day since the attacks began, a massive explosion rocked the city, destroying a number of Leman Russ Battle Tanks and other fortifications. Silhouetted in the flames were hulking shapes that quickly vanished back into the smoke as the residents tried to battle the blaze. Within hours of the explosion, the skies were filled with Ork Kroozers and death rained down upon the world. The battered and exhausted defenders were no match for the savagery of the onslaught that was unleashed upon them. When the Imperial Navy arrived in system to answer the Feldarran distress calls, they found a blasted and burnt-out world crawling with xenos invaders.

Kommando

WS	BS	S	T	Ag	Int	Per	WP	Fel
37	19	46	44 (8)	35	24	38	26	21

Movement: 3/6/12/18 **Wounds:** 15
Armour: Flak armour (Body 2). **Total TB:** 8
Skills: Concealment (Ag) +10, Intimidate (S), Shadowing (Ag) +10, Silent Move (Ag), Survival (Int).
Talents: Bulging Biceps, Crushing Blow, Furious Assault, Hardy, Iron Jaw, True Grit.
Traits: Brutal Charge, Make it Work, Mob Rule, Size (Hulking), Sturdy, Unnatural Toughness (x2).
Weapons: Slugga (20m; S/3/-; 1d10+4 I; Pen 0; Clip 18; Reload Full; Inaccurate, Unreliable) or Shoota (60m; S/3/10; 1d10+4I; Pen 0; Clip 30; Reload Full; Inaccurate, Unreliable), Choppa (1d10+7 R; Pen 2; Unbalanced).
Gear: 2 Ammo clips, Shiny bitz, 1d10 Ork teeth ("teef"), gas mask.

MAD DOK

To say that Ork physiology is resilient would be something of an understatement; missing limbs, gaping holes, and even smashed heads can all be repaired by the insane science of the Mad Dok. These masters of the saw and stitch have perfected the art of putting an Ork back together again after it returns from the battlefield.

A Mad Dok is one of the Odd Boyz—Orks who embrace one of the paths of their society focused on something other than warfare (though even then, almost all Odd Boyz inventions and achievements are used solely for war). From the earliest days of sentience, the Dok spends its time experimenting on other greenskins. He usually begins his tinkering on Snotlings, as they are the easiest to capture, but he then quickly moves on to Grots and other Orks. As the Dok gains more and more notoriety, he soon finds himself with willing volunteers instead of having to seek out and capture subjects. When these "'eksperimentz" are complete, an Ork considers itself to be vastly improved over its regular brethren. Many of Orks sport shiny metal skulls, cyborg bodies, integrated weapon arms, and other upgrades thanks to the Dok's tinkering; those who did not fair so well on the operating table are often left mindless and drooling hulks.

Most Kaptins tend to keep a personal Dok in their Nobz retinue to tend to their battle wounds. While patching up the Kaptin, this personal "physician" is often overcome with an inexplicable need to enhance his leader in addition to ministering to his wounds. Most Kaptins view their new additions with a sense of pride; if, that is, they survive to become conscious of these modifications.

Mad Dok

WS	BS	S	T	Ag	Int	Per	WP	Fel
40	19	(8) 49	(10) 50	39	29	34	32	34

Movement: 3/6/9/18 **Wounds**: 25
Armour: Flak (Body 2). **Total TB**: 8
Skills: Command (Fel) +10, Intimidate (S) +10, Medicae (Int) +10, Tech-Use (Int) +10.
Talents: Air of Authority, Bulging Biceps, Crushing Blow, Furious Assault, Hardy, Iron Discipline, Iron Jaw, Lightning Reflexes, Master Chirurgeon, True Grit.
Traits: Brutal Charge, Fear 1, Size (Hulking), Make it Work, Mob Rule, Sturdy, Unnatural Strength (x2), Unnatural Toughness (x2).
Weapons: Slugga (20m; S/3/–; 1d10+4 I; Pen 0; Clip 18; Reload Full; Inaccurate, Unreliable) or Shoota (60m; S/3/10; 1d10+4I; Pen 0; Clip 30; Reload Full; Inaccurate, Unreliable), Dok's Tools (1d10+8 I; Pen 2; Tearing), Urty Syringe (1d10+4 R; Pen 3; Tearing, Toxic).
Gear: 2 Ammo clips, 2d10 Ork teeth ("teef"), Grot Orderly (adds +5 to any Medicae Skill Tests).

Enhanced Boyz

When a Mad Dok takes the field of battle, he is almost always accompanied by a group of fanatically loyal Ork Boyz who he has performed a number of procedures on. Dok's Boyz are standard Ork Boyz with the addition of two Enhancements from the following Table. Roll twice on the table to see what upgrades each Boy gains. If the same result is rolled, the "Job's a Bad 'Un" instead! That Boy instead loses 1d5 wounds and 1d10 Toughness, and gains one Poor Quality Bionic Limb.

Table 3-3 Mad Dok Enhancements

D10 Roll	Enhancement
1-3	+d10 Wounds (may only be take once)
4	Swift Attack Talent
5	Frenzy Talent
6	Lightning Reflexes Talent
7	Fearless Talent
8	Regeneration (2) Trait
9	Bionic Upgrade (gains Bionic arm, leg, etc.)
10	Cybork Body (gains +5 Wounds, +5 Strength, +10 Toughness)

MEKBOY

"Nah, ya grot, ya don'tz need ta stop shootin' just 'cause I'z gonna fix up yer shoota. Just 'old dat bit for a second, and den I'z can stick in dis 'xtra 'splodey bi-"

–Rekrench da Unlucky, Ork Mekboy

Ork technology has been the subject of much study and debate throughout the Imperium, and entire teams of the Adeptus Mechanicus have dedicated years of their lives to researching it. How it functions—when all laws of science say it should not—is something that only the Mekboyz can ever truly know.

The life of a Mek is a perilous one filled with excitement, danger, and often death—for one cannot have amazing technological advances without risks. Ork Kaptins and Warbosses know this fact all too well and make sure that Mek workshops and foundries are located a safe distance from the rest of the warband. The hustle and bustle of these areas in an Ork encampment are both fascinating and terrifying at the same time as hundreds of Grots scurry to and fro dragging supplies to their masters. The crackle of electricity, the hum of the plasma coils, and the whine of the saws all blend together into a symphony of crazed invention. The machines of war created by a Mek are truly unique creations embodying the Ork way of life.

Mekboy

WS	BS	S	T	Ag	Int	Per	WP	Fel
35	19	(8) 40	(8) 46	30	39	34	34	25

Movement: 3/6/9/18 **Wounds:** 22
Armour: Kustom Flak (Body 3). **Total TB:** 8
Skills: Command (Fel) +10, Intimidate +10 (S), Tech-Use (Int)+20.
Talents: Air of Authority, Bulging Biceps, Crushing Blow, Furious Assault, Hardy, Iron Discipline, Iron Jaw, Lightning Reflexes, Rapid Reload, True Grit.
Traits: Brutal Charge, Fear 1, Size (Hulking), I Can Fix Dat†, Make it Betta!††, Make it Work, Mob Rule, Sturdy, Unnatural Strength (x2), Unnatural Toughness (x2).
†I Can Fix Dat: A Mekboy's knowledge of Ork Tek is second to none. A Mek can clear any jam in an Ork weapon as a Full Action.
††Make it Betta!: Tinkering with the weapons in a Mek's Retinue is very common and any of the Ork Boyz travelling with him has an upgrade to his Shoota or Slugga from **Table 3-4: Make it Betta!** below. Each weapon may only be upgraded once this way.
Weapons: Slugga (20m; S/3/-; 1d10+4 I; Pen 0; Clip 18; Reload Full; Inaccurate, Unreliable) or Shoota (60m; S/3/10; 1d10+4I; Pen 0; Clip 30; Reload Full; Inaccurate, Unreliable), Kustom Blasta (Basic; 100m; S/2/-; 2d10+5 E; Pen 6; Clip 10; Reload 1 Full; Inaccurate, Scatter, Tearing), Power Hamma (1d10+10 I; Pen 6; Power Field, Unwieldy).
Gear: 2 Ammo clips, 2d10 Ork teeth ("teef"), Kustom Force Field†††, Mekboy tools, Grot Assistant (carries 3 extra ammo clips).

†††Kustom Force Field: Many Meks construct Kustom Force Fields to better protect them whilst they tinker away. This has a Protection Rating of 45. Each time the Mekboy or anyone within two metres of him is hit by a ranged attack, roll a d100. If the result is lower than or equal to 45, the attack has no effect on those within that two-metre-radius protective field around the Mek. If the roll is a 5 or less, the field has overloaded and ceases to function until it is recharged or repaired (requiring a successful **Very Hard (–30) Tech-Use Test**).

TABLE 3-4: MAKE IT BETTA!

D10 Roll	Weapon Upgrade
1-3	+3 to Weapon's Damage
4	+2 to Weapon's Pen Value
5	Weapon gains Tearing quality (re-roll if already possesses this quality).
6	Weapon's Range is increased by 20m.
7	Weapon's Reload time is halved (to a minimum Half Action).
8	Weapon's Clip value is increased by 10.
9	Weapon gains Blast (2) quality (add +1 to Blast radius if weapon already has this quality).
10	Job's a Bad 'Un! The weapon has the same Damage and Penetration as a Grot Blasta.

SPEED FREAK

"Now, where'z we gunna get enuff red paint ta make a sumfing as 'uge as dis Kill Kroozer go fasta...?"

–Chor "Da Bluddrokk," Speed Freak Pilot,

If the life of an Ork is filled with fighting, noisy weapons and equipment, and headfirst charges regardless of circumstance, then the life of a Speed Freak is all that times one hundred. These xenos have dedicated their entire being to the extreme; whether that is barrelling into combat on the back of a warbike or piloting a voidship at full speed through an asteroid field.

Speed Freaks are members of the Ork Kult of Speed, a collection of fanatical greenskins who value extreme velocities in all that they do. Everything in their life revolves around this principle. From this group the most skilled (and insane) voidship pilots are chosen, always eager and ready to perform even the most reckless and dangerous manoeuvres their Kaptin might command. Most Speed Freak pilots actually perform them when they are not asked, or even if specifically commanded not to.

Throughout the Expanse, most consider Speed Freaks crazy even by Ork standards. They think nothing of sling-shotting a Kill Kroozer around a neutron star to give them an increase in speed for an attack run; never mind the lethal levels of radiation this exposes the crew to in this tactic. Voidship pilot Speed Freaks have also been known to begin slowly cackling as they approach a battle; this maniacal laugh grows in intensity as they get closer and closer to the combat. In the final stretch, all sanity

THE SHIPBREAKER RUN

Near the Frozen Stars on the far side of the Accursed Demesne lies a massive asteroid belt known as the Shipbreaker Field due to the number of catastrophic wrecks that have taken place in and near this hazard. The asteroids of the field are prone to flying off from the gravitational fields that hold them in place and have smashed into many passing ships over the centuries. Most human and other xenos vessels avoid it entirely, as the risk of catastrophe damage is too high. With less activity in the vicinity of the asteroid field in the past centuries, it has become home to an event that draws Speed Freaks from all across the Expanse: the Shipbreaker Run. Once every year (or thereabouts, as Orks are not the best at telling time), this suicidal race is held to determine the best pilot in the empire of the Undred-Undred Teef. Over the course of three days, these insane pilots run a route deep through the heart of the asteroid field; careening around the constantly moving rocks and often exploding off of them. At the end of the race, only the best pilots remain alive, as any Ork not skilled enough to complete the track has found a permanent home inside the Shipbreaker Field. The winning Speed Freak is given a place of great honour amongst the other Orks of the Empire and is heavily sought after by Kaptins.

is seemingly lost as the crazed laughter echoes throughout the ship's bridge and the pilot increases speed beyond any safe levels to ram his ship directly into an enemy vessel. Even with these behaviours well known, Kaptins go out of their way to recruit Speed Freak pilots for their ships.

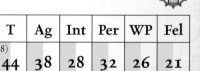

Speed Freak								
WS	BS	S	T	Ag	Int	Per	WP	Fel
37	19	46	(8) 44	38	28	32	26	21

Movement: 3/6/12/18   **Wounds**: 15

Armour: Flak armour (Body 2).   **Total TB**: 8

Skills: Drive (Ag) +10, Pilot (Ag) +10.

Talents: Bulging Biceps, Crushing Blow, Fearless, Furious Assault, Go Fasta!†, Hardy, Hotshot Pilot, Iron Jaw, True Grit.

Traits: Brutal Charge, Make it Work, Mob Rule, Size (Hulking), Sturdy, Unnatural Toughness (x2).

†**Go Fasta!**: A Speed Freak gains a +20 bonus to any Pilot or Drive Skill Tests that do not decrease the Speed of his vessel or vehicle (including any Tests to Ram), but –20 to any Tests that decrease his Speed.

Weapons: Slugga (20m; S/3/–; 1d10+4 I; Pen 0; Clip 18; Reload Full; Inaccurate, Unreliable) or Shoota (60m; S/3/10; 1d10+4I; Pen 0; Clip 30; Reload Full; Inaccurate, Unreliable), Choppa (1d10+7 R; Pen 2; Unbalanced).

Gear: 2 Ammo clips, flight helmet, goggles, 1d10 Ork teeth ("teef").

Transmission Aleph-Pattern, Occipital Vector
Origin: Hector Prinn, Savant Biologis
Eyes Only, Captain Rafielli Kanto, *The Wrath of Koronus*

…Our continued study of the Ork Warrior caste subgroups has yielded a number of results. From my extensive interviews with soldiers in the field, Imperial Guard Commanders, and even a lengthy discussion with members of the Adeptus Astartes we have compiled a list of the following warrior subgroups:

Tankbustas

The Orks who refer to themselves as Tankbustas specialise in the destruction of enemy armoured vehicles, and in breaching the hulls of ships during boarding actions. These xenos possess the same lack of fear and brazen nature as their brethren but when combined with their love of demolitions the lethality of these attacks become exponentially more dangerous. Tankbustas utilise a weapon known as a Tankhammer to deliver a massive explosive charge directly to the armour of a vehicle, often destroying themselves in the process.

Flash Gitz

Information regarding the ostentatious greenskins who call themselves Flash Gitz has been hard to come by. I have been able to discern that they are a subgroup of the Clan known as Bad Moons and favour heavily-modified weapons that fire energy bolts, solid rounds, and other more esoteric forms of projectiles. It is not known if these "Gitz" modify the weapons or if they employ a Mek to carry out the adjustments. In the one battlefield engagement that I personally witnessed these xenos in action, I noted that their dress and other equipment is also very elaborate, to match their weaponry. They tend to sport elaborate headwear, long coats, jewelry, and other affectations. Do not let their appearance fool you—they are extremely deadly on the field of battle.

Lootas

Of all the various subgroups of Ork Boyz, I consider the xenos known as Lootas to be the most terrifying opponents facing the soldiers of the Imperium. These Orks have an amazing and unknown ability over technology that rivals the best Mek Boyz. They can take enemy armaments and create amalgamations of many different weapons into what they refer to as "Deffguns." This shoulder-mounted weapon can lay down a withering barrage of fire capable of dealing serious losses to enemy infantry and vehicles. The bizarre nature of the gun's construction seems to produce a varying level of firepower with each gun; perhaps this is due to the Mekboy's unique vision for each weapon. I am continuing to attempt to secure one of these for further study.

Stormboyz

Some Orks have an unnatural fascination with Imperial troops (see ref: XJH-3564.09EX) and tend to copy many of the battle tactics and equipment utilised by our fighting forces. On the world of Naxxurrus in the Foundling Worlds, I was accompanying a detached force of Brontian Longknives as they eradicated an Ork infestation from the southern deserts. While we were entrenched in a series of Imperial Bastions, we heard a strange whine approaching over the massive rock formations to our flank. As the first soldier fell to a slug through his helmet we could see the cloud of dark smoke quickly approaching us. I trained my auspex on the cloud and could not believe my augmentics—Orks were furiously flying through the air toward our position with massive rockets strapped to their backs. These strangely-constructed thrusters served as a form of jump pack to quickly propel them into battle while overcoming the intervening barricades. Once these rocket-pack Orks landed inside the perimeter, they quickly charged into combat with the Brontians, taking advantage of the surprise their arrival had caused. Luckily for us, reinforcing units of these Stormboyz (as I later learned they were called) crashed into the side of the bastion, thinning their numbers and allowing us to repel the attack.

Burnas

The pyromaniac Orks known as Burnas are classified as Terror Troops by the Imperial Guard (see subsection 7, ref: 53-vh905) and are to be considered threat level Xenos Majoris. Burnas delight in setting everything in their path ablaze with their scorchas as they make their way across the battlefield. In addition, Burnas have recently been found by various Imperial Captains within the Koronus Expanse to be lethal boarding troops. According to a recent interview I conducted with Rogue Trader Vin Speng, these troops were responsible for the loss of the escort vessel *Indomitable Will*. It appears that these xenos are able to alter their flamethrowers to function as a high-powered cutting torch as well, and used them to bypass a number of decks on the ship after a successful boarding action during battle. The Burnas had made their way into the engine room and during a prolonged shootout, they managed to set fire to the fuel reserves and cause a catastrophic explosion that tore the ship apart.

ORK BOY

The untold masses of greenskins found throughout the Expanse are simply known as Ork Boyz; these are the warriors of the Kaptins that populate the many voidships, warbands, and tribes ready to unleash their destruction upon their enemies, which for Orks simply means everyone else.

Boyz (or Da Boyz, as they commonly refer to themselves) are always ready for a fight and usually spend their time looking for one. It is not uncommon for the bowels of a Kroozer to be filled with fighting pits and other areas where Da Boyz duke it out to find the biggest and best fighter in the warband. These dust-ups are brutal and bloody, but seldom lethal thanks to the amazing constitution of an Ork; the xenos just batter each other until the winner is clear (and the loser can't stand up any longer).

In battle, a Nob leads the mobs of Boyz, keeping them in line and following orders on the battlefield. A Nobz' crew reflects his own personal style and past glory. Individual mobs sport various heraldry and totems based on past achievements and conquests; it is not uncommon for Orks to have all manner of grisly trophies on their armour, such as enemy helmets, skulls, banners, and other items. Another way these bands set themselves apart is based on any Clan affiliation that they have. For example, members of the Evil Sunz have red paint jobs and the grinning sun icon on their armour and weapons while Bad Moons have garish yellow armour and black flames as accents.

Ork Boy

WS	BS	S	T	Ag	Int	Per	WP	Fel
37	19	46	(8) 44	30	24	32	26	21

Movement: 3/6/12/18
Wounds: 12
Armour: Flak armour (Body 2).
Total TB: 8
Skills: Intimidate (S).
Talents: Bulging Biceps, Crushing Blow, Furious Assault, Hardy, Iron Jaw, True Grit.
Traits: Brutal Charge, Make it Work, Mob Rule, Sturdy, Unnatural Toughness (x2).
Weapons: Slugga (20m; S/3/-; 1d10+4 I; Pen 0; Clip 18; Reload Full; Inaccurate, Unreliable), Shoota (60m; S/3/10; 1d10+4I; Pen 0; Clip 30; Reload Full; Inaccurate, Unreliable), Big Shoota (80m; S/3/10; 1d10+6 I; Pen 1; Clip 40; Reload Full; Inaccurate, Unreliable), or Choppa (1d10+7 R; Pen 2; Unbalanced).
Gear: 2 Ammo clips, shiny bitz, 1d10 Ork teeth ("teef").

KAPTIN VOGRUD'S SQUIG CANNON

The Freebooter ship *Gork's Klaw* is known throughout the Expanse for its ability to plunder vessels quickly as well as its more arcane weaponry devised by Kaptin Vogrud's insane Mek Boyz. Amidst the vast arrays of Lifta Droppas, Pulsa Rokkits, and other weapons that coat the hulls of his ship, there is one that sends more shivers down the spines of enemy captains than the others—the rumoured Squig Cannon. Where most weapons simply destroy a ship and slaughter its crew, the Squig Cannon is said to be a weapon of pure terror as it unleashes terrible, agonising change upon its victims. If a ship's void shields are breached and an area of hull is exposed, Vogrud's favourite tactic is to order an immediate surrender or he "Turnz uze all into stinkin' squigs." According to the tales, inevitably when the enemy captain refuses, Vogrud fires the cannon and unleashes its horror.

How the cannon works is not said, but its rays evidently permeate the hull of the target vessel and anyone caught in the blast begins to transform as their DNA begins to mutate into something akin to that of a Squig. There is no actual proof of this weapon or its effects, but after losing several merchant barons and their valuable holds to the Kaptin, several Great Houses have jointly placed a bounty on *Gork's Klaw* that could keep many Rogue Traders living comfortably for many decades.

THE LOST BOYZ

Ork infestations can be notoriously hard to eradicate from a planet. At times decades, and even centuries, after an Ork invasion, bands of these xenos warriors who have been living in remote areas of the world or even underground may appear, often long after the initial attacks have been forgotten. These Lost Boyz can cause a number of problems for local defence forces tasked with dealing with the problem.

In the aftermath of the infamous Siege of Port Wander, slain Orks were everywhere in the damaged structure. A massive effort was undertaken to clean out the xenos corpses, and hundreds of press gangs were assembled to search through the station's untold number of decks. It took crews many weeks to even begin to clear the bodies from the station's labyrinthine decks and corridors. During this time, a number of crewmen disappeared in some of the lowest and most remote areas and many of the superstitious workmen began blaming these disappearances on the unsettled spirits of the masses who died in the battle for the void station. Nothing was ever found after extensive internal sensor sweeps of the port, however, and additional provost-lead searches found nothing more amiss than normal for the port. Most of the naval personnel reported that the missing crew had simply deserted their posts for imagined better lives in the underdecks, a not uncommon occurrence for those under the harsh conditions of pressment.

Several years later, though, a new rash of disappearances began across the station. Rumours and sightings of large, hulking creatures in the darkness began to make the rounds, as large as the common Ogryn dockworkers. Auspex readings of the station did not turn up any xenos life signs, but many areas are heavily shielded or blocked from internal sensors for a variety of reasons, rendering many of the scans inconclusive. Finally, after a Tech-Priest and a valuable team of repair servitors vanished in one of the deepest sectors of the station, a detachment of Naval proctors were sent to conduct a level-by-level sweep of the entire complex.

What they discovered in a forgotten storage bay shocked the detachment sergeant. Nearly forty Ork Boyz hid here, remnants of the invasion force or perhaps new Orks grown from the spores left behind in the attack. The fighting was intense and most of the proctors lost their lives purging the taint of the xenos from the station. In the end, nearly a decade after Gulgorg's massive Waaagh! brought it to the brink of destruction, the final Ork drew its last breath in the battle for Port Wander. To this day though, there are still tales passed across the tavern tables of unexplained murders and huge forms operating in the lower decks.

GRETCHIN AND RUNTHERD

Gretchin, or Grots as they are often known, are the most numerous of all the greenskins. These short, conniving, scheming, wretched creatures live only to be bullied and tortured by their larger masters. The Orks love nothing more than to kick, punch, punt, and generally abuse Gretchin at any chance they get. For all the pain and punishment they endure, Gretchin still seem to carry out what they are told to do with a mixture of fear and awe of the Orks, or at least until they can successfully scamper away to safety.

These small greenskins are similar in physiology to an Ork but stand less than half their height. Gretchin are bald with large pointed ears and sharp teeth (instead of tusks), with long gangly limbs and a hardy constitution for their small size. They also have a well-developed sense of self-preservation.

Gretchin are commonly found alongside Orks in any fighting, and are often used as a first wave of attack in combat so that the Orks can roughly gauge the strength and firepower of their enemy. Orks have no reservations about sending wave after wave of Grots to their death while they come up with "Da Kunnin Plan" based on the casualties, or more often simply for their own amusement. Orks also utilise Gretchin to be their weapon carriers, ammo porters, footstools, mine detectors, emergency victuals, and for other less appealing jobs not related to actually fighting the enemy. Some Orks even use specially-trained Gretchin as assistants in repairing vehicles or conducting medical operations.

Ork Runtherds specialise in corralling and training Grots, primarily to drive them forward into enemy fire. Needless to say, many Gretchin would rather avoid this, so the Runtherd applies encouragement involving weapons fire and application of their Grot Prods or grabba-sticks. Some Runtherds, realising that the Grots are more willing should they actually have a chance of surviving, outfit their herdz with ramshackle, blunderbuss-style weapons. In reality, this rarely helps them, but for a Grot in combat it is better than nothing. Despite what would appear as an odious chore at best, Runtherds are proud of their occupation and know they contribute greatly to the wellbeing of their tribe or ship. Maintaining a well-trained population of Gretchin is a respectable position for an Ork, and Runtherds do their best to keep the little Grots properly in line.

There are some Gretchin that can only take their downtrodden lifestyle for so long and eventually rise up and rebel against their cruel masters; the Ork Kroozer *Kill 'Em All* is a tale of one of these uprisings. According to legends and tales whispered amongst Grots to keep their spirits up, the Gretchin crew of the ship plotted for many months to take control of the vessel. When the Orks were about to undertake an attack on a seemingly crippled Eldar ship, the Grots managed to arrange for most of the Boyz to be loaded onto the Ramships while they remained behind. Once the attack began, the Grots stormed the bridge and killed the few remaining Orks there, while firing the thrusters and catapulting the ship far from the battle. Without the fire support of their Kroozer, the Eldar made quick work of the Ork raiders and the Gretchin had secured a ship. This voidship was the first (and only) ship of the Rebel Grot Armada in the Expanse.

Gretchin

WS	BS	S	T	Ag	Int	Per	WP	Fel
18	34	18	19 (2)	44	33	37	22	24

Movement: 3/6/12/18   **Wounds**: 7
Armour: None.   **Total TB**: 2
Skills: Awareness (Per), Concealment (Ag), Dodge (Ag), Search (Int), Shadowing (Ag), Silent Move (Ag).
Talents: Heightened Senses (Hearing).
Traits: Mob Rule, Size (Scrawny), Unnatural Toughness (x2).
Weapons: Grot Blasta (30m; S/-/-; 1d10+3 I; Pen 0; Clip 5; Reload 2 Full; Inaccurate, Unreliable) or Slugga (20m; S/3/-; 1d10+4 I; Pen 0; Clip 18; Reload Full; Inaccurate, Unreliable), sneaky boot knife (1d5+1 R; Pen 0).
Gear: 1 Ammo clip, shiny bitz, 1d5-2 Ork teeth ("teef").

Runtherd

WS	BS	S	T	Ag	Int	Per	WP	Fel
37	19	46	44 (8)	30	24	32	26	21

Movement: 3/6/12/18   **Wounds**: 15
Armour: Flak armour (Body 2)   **Total TB**: 8
Skills: Awareness (Per), Intimidate (S).
Talents: Bulging Biceps, Crushing Blow, Furious Assault, Grot Wrangler†, Hardy, Iron Jaw, True Grit.
Traits: Brutal Charge, Make it Work, Mob Rule, Sturdy, Size (Hulking), Unnatural Toughness (x2).

†Grot Wrangler: Runtherds are very good at getting Gretchin and Snotlings to perform their assigned tasks, no matter how dangerous or downright suicidal they might be. He has the Command (Fel) and Wrangling (Int) Skills, both with a +20 bonus, when used to direct these lesser orkoid beings.

Weapons: Slugga (20m; S/3/-; 1d10+4 I; Pen 0; Clip 18; Reload Full; Inaccurate, Unreliable), Choppa (1d10+7 R; Pen 2; Unbalanced), Grot Prod (1d5+8 I; Pen 0; Shocking).
Gear: 2 Ammo clips, shiny bitz, 1d10 Ork teeth ("teef"), Guard Squig.

SQUIGS

In addition to Orks and Gretchin, the lands of the greenskins are filled with smaller, stranger creatures—Squigs. These creatures are so varied in form and function that some believe cataloguing them all is impossible. While Squigs may vary in appearance and ability, they all serve a fundamental role in Ork society. Some are used as medicine, others are used to oil machinery, many are used as food, and some are even used cosmetically, but all are essential to the Ork way of life.

ATTACK SQUIG

In battle, the larger, most ferocious Squigs are used by the Orks in many ways. One of the most common is the Attack Squig. This creature is nothing more than a fanged mouth and a bad attitude that is unleashed on the enemies of its Ork master. There are many varieties of Attack Squig and breeding them is a favourite pastime of all manner of Orks. The most common type is known as the Ravenous Face-Biter, though others are growing in popularity amongst the Freebooterz of the Expanse including the Insatiable Armripper, the Gut-Growler, and the Large-Eyed Legsnapper.

Attack Squig

WS	BS	S	T	Ag	Int	Per	WP	Fel
40	—	36	(4) 25	33	10	32	28	––

Movement: 3/6/9/24 **Wounds**: 12
Armour: None. **Total TB**: 4
Skills: Awareness +10 (Per), Tracking +10 (Int).
Talents: Furious Assault.
Traits: Bestial, Natural Weapons, Unnatural Toughness (x2).
Weapons: Bite (1d10+6 R; Pen 0; Tearing).

BOMB SQUIG

One type of Squig that has become increasingly prevalent on the battlefield across the Expanse is the Bomb Squig. This is usually nothing more than an Attack Squig that has been loaded down with stikk bombs and other explosives and let loose. The Squigs chosen to become Bomb Squigs are usually the fastest ones in the pens, so that they can deliver their payload before being shot by an enemy. The Orks who have rigged these running bombs sometimes rig a crude device so that they can detonate the Squig when it is likely to cause the most damage, but most are happy to have the Squigs run rampant and explode randomly. Bomb Squigs are especially favoured by Tankbustas to aid them in blasting through enemy armour.

Bomb Squig

WS	BS	S	T	Ag	Int	Per	WP	Fel
35	—	32	(4) 22	33	10	32	28	––

Movement: 3/6/9/24 **Wounds**: 10
Armour: None. **Total TB**: 4
Skills: Awareness +10 (Per), Tracking +10 (Int).
Talents: Furious Assault.
Traits: Bestial, Natural Weapons, Unnatural Toughness (x2).
Weapons: Bite (1d10+6 R; Pen 0; Tearing); Bomb Harness†
(2d10+4 X; Pen 1; Blast).
†**Bomb Harness**: This device can be detonated by an Ork designated as the "Squig Handla" if he is within 20m of the Squig, and automatically kills the Squig (as well its target if all goes according to Da Plan). Obviously, it is one use only.

GUARD SQUIG

Ork Kaptins have been breeding a form of Squig known as a Guard Squig, or Squig Hound to some. This creature has all the ferocity of an Attack Squig, but is bred to be utterly loyal to its master and to stay by his side and protect him at all costs. Squig Hounds can be almost affectionate with their keeper and tend to lie at his feet like a contented dog unless danger arises.

Guard Squig

WS	BS	S	T	Ag	Int	Per	WP	Fel
37	—	38	(4) 25	35	12	32	28	––

Movement: 3/6/9/24 **Wounds**: 15
Armour: None. **Total TB**: 4
Skills: Awareness +10 (Per), Tracking +10 (Int).
Talents: Furious Assault, Guardian (only for his Master).
Traits: Bestial, Brutal Charge, Natural Weapons, Unnatural Toughness (x2).
Weapons: Bite (1d10+6 R; Pen 0; Tearing).

SNOTLINGS

Imperial scholars and Magos Biologis adepts have debated the nature of the Snotling since mankind first discovered Orks all those millennia ago. Some thought them to be juvenile Gretchin, but more evidence indicated they are separate variant sub-species of the basic Ork form. Where they come from and why they exist may always perplex those that study Orks, but one thing is for sure—Snotlings can quickly become a menace if not dealt with quickly.

A Snotling appears to be a miniaturized Gretchin. It stands roughly half a metre tall and has the same gangly appearance of a tiny Grot. Their small size means they cannot carry weapons beyond small daggers or sticks. Unlike Gretchin or even Orks, Snotlings also lack even a basic appreciation for violence, however, thus making them mostly unsuitable for combat. For the most part, these tiny creatures tend the many types of fungus and Squig-beasts that are omnipresent wherever Orks live for long, even aboard their ships. Many Orks keep Snotlings as pets, this being perhaps the pinnacle of Snotling achievement.

The danger that comes with Snotlings is their ability to infest an area and generally wreak havoc upon everything they come into contact with. A Snotling has no qualms about crawling into an intake tube or engine compartment to see what is inside, resulting in a messy end for the Snotling and a large amount of damage to the mechanism. These vermin also seem to reproduce quickly if left to their own devices, another link to their fungoid heritage it would seem.

On Ork ships and colonies, Snotlings are mostly left to themselves unless needed (especially by Mekboyz looking for Shokk Attack Gun ammunition). Runtherds are sometimes called in to gather the creatures when they get too numerous, too underfoot, or the ship's rations run too low, utilising a variety of means including specialised Squig Herding beasts, Grot Prods, frag stikkbombz, and other devices.

†**Snots Mob:** Snotlings are rarely alone and are normally found in uncontrollable mobs of ten or more at a time forming a tightly massed swarm. The Mob makes a single attack against every Explorer it is engaged with each round, until falling to 5 wounds, at which time it reverts to Size (Puny), loses the Fearless Talent, and immediately runs away. The Mob is immune to being Grappled, Knocked Down, or Pinned.

Weapons: Bite, claws, poking sticks, tiny knives (2d10 R; Pen 0).

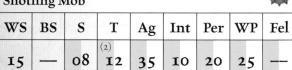

Snotling Mob

WS	BS	S	T	Ag	Int	Per	WP	Fel
15	—	08	12 (2)	35	10	20	25	——

Movement: 4/8/12/24   **Wounds**: 50
Armour: None.   **Total TB**: 2
Skills: Climb (S), Concealment (Ag).
Talents: Fearless.
Traits: Bestial, Natural Weapons (Bite), Size (Hulking), Snots Mob†, Strange Physiology, Unnatural Toughness (x2).

SNOTLING INFESTATIONS

If a group of Snotlings makes its way on board a Rogue Trader's vessel, it can cause all manner of problems for the crew and damage to the ship. Here are some possible ways a GM can have an infestation play out.

What's that sound? A group of Snotlings has made its way onboard, perhaps inside an unsecured cargo container. The miniature menaces quickly make their way inside access hatches and tunnels of the ship. For the first few days, the crew hears an occasional loud scratching, wild caterwauling, and other odd noises from inside the walls of the ship. The tiny creatures are too small for easy detection, and the ship may grow a reputation as being haunted by the warp-echoes of those who died aboard her.

Should that light be flashing? Eventually the Snotlings make their way to a critical system and their poking and prodding breaks something, causing the ship's engines to fail in interesting ways. This might happen when there are no other situations demanding the Explorers' attention, so that they can properly investigate and exterminate the creatures, but perhaps not.

It's getting away! While working to eradicate an infestation, a small number of the Snotlings escape and make their way elsewhere in the ship. This could be especially troublesome should there be visiting dignitaries or captured prisoners aboard.

A key to these encounters is keeping a fine balance between urgency and levity. At first glance, Snotlings are almost comical but the Explorers should soon realise that if they are not quickly dealt with they can become a major threat to a ship or ground installation. Snotlings can get almost anywhere, and the GM should not be hesitant in using them to infiltrate a ship's warp drive, Gellar Field, or other vital components should the players show complacency.

ORK ADVENTURE SEEDS

Orks can be an exciting opponent for Explorers to face. Unlike many of the xenos races that adventurers encounter, Orks can range from a desperate battle with a seemingly unstoppable force to an odd but tense encounter with wily Ork Freebooterz. The variety can be very rewarding to GMs looking for a new direction in their games. GMs should keep in mind, though, that while Orks are not the smartest species in the galaxy, they are not simple mindless brutes, either. They have motivations, goals, and plans like any other race—these desires just may be hard for the players to understand.

BREAKING THE ROK

As the Freebooter Kaptin Madrok's raids become more and more daring, the merchants have placed a large bounty on his head, drawing Rogue Traders from across the Expanse to hunt this elusive Ork. After much searching, the players learn of his hidden installation in the asteroids of Stompgit and set out to infiltrate his lair and bring the Kaptin to justice. Unbeknownst to the characters, the Kaptin has set up an elaborate game of cat and mouse to test his mettle against the best the humans have to offer. The players must successfully find the Rok, gain access, and survive Madrok's traps and challenges if they are to confront him.

THE MEK'S GAMBIT

Word has spread throughout the Expanse of a Mek Boy who builds the most amazing pieces of technology for his Kaptin and his warband. After a particularly harrowing encounter with a group of Orks armed with equipment far beyond that of normal Orks, the Explorers set forth to find this Mek and stop him once and for all. When rumours surface during the course of the investigation that the Mek possesses an ancient xenos artefact, the stakes are raised and the players must find this powerful device before the Orks unknowingly unleash a great devastation on the Expanse.

THE GREEN TIDE GROWS

Orks from many different warbands and ships are all making their way toward a desolate world in the Heathen Stars known as Bloodfane. What is calling these greenskins to this backwater world? Is this a new tide of Orks moving into the Expanse, or are they tribes formerly occupying Undred-Undred Teef? If a major Waaagh! is about to be unleashed, it may bring destruction throughout the Koronus Expanse.

THE GREAT SQUIG HUNT

A Magos Biologis researching on Footfall claims a select breed of Squig has amazing healing properties and can be used to wipe out many different forms of illness. When a horrific disease strikes a pleasure world deep in Winterscale's Realm, the Explorers are asked to find these Squigs in hopes of coming up with a cure for this plague before millions of lives are lost. They may find the Squigs do indeed aid in a cure, or they may find it all an elaborate trap designed to snare an unsuspecting Rogue Trader's ship.

A MYSTERIOUS TRANSMISSION...

While travelling near the Accursed Demesne, the mercantile frigate *Light of Macharius* intercepted the following transmission. After filing the report with their House, the frigate resumed regular operations in the area. Below is an excerpt of this transmission.

...iz dis ting on? Attention all Orkz and'umies! Wez iz da Rebel Grot Armada and wez have claimed dis part of spazz as our own. Wez are not to be messed wit az we are unstoppable... What? I iz making a threat 'ere. Leave me alone! (sounds of scuffle and punching)

(new voice)... *I is Robgratz and wez iz da Rebel Grot Armada. Wez are an unstoppable force and wez are not to be messed wit...*

THE BLACK FIRE

For centuries, Rogue Traders and other captains have reported sightings of a massive ship just on the edge of their auspex ranges. This vessel appears briefly and vanishes before it can be identified or tracked. The only thing that is consistent in these sightings is that when this mystery ship appears, Astropaths on board report horrible visions of an Ork skull surrounded by black fire. Captains have considered this ship an ill omen; a ghost ship that brings bad luck and danger when it is seen. Is the vessel real, and if so where does the ship hail from and where is it going? Why has it not engaged in piracy and plunder like so many other Ork voidships?

UNLIKELY ALLIES

An Ork Freebooter Kaptin seeks out the Rogue Trader and his crew with a strange request—another Rogue Trader who the Explorers have an enmity toward has double-crossed the Ork Kaptin and stolen his prized Snazzgun. Unable to locate the scoundrel on his own, the Ork proposes an alliance, as he knows the Rogue Traders have a longstanding rivalry and this would be a chance to get back his personally kustomized weapon. There is something else at work here, though, as the Ork is extremely knowledgeable of the Explorers and their history. How has he learned so much about them and why is he so anxious for this alliance?

THE RAK'GOL

"They descend from the heavens like a maelstrom of destruction. Everything they seek and everything that they find lies in ruins, for they are of a lost age. Though if they do find the treasure they seek, a new Age of Strife may come upon us all."

–The Witches of Footfall, prior to the first sighting of the Rak'Gol

Last night, we completed our pursuit, but the bounty escaped us once more. I cannot deny that the offer put out by the Magos Biologis is a generous one. I also understand my Rogue Trader's lust for the glory that comes with such a triumph. However, I now hope that Tallen is sincere in his oath to give up on this task. Neither our vessel nor our crew are well suited for confronting the Rak'Gol—in truth, I begin to wonder if any Imperial craft could be.

Our ambush of the xenos craft began perfectly. The mindless wretches assaulted the apparently defenceless transport like stinkbugs on corpse-starch. They closed just as we expected, and within minutes the xenos had greedily taken the bait, filling the void with hundreds of their assault craft.

Alberse commanded our ship to leave silent running and launch an all out attack on the Mauler's weaker aft armour. Within two salvos, our attacks shattered the vessel, leaving the xenos no hope for retreat. It was only moments later that the plan began to come apart. We had hoped that with their only chance for escape destroyed, the xenos would negotiate some plan for survival. After all, any sane being should prefer survival over certain death. It's now obvious that our only mistake was assuming these creatures were sane. They are not even predators, only destroyers—a predator makes use of what it kills.

Within moments of the xenos realising that their vessel had been destroyed, they threw themselves at the transport with renewed fury. Over the vox, I heard the sounds of battle interspersed with cries for reinforcements and xenos howls of fury.

As the battle continued, I admit I chaffed under Alberse's request that I remain aboard the *Aureus*. It sounded as if quite the combat took place between our stalwarts and the foul creatures, and I wished I could have been there to direct things personally. Then, the signal stopped abruptly and beyond our viewports we watched the transport explode. I'm not sure how the monsters managed to destroy her (yet another reason I resent Alberse keeping me at his side—I'm sure I could have helped stop them), but Alberse's dynasty can ill afford the loss.

BEASTS PROWLING THE EXPANSE

Nothing within the Koronus Expanse embodies mindless brutality and unrestrained savagery like the Rak'Gol. Their actions seldom follow any pattern other than that of violence. Huge swaths of destroyed vessels, stations, and even colonies are often the only indications of their passage. The methods by which they select their targets are as yet unfathomable or perhaps may be entirely at random. Only the most focused and the least sane adepts have dared attempt to see a pattern within the activities of these wretched xenos. Their ways remain a mystery, and it is unclear if the answers are crafted in cunning or buried beneath insanity.

HISTORY AND CULTURE

Since the discovery of the Maw, relatively few Imperial vessels have ventured into the Unbeholden Reaches. Far fewer have successfully made such journeys and returned to tell of them. However, in 710.M41, an attack on the merchant brig *Solace of Dawn* revealed this new threat; possibly the most dangerous in that region of the Koronus Expanse.

Adeptus Mechanicus Explorators from the Disciples of Thule discovered the *Solace of Dawn* a drifting wreck. Her crew were all slain and the records only began to hint at the savagery involved in the assault. Since that time, dozens of additional confirmed losses have been attributed to Rak'Gol attack. The Rak'Gol may have victimised countless more, but limited communications and the lack of any remains means that any numbers would be speculative at best. Over the decades, Rak'Gol sightings continue to occur throughout the trailing and rimward portions of the Expanse. In recent years, other human craft have also confirmed encounters with these marauding terrors in the Cauldron and Heathen Stars, indicating their spread across the Expanse. Unfortunately, very few have survived an encounter with these xenos to tell the story of their conflict. Even fewer have retained sufficient sanity to make the stories believable.

With their continued expansion, the Rak'Gol have eradicated the sentient life on dozens of planets. In some instances, these were isolated populations of primitive xenos. In others, the creatures destroyed larger human settlements, including the one on Nypson's Prize. Throughout this time, no known humans have ever established a meaningful dialogue with the species. Rather, attempts at communication have always ended with violent conflict as the xenos continuously attack any whom they encounter. As a consequence, little is directly known of their culture, philosophy, or language—or even if they possess any of these traits. Suppositions have been made regarding all of these matters, particularly in concert with information obtained from other xenos species concerning encounters with the Rak'Gol.

Even prior to the first confirmed human losses, races such as the Stryxis and the Vyrkeen mentioned the Rak'Gol when dealing with human cultures. Ancient legends from several cultures spoke of a race that travelled the stars, purging planets as they went. The capabilities accorded to these xenos varied from world to world, but a few factors were consistent with modern reports from Imperial sources. The first of these issues is the clear fact that the attackers were relentless and merciless. The aliens were known as the Scourge of the Expanse, and the legends described them as relentlessly cleansing planets of all life and culture.

Similarly, these mythical terrors were described as corrupted and armed with fell mechanical enhancements. The legends disagree on the reason for this, but all clearly indicate their mechanical components were designed to increase their combat capabilities. Some of the tales said the creatures hated themselves as much as they hated other life, and thus replaced components to distance themselves from their physical form. Others suggest that the Rak'Gol were a race created from nothing by another god-like race and that the mechanical components were simply used to finish the job, replacing those parts that could not be crafted biologically. Additional stories suggest that the implants might be associated with status, purity, or serve as a requirement for reproduction. However, the truth is likely to remain unknown until Imperial agencies capture and interrogate one of these xenos.

Most confirmed knowledge of Rak'Gol cultural activities has been discovered through the analysis of combat sites. Since the earliest known encounters with these xenos, those few humans who survived have often been thoroughly questioned, whether by a Rogue Trader who wants to see the Rak'Gol destroyed, a renegade Magos Biologis, or even the Inquisition. However, such questioning often proves largely futile—as the survivors are often plagued by horrible mental trauma. It is unclear if this damage was a consequence of the horrors that they faced or if it is a direct consequence of any psykers that may be found among the Rak'Gol. Astropaths used in the investigations have only returned inconsistent reports after analysing surviving victims. Some insist that the degree of mental scarring could only be a consequence of mental assault, while others argue that the damage is more likely due to a combination of visceral reactions to extreme terror and possible warp taint.

While individual reports are rarely particularly informative, members of the Ordo Xenos have recently shed additional light upon the Rak'Gol through comprehensive analyses of compiled studies. It is clear that the creatures possess a hierarchical society. Their command structure appears to be based upon a combination of martial prowess and cybernetic enhancement. Currently it remains unclear if these enhancements are attained only after their wielders have obtained a certain degree of success or if those who possess such enhancements build up the necessary combat capability to advance within their ranks.

RAK'GOL PHYSIOLOGY

The dual taints of the warp and radiation are commonly found among the Rak'Gol. The radiation may be a consequence of the "fission-pulse" drives found in their vessels. However, it may be that the species seeks this out as a means of inducing additional mutations among their ranks. The seneschal and information broker Nathin Thsanthos has observed that he is unsure which option is more terrifying—that the Rak'Gol deliberately seeks out corrupting mutation, or that the species is so consumed by bloodlust and rage that they no longer have the interest or ability to conduct basic maintenance on their vessels.

While some mutations are clearly due to the depredations of the warp, others seem more consistent with those developed following extended radiation exposure. The combination of these two influences clearly affects the species' gene pool, which has resulted in substantial variation between specimens found in different regions of the Expanse. At the same time, Imperial reports have not identified any tribal or cultural iconography that associate with any of these genetic variants. This suggests—but does not confirm—that the Rak'Gol may lack the necessary cultural sophistication to develop tribal cultures.

Members of the Magos Biologis have marvelled at remains recovered from Rak'Gol conflicts. Studies indicate that the species is egg-laying and that Rak'Gol undergo extensive physiological changes over the course of their maturation. Further, their reproductive methods appear to involve a trinary breeding scheme that is dependent upon the age and stature of the individuals involved. Some reports suggest that biochemical and physiological changes may occur in the Rak'Gol based upon their social standing within their communities. As the xenos attain specific levels of authority, this may trigger shifts in their reproductive mode. However, these factors cannot be confirmed until live specimens are studied over an extended period.

Astropaths have been unable to consistently divine future attacks, even with the assistance of the Emperor's Tarot, as the simple brutality occurs at unpredictable intervals across a huge range of locations. The xenos infest the Unbeholden Reaches more so than others, but attacks have occurred inconsistently in many other locations. Among voidsmen, many legends have circulated that the warp itself often places the xenos vessel in ideal locations to launch an attack at the most inconvenient time possible. These legends are most common within the regions of space where the Rak'Gol are most active—a factor that is hardly coincidental.

In sharp contrast, based upon their exploration patterns through the Koronus Expanse, there may be more of a pattern to at least some of Rak'Gol attacks than first appears. A number of these assaults occurred on worlds where xenoarchaeologists have identified the remains of civilizations lost long before the first Rogue Traders passed through the Maw. This suggests that the seemingly mindless Rak'Gol have the motivation and abilities necessary to carry out a search for something lost. Thus far, however, no researcher has been able to discover what could be valuable enough to send them out across the Expanse.

This presents a challenge to Imperial forces attempting to constrain the Rak'Gol. Without a known target, it is far more difficult to provide consistent protection against the alien incursions. Their volatile and unpredictable natures only exacerbate the problem. Ultimately, there are far too many worlds containing the remains of shattered cultures within the Koronus Expanse to hope to protect them all. The most prominent Rogue Traders in the Expanse—Winterscale, Chorda, and Saul—have promised great rewards to the persons who discover the source of these foul aliens, so that they might descend upon their world and cleanse it with the wrath of their considerable fleets. However, thus far no one has managed to accomplish this.

TABLE 3-5: RAK'GOL WEAPONS

Ranged Weapons

Name	Class	Range	RoF	Damage	Pen	Clip	Rld	Special	kg	Availability
Rak'Gol Razor Gun	Basic	40M	S/–/–	1d10+5 R	0	10	Full	†	4	Very Rare
Howler Rifle	Basic	30M	–/–/12	1d10+3 I	4	600	2 Full	Storm	35	Very Rare
Rad-beam Cannon	Heavy	150m	S/–/–	4d10+5 E	8	10	2 Full	–	90	Very Rare

Melee Weapons

Name	Class	Range	Damage	Pen	Special	kg	Availability
Rak'Gol Rad Axe	Melee	—	1d10+8 E	7	Power Field, Toxic, Unbalanced	15	Very Rare
Rak'Gol Intimidator	Melee	—	1d10+4 E	2	Shocking	5	Extremely Rare

†Razor guns fire barbed slugs that augur their way through flesh and other soft tissue, leaving horrid wounds. Those taking five or more Damage from this weapon after Armour and Toughness suffer the Blood Loss Critical effect.

WEAPONS AND GEAR

"Effective, but poorly optimised. Ammunition is expended too quickly for effective use in an extended firefight. Unmodified humans are incapable of carrying sufficient ammunition for maximal utility."

—Magos Trosk, Weaponsmith of Leveen Rho

The Rak'Gol appear to care little for their gear, as is readily evidenced after every raid they conduct. They casually leave weapons and armour behind, as well as their dead. In those instances where a defender successfully survives a Rak'Gol assault, they always have samples of the xenos tech to use or provide to the Adeptus Mechanicus for analysis. Similarly, in those cases where a vessel at least put up an effective defence against the Marauders, the ship's ruins always contain samples of Rak'Gol technology for those that salvage the remains. Consequently, Inquisition and Adeptus Mechanicus agents have successfully assembled far more information about Rak'Gol technology than they have managed to glean of their history or culture.

In the years since the Rak'Gol emergence, various xenographers and Adeptus Mechanicus explorators have undertaken exhaustive studies of Rak'Gol technology at their own initiative or at the behest of those Rogue Traders who want to see the Rak'Gol destroyed. The results of those studies reveal a race possessing an inferior technological base to humanity, though the beasts seem able to compensate for this somewhat with their hyper-aggressive demeanour. Rak'Gol energy production seems firmly rooted in primitive atomics, meaning their ships' motive power comes from dangerous and inefficient fission pulse engines, rather than the mighty plasma drives of Mankind. Though they can reach an impressive speed, their turning and acceleration is greatly limited.

The rest of their technology shows the same limitations. The Rak'Gol have little skill with the arcane sciences of energy weapons. While the few such devices they do possess are potent atomic beam weapons, they are also bulky and unwieldy. The "roarer beams" mounted on their starship are spinal weapons running the length of the hull, and the few beam weapons used by individual Rak'Gol suffer similar limitations, their bulk requiring them to be wielded by the largest and strongest of the xenos race.

Simple projectile weapons make up the majority of the Rak'Gol armoury. Some of these weapons are very similar to human heavy stubbers or autoguns, though this is more likely a quirk of similarly evolving technologies. Another common variant of projectile weapons fire barbed razor shells that shatter into sharp fragments on impact, ripping through a target's body and causing massive and usually fatal tissue damage.

Cybernetic enhancements are a clear hallmark characteristic of the species, though again, these are almost always bulkier and cruder than their human equivalents. Virtually every combat-capable specimen has at least one mechanical modification, and many of the bodies recovered possessed more than a dozen different implants. Rak'Gol cybernetics tend to be simple but robust, able to withstand a great deal of punishment before failing, and sometimes operating long after their owners die. It remains unclear if these devices are still manufactured by the Rak'Gol, recovered from their fallen brethren, or simply ancient devices that remain from a time when the race might have possessed a greater level of sophistication and technical aptitude.

Clearly there are individual members of the species that possess sufficient technical acumen to implant these devices within the bodies of their brethren. Most of the devices' purposes are fairly obvious—cybernetic limbs, bionic replacement organs, and implanted weapons. However, some served no discernible purpose, even when subjected to detailed analysis. At least one Magos employed by Aspyce Chorda attempted to learn their function by implanting the devices in a number of the Rogue Trader's indentured workers.

Initially analysts believed that the Rak'Gol implants were non-functional as the installed devices appeared non-responsive to standard query protocols. Further analysis showed little evidence of any energetic flow within the devices, suggesting that the alternative hosts were incapable of activating and controlling these implants. However, the test subjects soon discovered that these preliminary results were not consistently accurate. In all cases, if the human body did not fatally reject the unknown implants, severe mental degradation followed within a week. It is unclear if this was a consequence of the implant's unusual biochemical interface or if the implants affected the brain directly. None of the test subjects survived beyond two weeks—and the three that possessed some rudimentary psychic abilities perished in screaming agony within hours. It is said that Chorda sold the results, as well as the services of the Magos who conducted the experiments, to an agent of the Ordo Xenos in Footfall.

One point of note about Rak'Gol technology is that a small but significant percentage seems to incorporate technology that bears the hallmark crystalline and bone structure associated with the Yu'Vath. This suggests that the Rak'Gol may have an association with that dead species. Some of those who have had the misfortune of encountering one of the Rak'Gol "Abominations"—the xenos' leadership caste—note that they are more likely to possess Yu'Vath technology, indicating that it may be some sort of status symbol amongst them.

Rak'Gol have been encountered possessing Yu'Vath symbols, as well as symbols that learned scholars of the arcane and the forbidden claim are debased and simplified symbols of the Ruinous Powers of the warp. Clearly, the Rak'Gol have some sort of ties to the Immaterium, possibly through their covetous desire of Yu'Vath technology.

RANGED WEAPONS

Most Rak'Gol seem to disdain ranged weapons, exhibiting a clear preference for melee combat. In several instances, survivor reports have indicated that Rak'Gol wielding ranged weapons tend to use them as melee weapons once their ammunition is depleted, rather than reloading.

Rak'Gol Razor Gun

The most common ranged weapon among these xenos, these weapons use chemical propellants to hurl finely barbed slugs at their targets. These weapons are most effective against lightly armoured targets and often inflict savage wounds upon their victims. The slugs create a distinctive high-pitched whine as they corkscrew through the air at hypersonic speeds. The combination of the sound and the savage howls of the marauders haunt the nightmares of nearly all who have survived encounters with these savages.

Howler Rifle

Rak'Gol wielding Howler Rifles are easily identified by the large packs of ammunition that they must wear strapped to their torso to supply these chain-fed weapons. The rounds are made of a dense, ceramic-like material fired by highly volatile propellent. The tri-barrelled weapon spits out thousands of these rounds per minute with great gouts of flame, yielding a characteristic wailing noise as it showers unlucky targets with lead.

Rad-beam Cannon

The massive Rad-beam Cannon is only rarely seen among Rak'Gol units. The cannon discharges a blast of high intensity atomic radiation that voraciously breaks down armour and materials and kills living tissue. The radiation is focused

through an unstable ionisation field, meaning the wielders often suffer doses of radiation whenever it fires. While an extremely effective weapon, the Rak'Gol wielding it often show little patience for getting it aligned and waiting for it to recharge after each burst. Only the Abominations seem capable of restraining the bearers from throwing themselves into melee combat instead.

MELEE WEAPONS

Many Rak'Gol choose to employ only their natural claws and massive teeth as their weapons of choice in close combat. Others use a vicious collection of implanted mono-blades and armoured, razor-edged gauntlets designed to rend and tear flesh with maximum carnage.

Rak'Gol Rad Axe

The massive blade on this pole-arm is characterised by an ionisation field that focuses a massive radioactive discharge. When these weapons are used, the battlefields often suffer from substantial levels of radioactive contamination.

Rak'Gol Intimidator

Only a few of these handheld devices have been recovered, but no eyewitness reports indicate their use in combat. Adeptus Mechanicus agents believe that the Intimidators are primarily used as torture devices, but records indicate most Rak'Gol Abominations carry them. This may be an indicator of status or a means to maintain discipline among their crew.

NYPSON'S PRIZE

This world was once held by human colonists, lost to the Imperium for several millennia. The inhabitants lived a simple, agrarian lifestyle on a planet that possessed long growing seasons. Most of them lived contented, peaceful lives of quiet contemplation and farming. Their technology regressed and stagnated, to the point that their agricultural equipment was primarily powered by native animals.

Vessels associated with House Ma'Kao re-established contact with Nypson's Prize in 784M41. At that time, they created agreements to exchange substantial portions of the world's agricultural output in trade for off-world communications, information, and a selection of Imperial supplies. The arrangement worked effectively for just over a decade of regular shipments and communications. Then, the Sacred Testament arrived to find the world a toxic wasteland, its population completely eliminated, its landscape devastated with huge craters, and its atmosphere a radioactive hell. Ship's sensors suggest that a Rak'Gol vessel may have crashed into the surface of the planet, unleashing the scouring radiation. No further details have been recovered, though rumours suggest House Ma'Kao has made several failed attempts to recover the remains of the crashed xenos ship.

ABOMINATION

Only rarely observed, Abominations are believed to be the highest known rank of Rak'Gol active within the Koronus Expanse. Examples of these creatures are most often seen during the latter stages of a Rak'Gol attack. All instances where survivors described specimens occurred on planetary surfaces. While analysts believe these creatures play a role in shipboard combat, they hypothesise that by the time they join the battle the outcome is virtually certain and survivors are tremendously unlikely.

Analysts have concluded that Abominations typically command Rak'Gol vessels and—in the rare instances where multiple Rak'Gol ships co-operate—small fleets. Reports indicate that their approach to close combat mirrors their shipboard tactics. These xenos embrace all out assaults and prefer to manoeuvre so that they might engage in melee combat at the earliest opportunity. While these massive specimens are always willing to engage in conflict, they are never alone. Abominations are always accompanied by other exceptionally large Rak'Gol specimens. Agents of the Ordo Xenos suggest that these guardians are Broodmasters that have been tasked with a specific responsibility to protect their overlord.

Abominations are typically slightly larger than other Rak'Gol. This may be due to physiological changes associated with their cultural status, but it is more likely that this is a direct consequence of the extensive implants present within these specimens. Many (though not all) reports of Abomination sightings indicate that the specimens exhibit extensive decorations upon their cybernetic exoskeletons. The patterns described were complex—several witnesses suggested that they also played tricks upon the eye. Others have stated that the symbols were identical to patterns found among Yu'Vath ruins. The patterns could be specific iconography associated with these individuals or it could be that they are present to indicate specific links to the Ruinous Powers.

If Imperial analyses are correct, then it is likely that the Abominations are involved in selecting the places where the Rak'Gol launch their attacks. Consequently, it is likely that they are familiar with their overarching goals. Abominations may even be associated with different combat groups or in direct competition for some unidentified resources present within the Koronus Expanse. Ordo Xenos agents as well as individuals associated with groups victimised by the Rak'Gol remain extremely interested in discovering such information. In such a case it is likely that eliminating a single Abomination might thoroughly disrupt Rak'Gol activity within a region, or it might refocus internal struggles as the species reacts to the new power vacuum.

Alternatively, it is possible that there might be a higher-ranking unknown entity responsible for coordinating Rak'Gol actions. Such a being or group of beings might easily be unknown due to the lack of communication and confirmed reports of Rak'Gol activity. Some even suggest that it might be another species of xenos entirely, though since the Rak'Gol response to every xenos they encounter has been murderous frenzy, this is unlikely.

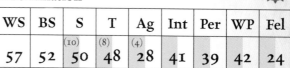

Abomination

WS	BS	S	T	Ag	Int	Per	WP	Fel
57	52	(10) 50	(8) 48	(4) 28	41	39	42	24

Movement: 5/10/15/30 **Wounds**: 35
Armour: Implanted ceramic plates and stone-like hide (Body 9, Head 7, 6 Arms, Legs). **Total TB**: 8
Skills: Awareness (Per), Climb (S) +10, Command (Fel) +10, Demolition (Int) +10, Dodge (Ag)+10, Intimidate (S) +10.
Talents: Bulging Biceps, Combat Master, Die Hard, Fearless, Hard Target, Lightning Reflexes, True Grit, Sprint, Swift Attack.
Traits: Fear (3), Hunting Frenzy†, Multiple Arms, Size (Hulking), Quadruped, Sturdy, Unnatural Strength (x2), Unnatural Toughness (x2).
†**Hunting Frenzy**: Rak'Gol tend to go into a frenzied berserker rage once combat begins. Treat this as the Frenzy Talent, except that the Rak'Gol may enter it immediately as a Free Action.
Weapons: Rak'Gol Intimidator (1d10 +14 E; Pen 2; Shocking) or Rak'Gol Rad Axe (1d10 +18 E; Pen 7; Power Field, Toxic, Unbalanced), Rak'Gol Howler Rifle (30m; –/–/12; 1d10+3 I; Pen 4; Clip 600; Reload: 2 Full; Storm) or Rak'Gol Razor Gun (40m; S/–/–; 1d10+5 R; Pen 0; Clip 10; Reload: Full), 3 frag grenades, 1 krak grenade.
Gear: Bionic respiratory system (Good Craftsmanship), implanted vox, photo-visor, suicide device (as bomb collar, self-detonated), bomb-collar remote detonation system (for underlings).

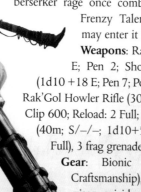

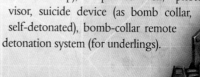

RENDER

The Rak'Gol, as a race, have deeply embraced the ways of the warp. However, even among these blood-crazed savages, there are those who go too far in their pursuit of additional power. Mercifully rare, these Renders are larger and even more violent than typical Rak'Gol. They are easily recognised, even in isolation, as they never carry any additional armaments and typically are almost totally covered with protruding cybernetic modifications.

The most comprehensive study of these comparatively rare xenos-forms took place after the Rogue Trader Joquin Saul came under attack. Saul was able to fight off the marauding Rak'Gol vessel that ambushed his *Necessary Expenditure* off the Lethe Clouds, though not before his ship fought several desperate boarding actions. In the wake of the combat, a representative of an Inquisitor approached Saul, requesting the corpses for research. Saul acquiesced, and a year later, a report concerning certain Rak'Gol xenosforms arrived at the Tricorn on Scintilla. Though the studies were incomplete due to the damaged condition of the subjects, they revealed that the Rak'Gol known as "Renders" were extremely different from that of typical Rak'Gol Marauders.

Renders universally showed a thirty to forty-five percent increase in muscle mass when compared to Marauders with a comparably sized skeletal structure. Renders also showed a marked structural change in overall neural structure. Sensory organs showed a marked increase from the norm in other Rak'Gol corpses. Further, the neural pathways connecting the specimens' auditory and visual organs showed a substantial thickening. In contrast, the neuronal regions believed to associate with cognitive processes showed a marked decrease. It is believed that these changes offer a biological explanation for the specimens change in role to that of a devoted hunter as opposed to the more generalised neurophysiology of the Marauders. A potential side effect of these changes is that this subspecies appears to have lost some degree of control over their characteristic combat rage, sometimes requiring a greater time to build up to that desired state.

Renders also exhibit an increase in the overall number and type of cybernetic enhancements. It is unclear if these enhancements are all fully functional within the specimens examined; it may be that some of these implants served only as additional armoured protection. Few of the implants present in the examined specimens appeared functional, though these components might have been damaged as part of the events that led to the user's death.

Alternatively, it might be that some of the additional cybernetics were used to transform a Marauder into a Render. Previous studies suggest that Rak'Gol may be capable of biological change in response to cultural pressures. It may be that the presence of so many cybernetic components—particularly those associated with increased sensory awareness—could trigger a physiological change comparable to that associated with the Abomination variant. It is unclear if Renders might be created deliberately in this manner or if their presence could be an inadvertent side effect involved in developing additional Abominations.

Reports indicate that these specimens are almost universally encountered at the forefront of Rak'Gol voidship attacks. In most instances, fewer than ten Renders are present. Their additional implants and muscle mass serve them well as they present the largest targets in such conflicts. However, the Renders seem to have less technical aptitude than even the most primitive of Rak'Gol. These savage beasts appear capable of little more than melee combat and may be incapable of such basic tasks as opening an unlocked portal to continue pursuit of their prey. This might be a significant vulnerability if it were not for the fact that these xenos are typically capable of smashing their way through most walls.

Render

WS	BS	S	T	Ag	Int	Per	WP	Fel
58	24	(15) 50	(10) 50	(4) 20	24	39	15	03

Movement: 5/10/15/30 **Wounds**: 33

Armour: Implanted plates and stony hide (Body 9, Head 6, Legs 5, Arms 5).

Total TB: 10

Skills: Awareness (Per), Climb (S) +10, Dodge (Ag), Intimidate (S)+10.

Talents: Bulging Biceps, Combat Master, Die Hard, Fearless, Frenzy, Hard Target, Lightning Attack, Lightning Reflexes, True Grit, Sprint, Swift Attack.

Traits: Fear (2), Multiple Arms, Size (Hulking), Quadruped, Sturdy, Unnatural Strength (x3), Unnatural Toughness (x2).

Weapons: Implanted mono-blades (1d10+15 R; Pen 4; Tearing).

Gear: Bionic respiratory system (Good Craftsmanship), implanted vox, photo-visor, and suicide device (as bomb collar, self-detonated).

RAK'GOL ADVENTURE SEEDS

As the bloodthirsty, rampaging terrors of the Koronus Expanse, the Rak'Gol can be easily added as an additional encounter in virtually every scenario. They can strike from hiding at any time and seldom need motives to rationalise their actions. In such a situation, their militant nature serves as the only focus of the encounter. However, this use neglects many of the possibilities presented by these savages. A few alternative approaches follow:

TECH-HUNT

In some instances—but not all—Rak'Gol scavenge a ship's contents after they complete their assault. The goods captured can vary from prisoners to technological devices essential for a vessel to survive within the void. Rak'Gol might alternatively seize basic sundries from a vessel while ignoring valuable archeotech or they might do just the reverse. The methods by which they determine value remain unclear.

After an attack, word begins to circulate throughout the region that a Rak'Gol ship has acquired a valuable piece of human archeotech that predates the Age of Strife. A rival Rogue Trader house owned the device previously and now offers a generous bounty for its recovery. While the Explorers might prefer to recover it for their own purposes, they must also compete with other groups that seek to return it for the generous reward. Of course, the threat presented by their human competitors pales next to the dangers involved in finding and assaulting a Rak'Gol craft. Even if the Explorers can successfully identify the craft that took the artefact, they must still defeat it and recover the device. This may mean assaulting the xenos vessel with hit-and-run attacks, or even battling their way through it while their own vessel attempts to stay within support range. Of course, if the Rak'Gol have deciphered how they might use this ancient device, the matter could be further muddied as the Explorers try to avoid having it used against them.

TREASURE IN THE DEPTHS

The worlds of the Koronus Expanse are unquestionably ancient and have seen the growth and collapse of countless civilisations. Humanity has come to the region comparatively recently. Many of the worlds that they have settled served as homes to other species across the aeons. The remains of these lost cultures are often buried miles beneath the planet's surface, but the Rak'Gol seem capable of identifying some of these sites in spite of the difficulty. It could be that they have access to unbelievably ancient maps, or they have some other connection to one of these extinct civilisations. In either case, once they have identified a target, they pursue it mercilessly.

The survivors of a planet under Rak'Gol assault send a desperate plea for assistance out to the stars. The Explorers receive the distress signal and must choose to offer assistance or flee before the might of the Rak'Gol forces. When they investigate the message, they discover that the planet is a world rich in natural resources with a relatively low population density. Such a planet could offer substantial compensation for a Rogue Trader that might come to their aid. When the Explorers reach the world, they discover that the Rak'Gol have uncovered an ancient archaeological site and are busily searching the site for something, completely ignoring both the planet's inhabitants and the Explorers as they do so. This offers an opportunity to eliminate the Rak'Gol, but it might destroy the ancient site and its treasures as well.

CAPTURE

Thus far, no person is known to have successfully captured a Rak'Gol alive. The beasts are utterly savage and refuse (or are completely incapable) of engaging in any communication with their foes. Many bear suicide devices that they are willing to use if they are captured. Even if they are stopped from triggering such a device (which a few skilled hunters have managed to do), a captured Rak'Gol always throws itself into a murderous frenzy in captivity, until it either escapes, kills itself in the attempt, or forces its captors to terminate it.

Even for a successful Rogue Trader household, the bounty offered for the live capture of a Rak'Gol is a substantial sum. This could also represent a major accomplishment that might be recognised by others who could otherwise question the individual's martial prowess. As Rak'Gol seldom work alone, capturing a single individual likely represents a situation that could involve encountering hundreds of the xenos simultaneously. The Explorers must consider a variety of different strategies in order to identify one that could be effective under extremely dangerous conditions.

Once captured, the Explorers must figure out a means by which to keep the Rak'Gol alive in captivity. Considering the creature's considerable size and strength, conventional restraints may not be successful. The Explorers might have to invest in more esoteric devices, such as a stasis field, in order to accomplish their goal.

THE SSLYTH

"Snakes that try to act and dress like men—how could anyone trust such a creature?"

—Arch Militant Kestral Overmears

Alberse had decided to take the *Aureus* to Adulia's Narrows, a backwater world near the Naduesh system. It seems he heard of a planet that contained vast amounts of a certain metal valuable in cogitator production. The rumour spoke of a cabal of merchants making an agreement with some less-than-reputable traders for mineral rights of the world and protection while there. Alberse knew he would have to move quickly if he wanted to set up a mining claim before the merchants could get to the planet and begin operations. The world was no more than chains of islands on a vast sea that occasionally harboured odd xenos structures, monoliths and ruins; it was on one of these islands that Alberse decided to start the prospecting, with hopefully a full extraction vault to follow.

They came upon us as we landed, before we could even set up a perimeter, crawling out of the trees surrounding the beaches. Their forms were humanoid but only in the loosest sense of the word, with snakelike bodies and four long arms holding long blades. Each wore a familiar style of plated xenos armour on its torso and arms, all in dark colours that contrasted with the bright scales covering the rest of their bodies. My first thought was Rak'Gol, but I quickly realised that these attacked only with sibilant hisses, not the howling warcries of those foul xenos. These also brought scents of cinnamon and incense on the morning breeze, something odd that has always stuck in my mind when I think of them.

The lead creature tried to speak to us in a chattery, raspy language that none of us could make out while I herded Alberse behind me. At first I thought Alberse was going to try to communicate, but instead he signalled us all to go to arms. We raised our weapons upon seeing his sign and not a moment too soon. The xenos creatures reached behind their backs to draw

larger spiked rifles, and I fully recognised them as belonging to those cruel Eldar pirates I've had the misfortune of encountering. Alberse shouted as well to look to the rear, where several more of the xenos had silently taken positions. I managed to get off a shot but Adept Everson was caught in their opening salvo, ripped apart by shards of razor-sharp material.

I threw Alberse to the sand looking for any cover I could get him into while firing my bolter wildly at the things. As I fell atop Alberse, trying to shield him as best I could, Armsman Korham rushed forward. The xenos swung his rifle at Kolberse, which he blocked easily. He forgot the other arms though, and poor Korham fell to a pistol shot in his chest even as the creature opened his throat with a wicked blade.

Despite our position, our heavier weapons managed to put down the creatures. They fought well, I must admit, only retreating when bloodied beyond my expectations. We limped back to the lander to make our escape, Alberse stopping of course when he noticed a fallen blade in the thick trail one left in the sand, xenos blood mixed with the grains. I have seen him use it from time to time to cut the thick seals on secured slates as well as to impress visiting traders, both to equal effect. I'm wondering if he is keeping it just so he can give it back to those snake-creatures should we meet again.

XENOS MERCENARIES

The Sslyth are a sentient race of reptilian creatures with a snake-like lower body and vaguely humanoid torso, though they sport multiple arms and a head more serpentine than human. This xenos has two pairs of strong arms which work independently of one another, meaning a Sslyth has a great deal of dexterity and can even use multiple weapons at the same time. Sslyth are hairless and covered with thick, iridescent scales, and while the head is vaguely human there are no visible signs of ears outside of a small hole on each side of the Sslyth's head. The creature has large, wide-set eyes and instead of a nose, it has a pair of nasal pits. The Sslyth's lipless mouth holds a set of huge fangs that protrude from the upper jaw, along with a host of smaller sharpened teeth. A thin forked tongue flickers from its mouth, constantly tasting the air for prey. The senses of the Sslyth are overall quite advanced, displaying a far better sense of smell than humans, but with less-developed hearing.

The Sslyth's lower body provides locomotion, with wide flat scales that allow the creature to grip the ground and pull itself along. They can move quickly and with good speed over most types of terrain, and their multiple arms along with their lengthy torso allow them to climb rapidly when needed. The scales are larger on its back and sides, and the roughly textured arms host strong hands able to easily crush a man.

SSLYTH IN THE EXPANSE

The Sslyth are intelligent and most xenologists believe they can understand and even communicate in various languages. They have been known to work with other xenos species, especially the enigmatic Eldar. When questioned about the Sslyth, the Eldar however do not discuss them or any bargains they have made with them. Some more infamous trader captains have been reported to be trying to hire Sslyth as mercenaries, but as far as anyone knows, none have as yet succeeded. Given the nature of the Expanse, though, it is very possible these captains have kept the matters as private as possible, lest the actions of their xenos employees be traced back to them. The Sslyth would make excellent hired fighters if such a bargain could be struck, as they are tenacious in combat, seemingly able to disregard enemy distractions as they go about their duty. Many Explorers hold that this could be the result of conditioning programs implanted by their masters, but others who have watched the creatures in action hold their behaviour more resembles that of debauched addicts, too fallen to their excesses to mark what happens around them.

The Sslyth have been found on several different planets and regions in the Expanse, usually in small packs of no more than six, but occasionally larger groups have been sighted as well. If they are seen with any technology, it is always of another race's make. They seem to prefer the vicious shard weapons favoured by Eldar pirates, but it is unknown if this indicates they are a subservient race to those cruel xenos or simply have greater access to their weapons. There are also no records of actual Sslyth voidcraft either, and many xenologists hold the Sslyth can only travel through the stars at the whim of their employers.

Storytellers in the Expanse tell that they are an ancient xenos culture that fell to darkness long ago, but then that is a common way to speak of almost every xenos race in these unlawful regions. There are those who speak of the Sslyth in the same breath as the Rak'Gol and whisper their name alongside such foul things as the Yu'Vath, but this would seem an overly aggressive assessment of the threat they pose. Though there are few properly documented accounts, the Sslyth seem to function as dedicated fighters, well able to defend their employers in combat. Several pic-captures show them using multiple weapons at the same time and even reloading one weapon whilst firing another. In close-quarters fighting, their extra limbs can wield several barbed swords in a whirling shield of blades that few can penetrate. Most importantly, they are either well paid or extremely loyal; some accounts have them fiercely holding ground to allow their masters to safely escape a conflict.

There is little data concerning the race's origins, or how they came to be in the Koronus Expanse. To date they have not been sighted in the Calixis Sector, though it is very possible that none have survived such encounters to report them. Their presence in this area, like their motivations, remains yet another mystery of the Expanse.

Sslyth Mercenary

WS	BS	S	T	Ag	Int	Per	WP	Fel
35	42	51	48	47	31	38	23	28

Movement: 4/8/12/24   **Wounds**: 25

Armour: Scales (Head, "Legs" 3), Eldar Carapace Armour (Arms, Torso 4).   **Total TB**: 4

Skills: Barter (Fel), Carouse (T), Climb (S) +10, Commerce (Fel), Concealment (Ag), Contortionist (Ag), Dodge (Ag), Forbidden Lore (Pirates, Xenos) (Int), Silent Move (Ag) +20, Speak Language (Eldar, Low Gothic) (Int), Survival (Int), Tracking (Int).

Talents: Sprint, Ambidextrous, Blademaster, Crack Shot, Dual Shot, Guardian, Gunslinger, Heightened Senses (Smell), Improved Natural Weapons, Last Man Standing, Nerves of Steel, Two-Weapon Wielder.

Traits: Crawler, Multiple Arms, Natural Armour (Scales), Size (Hulking), Sturdy, Unnatural Senses (Smell).

Weapons: Shard Carbine (60m; S/3/10; 1d10+2 R; Pen 3; Clip 80; Rld 2 Full; Toxic), brace of Splinter Pistols (25m; S/3/–; 1d10+2 R; Pen 3; Clip 120; Rld 2 Full; Toxic), xenos blade (1d10 R; Pen 2; Tearing, Toxic), punch claw (1d10 R; Pen 1), Fangs (1d10+3; Pen 0).

Gear: 2 ammo clips, decadent xenos charms.

THE STRYXIS

"Advantage is a fleeting thing, honoured biped. Its comings and goings few can predict. Best take action when advantage smiles in your direction, before it should smile on another."

–Drine Miir, Stryxis Nomad

We found ourselves the "guests" of the Stryxis following a brief encounter with one of their less than reputable kind whilst orbiting Lacristy. The leader of their caravan had promised Alberse mounds of goods and esoteric information if we would but accompany them to their base of operations and part with a few paltry icons. I advised against it; however, Alberse had his mind set on the deal. He said it would be foolish to pass up such an opportunity. However, I feared we were the foolish ones.

The *Aureus* set upon the coordinates relayed to us by their representative and we travelled for several days before arriving at their home, a collection of hollowed asteroids towed by a salvaged vessel of some unknown, possibly xenos, origin. We were greeted by the xenos from our previous encounter, Fai Taarn. It asked in Low Gothic (it spoke our tongue well enough, but the wet burbling of its voice was more than enough to remind me of its xenos nature) for us to send a small party to survey the wares that the Stryxis meant to trade.

Upon docking within one of the asteroid hives we were greeted by a cabal of the robed creatures who greeted us as a lowly merchant factor might have welcomed an Ecclesiarchy Cardinal on Veneris. Fai Taarn showered us with praise, calling Alberse "esteemed merchant liege" among other archaic and ancient labels, and the rest of the creatures behaved in a toadying manner that left me quite uncomfortable. It led us on through a maze of corridors talking excitedly, pausing at times to examine work that was being done to the passages. The workers resembled Imperial servitors; however, they were of a slab-like build and seemed specially designed for the labour they were performing. Fai Taarn said something in passing about the additional goods he would include in the deal if I were but to part with my hat. Despite Alberse's glare, I only stated I would consider the offer, and pushed it down more firmly on my head.

After what seemed like hours of twisting through the complex tunnels we emerged into a vast open space which was filled with many rows of silent, motionless beings. They stood there looking forward and never blinking, their smooth featureless faces expressionless. The feeling that hung about the room was like that of a hospice-ship or gene-factory, very sterile and purposeful. Fai Taarn made a gesture toward the rows of inanimate bipedal frames as though indicating that this was the treasure that the Stryxis merchant meant to trade.

The look on Alberse' face said it all. He had anticipated mountains of precious metals and resources, perhaps xenotech or star charts, not bio-crafted labour units. He had no use for these, and we all knew it. Alberse began saying something about expecting goods of a more dynamic nature. It was when Fai Taarn curiously asked if we preferred to inspect the slave pens that my suspicions of its motives were confirmed; at that point I proceeded to survey our surroundings, looking for exit strategies.

CRYPTIC WANDERERS OF THE VOID

The Stryxis are an utterly alien xenos, devoid of what a rational Imperial citizen might consider logic. They traverse the endless void in nomadic groups that they term Pacts, always searching for the next great trade. Their society is one based heavily on commerce and the attainment of knowledge, although the values that they assign to items can baffle even the most experienced of Explorers.

To encounter the Stryxis is to encounter enigma incarnate, for it is never certain if the creatures are going to attack or flee. However, it is almost guaranteed that the Stryxis attempt to barter with almost anyone they come across, save for the Eldar whom they hate, and the Rak'Gol whom they fear (along with the rest of the Expanse). The Stryxis are an uncommon sight in the Koronus Expanse. Their mark upon it, however, is undeniable.

Humanity has learned very little concerning the ways of the xenos now known to the Imperium as the Stryxis. The infrequency of encounters with these enigmatic voidfarers has lent them a nearly mythical reputation. Many believe that they are native to the Koronus Expanse, and more than one Inquisitor of the Ordo Xenos made it their mission to discover the location of a Stryxis homeworld. These endeavours have thus far proven fruitless.

The Stryxis have baffled mankind for centuries; their odd sense of value—and even more peculiar anatomy—make them one of the strangest xenos known to the Imperium. Members of this inscrutable race have almost always been encountered living in fleets of oddly constructed caravan ships known as Xebecs, and are almost always interested in trading with those whose paths they cross. Their mercantile ways have given them access to uncountable goods and relics. Their extensive travels have provided them with unfathomable amounts of priceless information; information that they shroud in secrecy, and do their best to protect.

These crafty, somewhat aloof creatures are experts at bartering and gathering information. They hold knowledge in high regard and are very careful about divulging anything in too much detail. Their secretive ways have led many to question if the information that they possess holds any truth, or if it is all merely fanciful tales told by unscrupulous merchants for a better return on their goods. The Stryxis only part with information that pertains to other species or areas of the Koronus Expanse that they have little personal interest in. They are notorious for being protective of their origins and secrets; many an Explorer who has strayed too close to these secrets has disappeared, or been found dead. The Stryxis appear supremely self-serving and notoriously do anything in their power to preserve their own lives.

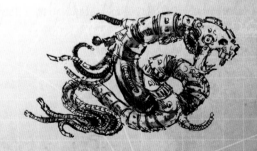

The Stryxis can be encountered anywhere within the Koronus Expanse; although they are most frequently spotted in the vicinity of The God-Emperor's Scourge or around the vast warp anomaly known as the Cinerus Maleficum. This has led to the genesis of many myths pertaining to the origins of the Stryxis. Some even speculate that their homeworld was on the coreward edge of the spectacular warp anomaly known as The Cauldron, and that the planet was swallowed by that storm many millennia ago. Others believe that it was possibly destroyed by the Eldar, a xenos that the Stryxis are known to violently avoid dealing with. Most researchers surmise that these two xenos share a hatred for one another, but none truly understand this perceived enmity. Others postulate that the strange creatures are but an advanced scouting or surveying wave of Stryxis and that their origins lie beyond the Rifts of Hecaton out on the farthest rim of the Galaxy.

Whatever the truths behind these stories are, the only clear things about the Stryxis are that they remain completely inscrutable, completely untrustworthy, and yet all of this they are often extremely profitable as trading partners.

Stryxis Anatomy

To be in the presence of a Stryxis is rather disconcerting; their twisted bodies, which are oddly elongated and covered in an exceedingly moist membrane, often make the less disciplined lose their nerve. This is said to be the reason behind their choice of attire, as they are almost always encountered wrapped in heavy robes that cover them from head to foot.

It is theorised that they augment their vocal organs with alien devices that provide a precise control over tone and pitch, allowing them an amazing range of communication. They are thought to be some of the most linguistically capable xenos in the Expanse. This grasp that they seem to possess over language has also been attributed to their immense lust for knowledge.

They are a bipedal species that can reach up to two metres in height; however, they tend to slouch and rarely stand fully erect. Their frames are exceptionally slender and each of their appendages ends in three prongs, their fingers elongated and claw-like, and their feet stubby and cushioned. Although the Stryxis seem to weigh very little, it is unlikely that one weighs less than 90 kilograms. The Stryxis have also evolved four small, inquisitive eyes and many believe these to be their most defining feature. These eyes scan and blink individually which gives them an even greater alien appearance. It is thought by many that their understanding of light and even their knowledge of warp travel is a result of their extremely unusual ocular capabilities.

The Imperium has never had reason to believe that the Stryxis possess gender traits. They do not exhibit any clearly definable gender specifying features and there is no recorded evidence pertaining to their mode of reproduction. Such physiological hypotheses are nearly impossible to prove, however, due to the shortage of Imperial autopsies of viable Stryxis corpses.

Pacts and Provenance

Ancient Thulean records are said to contain many possible interpretations of Stryxis culture. These records state that the groups of Stryxis who nomadically wander the void are known as Pacts; and that these Pacts are led by what are referred to as Masters. These sparse records hint that the most revered and powerful of

the Stryxis are known as Slave Masters—though many believe this to be a misnomer. Whatever the case may be, these shrouded leaders have vast convoys of spacefaring craft, asteroid hives, and armies of slaves and genetically-crafted labourers at their disposal. However, no researchers claim a definite comprehension of the minute complexities of Stryxis society.

They are notoriously fickle in their dealings with humans; one minute a trade is good, the next it simply does not suffice. This racial quirk has led to several reported clashes between the Stryxis and those whose offers are deemed unacceptable. To the Stryxis, everything has purpose and value, however the scales they use for such determinations are impossible for humans to decipher. Items deemed mere trinkets or trash by humanity are sometimes held in high value by these mysterious creatures; the reverse is also common. "One man's detritus is Stryxis gold" has been a phrase used for centuries amongst those who ply the warp routes of the Koronus Expanse.

STRYXIS WEAPONS AND GEAR

"I asked it what it would trade for its fascinating blade. It only looked at my young heir beside me and beckoned its claw..."

–Valen Surbaet, Chronicler

The sheer lack of Stryxis weapons or tools found in the hands of the Emperor's faithful means they are highly sought after by covetous Rogue Traders and xenographers, as well as agents of the Ordo Xenos. However, if convincing a Stryxis merchant to trade information about their species is a nigh-impossible feat, then doing the same in regards to their technology is even more difficult.

Although the Stryxis are consummate scavengers, they tend to use weapons that appear to be completely based on native technology. Though a Stryxis has never admitted as such, certain savants note that their weaponry often possesses certain consistent and very anomalous qualities. The most curious of these weapons are their Æther weapons. Few humans have ever been reported to be in possession of one of these eerily beautiful, ghostly weapons, and it is speculated that the humans lack the unique Stryxis ocular anatomy necessary for seeing the weapon's true qualities.

Æther Weapons

These exceptionally rare weapons glow with an otherworldly energy and none, save the Stryxis themselves, understand their full range of capabilities or origins. They have been reported to use several different design templates; blades and lances are the most common, though rarer rifles and whips have also been sighted. This technology is theorised to be incapable of penetrating energy shielding and nearly useless when pitted against a psyker's abilities. Æther weapons are often considered a myth by all but the most experienced of traders, and the scant reports of devices are vague and contradictory. They are also known as "ghost-light" weapons to the superstitious voidsmen who travel the Expanse, and the tales told of such weapons' horrible effects describe crewmen and even entire ships vanishing in a pale, misty glow.

TABLE 3-6: STRYXIS WEAPONS

Name	Class	Range	RoF	Damage	Pen	Clip	Rld	Special	kg	Availability††
Ranged Weapons										
Light Pistol	Pistol	30m	S/–/–	1d10+5 E	0	30	Full	Reliable, Accurate	2	Near Unique
Light Rifle	Basic	90m	S/–/–	1d10+6 E	3	15	Full	Reliable, Accurate	5	Near Unique
Lightburner Cannon	Heavy	240m	S/–/–	3d10+10 E	5	5	2 Full	Accurate Overheat	50	Near Unique
Æther Rifle	Exotic, Basic	90m	S/3/–	1d10+2 E	†	40	Full	Special	3	Unique
Melee Weapons										
Æther Blade	Exotic	—	—	1d5+2 E	†	—	—	Special	3	Near Unique
Æther Lance	Exotic	—	—	2d5	†	—	—	Unwieldy	5	Near Unique
Æther Whip	Exotic	4m	—	1d10+4 E	†	—	—	Special, Flexible	2.5	Unique

†Æther Weapons bypass conventional armour and toughness to strike the target for direct Damage. Physical contact with energy shields or psychic powers renders melee Æther weapons useless for 1d10 days. These weapons do not damage non-living targets (such as creatures with the Daemonic Trait) or targets with the Machine Trait (5+), and cannot be used to Parry due to their insubstantial nature. Æther Lances have a long hilt and thus may be parried, but at a –10 penalty. Æther Blades have smaller hilts and cannot be parried.

††Should a Stryxis Merchant be offering the item, the Availability is made one level easier (for instance, Near Unique goes to Extremely Rare).

Æther Whip

It is believed that these vicious weapons are used by only the most socially-advanced Stryxis. They resemble Æther Blades and Lances in that they are made of a solid grip and a long incorporeal lash that glows with ghostly energy. The flexible energy cords are mainly employed to keep the slave populations on board Stryxis vessels in line, or at least that is the most popular current conjecture.

Æther Rifle

These Æther weapons are very rare and peculiar. They follow slightly different design patterns than their melee cousins, but have very similar effects on stricken targets. They fire ammunition made from what appears to be Æther energy, which can be devastating because of its ability to pass through most forms of solid protection.

LIGHT WEAPONS

Although these weapons are similar to the Imperial Guardsmen's standard issue las weapons; the basic rifles, pistols and cannons of Stryxis design fire a continuous beam of energy and are extremely accurate. These weapons, however; burn through their charge quickly. They have multiple design templates, each of which is crafted by a TechSight Master to fire in different spectra. Every different design is capable of firing a focused energy beam that acts in accordance to its specific spectral output function. Each of these spectral outputs possesses its own peculiar capabilities. Many xenographers have come to refer to these weapons as "light-rifles" or "light-pistols."

These are employed by the majority of the rabble who fight for the Stryxis in their infrequent engagements.

Although slightly weaker than Imperial las weapons, some Stryxis weapons have the ability to fire a constant and focused beam at a target over a long period of time. These are sometimes referred to as "lightburner" weapons by those humans who have had the misfortune of being on the receiving end of their fire. Reports of these weapons' functions come from illegally procured Thulean records and are considered inaccurate at best, however.

Many other weapon templates are rumoured to exist. These weapons are highly sought after by agents of the Ordo Xenos and also by dangerously curious xenographers. Should a brave Explorer get their hands on one, the rewards would be substantial.

Light Pistol and Light Rifle

These ornate and archaic-looking las weapons are relatively similar to Imperial las weaponry. They tend to be more accurate, though human wielders find such weapons are difficult to fire if one has more than three fingers.

Lightburner Cannon

A much more powerful laser device, the so-called "lightburner cannon" is a Stryxis heavy weapon, and must be crew-served or mounted on a vehicle. It focuses a deadly laser beam on a target for a long period of time, until metal runs like hot wax, and flesh incinerates to a smeared black char.

Every consecutive turn after the first that a wielder fires a Lightburner Cannon at the same target and hits, the weapon deals an additional +2 Damage and gains an additional +2

Penetration, to a maximum of +10 to each value. This represents the wielder holding the beam on the target. If the wielder ever misses the target or loses line of sight to the target, the additional damage is lost and the wielder must start over.

OBEDIENCE DEVICES

The Stryxis employ a multitude of restraining techniques on their slave populations with the Slave Collar being the most commonly used device. These slave obedience devices can either be detonated through remote or proximity methods and also are triggered if the wearer attempts to remove it. The following slave submission mechanisms are a relatively common sight along the slave routes of the Koronus Expanse as the Stryxis are some of the most prolific slavers in the sector.

Bomb Collar

A crude collar with small explosive devices rigged to it, bomb collars are detonated if compliance is not reached. These are used for those strong enough to break free from a claw collar.

Claw Collar

Fashioned to look like a small Stryxis hand gripping the wearer's throat from behind; collars of this design are used to choke, strangle, and even kill their unfortunate wearers if they fail to be obedient to their Masters.

Excruciator

Once implanted into the cortex of a potential slave, Excruciators interface with the nervous system. Upon predesigned triggers, the Excruciator shocks the nervous system creating paralysing pain in its host. The implanting process is a complex one so these devices are saved for use on exceptionally valued or resilient slaves.

PERSONAL PHASE REALITY SHIFTER

The Stryxis have developed a technology that creates a barrier that conceals all items and life signs behind it. This effectively hides whatever the phase shifter's shield envelopes from all augury attempts save for those of the most powerful of psykers. No one, save the Stryxis TechSight Masters, claims completely certainty concerning the true workings of this xeno-tech. Those dubious Masters of Stryxis technology have developed these devices to work onboard ships as well as for individual, high ranking Stryxis; although, ship sized "shifting" devices are bulky and beyond rare. These devices cause Scrutiny Tests and Augury Sweep Tests to suffer a −30 penalty.

TABLE 3-7: STRYXIS GEAR AND IMPLANTS

Name	Class	Kg	Availability†
Bomb Collar	Special	3	Extremely Rare
Claw Collar	Special	5	Extremely Rare
Excruciator	Implant	0.5	Unique
Phase-Reality Shifter	Special	6	Unique

†Should a Stryxis be offering the item, the Availability is made one level easier (for instance, Extremely Rare goes to Very Rare).

STRYXIS NOMAD

"So many eyes... so many looking through me... what does it really want from me?"

—Intercepted vox-cast near Foulstone, origin unknown

The Stryxis are a wandering species, spending most of their existence tumbling through the cold and unforgiving void. They have proven to be exceptionally adept at this lifestyle, however. These xenos act as "friendly" merchants just as easily as underhanded pirates and can change from one to the other on a moments notice. Either way, it is almost guaranteed that a bargain can be found somewhere during encounters with this particular race, assuming an Explorer maintains a very cautious attitude at all times.

One of their most common representatives are the so-called Nomads, perhaps given this appellation as indicative of the race as a whole. Although from what xenos savants can determine, these Stryxis make up the majority of this elusive xenos' reported true population, their numbers are dwarfed by those of the slaves and Vat-Born that inhabit Stryxis vessels.

The standard Nomad tends to be a basic pilot or salvager, standard trades for the race, though some lean more toward more extremes of exploration or piracy. This usually depends on the particular habits of their Pact leaders, though like all Stryxis they can easily shift their disposition as the circumstance requires. Nomads are very adaptable and can perform well in almost any situation that may arise, making them useful in a variety of ship-board roles and dealings with other races. They are rarely effectively armed for conflict, however, and almost universally flee any situation that does not favour them heavily.

Stryxis Nomad

WS	BS	S	T	Ag	Int	Per	WP	Fel
33	33	30	35	40	47	(6) 35	32	28

Movement: 4/8/12/24   **Wounds:** 13
Armour: Robes (All 3).   **Total TB:** 3
Skills: Awareness (Per), Barter (Fel), Deceive (Fel) +10, Gamble (Int), Scholastic Lore (any one) (Int), Forbidden Lore (any one) (Int), Inquiry (Fel), Navigation (Int), Pilot (Ag), Search (Per), Speak Language (Low Gothic, High Gothic, Xenos), Survival (Int), Tech Use (Int), Tracking (Per).
Talents: Ambidextrous, Basic Weapons Training (Las) Heightened Senses (Sight), Hard Target, Hatred (Eldar or Rak'gol), Jaded, Pistol Training (Las), Paranoia, Polyglot.
Traits: Dark Sight, Unnatural Perception (x2).
Weapons: Light Pistol (30m; 1d10+2 E; Pen 0; Clip 30; Reload Full; Accurate), Truncheon (Melee; 1d10+3; Pen 0;) or Parrying Dagger (1d5+3 R; Pen 0; Defensive).
Gear: Assorted trinkets from other races, three ammunition clips, and xenos ration packs.

STRYXIS MASTERS

To the Stryxis, few things are as important as knowledge, for knowledge leads to leverage in most endeavours. Those who possess the greatest knowledge are said to attain the rank of Master. These Masters are considered by many to be the leaders of their Pacts and there may be several Masters within a single Pact who each captain a vessel or control a large portion of a ships population. This puts them in a position as acting heads of the Pacts in which they reside. In many Pacts it is not unheard of for there to be multiple Stryxis Masters vying for power; and most postulate that there are bitter rivalries between those who share this control.

These beings are those Stryxis who have navigated the complex Stryxis social webs through cunning, trickery, trade, and slave acquisition and have attained what appears to be the highest rank amongst the Stryxis. Pacts vary wildly in their makeup and power structure but are almost exclusively lead by these Stryxis Masters. Each Master usually maintains ancient and esoteric information that pertains to a particular aspect of Stryxis purists. One may be a Master Raider, a Master Merchant, a TechSight Master, or a Vat Master to name a few; however, the most feared of these elite Stryxis are the Slave Masters of Pacts Siennes and Vagrae, whom speculations suggest control the majority of encountered Stryxis society. Few have seen a Stryxis Master, as they tend to use agents when dealing with non-Stryxis.

The massive populations of slaves within Stryxis Pacts is said to be one of the major factors behind the Slave Masters dominance of Stryxis society. However, this cannot possibly be the only reason as the Vat-Born, who are controlled by the Vat Masters, make up the vast majority of any Pact's population.

The dress of these vaunted Stryxis is much more refined then that of the common Nomads, their robes are more ornate and covered with all manner of ancient icons and shimmering trinkets. They wear loose hoops made from a plethora of precious materials around their exceptionally slender wrists, perhaps as a show of position and standing.

Below is the basic Master profile template as well as modification packages to create specialised Stryxis Masters.

Stryxis Master

WS	BS	S	T	Ag	Int	Per	WP	Fel
38	38	33	41	46	60	38 (6)	42	48

Movement: 4/8/12/24   **Wounds**: 16

Armour: Stryxis Ghost-Field† (All 3).   **Total TB**: 4

Skills: Awareness (Per), Barter Fel) +20, Contortionist (Ag) +10, Deceive (Fel) +30, Evaluate (Int), Command (Fel), Common Lore (any two) (Int), either Scholastic Lore (any one) (Int) or Forbidden Lore (any one) (Int), Scrutiny (Per), Search (Per), Speak Language (any two) (Int), Tech Use (Int).

Talents: Ambidextrous, Heightened Senses (Sight), Hard Target, Hatred (Eldar, Rak'gol and one other), Jaded, Paranoia, Polyglot.

Traits: Dark Sight, Unnatural Perception (x2).

Weapons: Light Pistol (30m; 1d10+2 E; Pen 0; Clip 30; Reload Full; Accurate), Digi-Laser (3m; S/–/–; 1d10+3 E; Pen 7; Clip 1; Reload Full, Reliable), Æther Blade (Exotic Melee; 1d5 +2 E; Pen Æ; Special).

Gear: Many Exotic Trinkets, Badges and Insignia, High Quality Robes, Maps and/or other assorted items of information, Ammunition, Rations, Respirator, vox-translator.

†Stryxis Ghost-Field: These create a barrier that saps the strength of most attacks. A Ghost-Field's armour points are unaffected by the penetration of all weapons except those with the Blast or Flame qualities, Æther weapons, or effects generated by psychic abilities.

MASTER RAIDER

Those humans who have encountered a Stryxis raiding armada have almost universally been the target of their cripple-and-loot tactics. These tactics are employed to great effect by the underhanded Master Raiders within Stryxis society. A common scheme employed by these leaders of the more piratical of the Stryxis Pacts is said to use several phase-shifted, or otherwise hidden, assault craft lurking near a star system's entry point. A more docile-looking caravan then proceeds to hail and attempt to trade with ships as they drop back into real space. Once the target is deemed distracted or weak enough to attack, the assault crafts reveal themselves and quickly batter the unsuspecting vessel with crippling fire. The Raiders then swoop in and proceed to assault the decks of the now-crippled target with massive groups of slaves or Vat-Born at the fore, taking as many prisoners and valuables as they can escape with.

Stryxis Master Raiders are more combat-oriented Stryxis are exceptional in ship-to-ship combat as well as savvy with long-range firearms and Aether weapons. Seldom, if ever, do they engage targets that can put up a significant fight, however.

Skills: Add any two of the following: Demolition, Dodge, or Tracking (Int) +20.

Talents: Add Void Tactician.

Weapons and Gear: Add Xeno Mesh Combat Cloak (All 4); Light Rifle or Æther Rifle.

VAT MASTER

The creation of the Vat-Born is overseen by these incredibly knowledgeable genetic manipulators. They are thought to experiment endlessly with different designs and have quite possibly amassed small fortunes selling armies of Vat-Born to the highest bidder. Their exposure to all manner of chemicals has created in them a resistance to most intoxicants and poisons. Most Vat Masters are said to reside in Asteroid Hives although there are rumours that report large Xebec's that have been fully modified to carry out genetic growth experiments and Vat-Born production. These vile bio-engineers are some of the most revered individuals in Stryxis Pacts; this is most likely due to their control over the Vat-Born themselves which make up over half of most Pacts population.

Skills: Add Medicae (Int) +20, Trade (Chymist) (Int) +20.

Talents: Add Decadence, Resistance (Poisons), Master Chirugeon, Talented (Medicae).

Weapons and Gear: Add Vat-Born controller devices.

TechSight Master

Stryxis technology is closely guarded and the TechSight Masters are rumoured to be in possession of the secrets of this mysterious science. Although they are amongst the rarest of Stryxis, TechSight Masters have been reported to be capable of repairing and rigging almost any technology that is found in the Expanse. These masters of Stryxis technology are said to speak their own secret language and it is assumed that this language contains the intricacies of Stryxian technology. Agents of the Ordo Xenos are reportedly scouring the region to locate and capture one of these high ranking Stryxis, believing that their knowledge of Stryxis technological design is integral in the destruction of that foul xenos once and for all. No expeditions have been successful in this endeavour, at least none that have been reported.

Skills: Add Secret Language (TechSight) (Int), TechUse (Int) +20, Trade (Technomat) (Int)+20.

Talents: Add Infused Knowledge, Rapid Reload, Talented (Tech Use).

Weapons and Gear: Add any single additional melee Æther weapon or Stryxis ranged weapon; multi-tools, magnifiers.

Slave Master

A Slave Master is exceptionally adept at creating fear and compliance in the slaves and nomads that serve it. It is rare that a Slave Master is ever encountered alone, as they are almost always accompanied by large groups of slaves. The names of some of the more infamous Stryxis Slave Masters are whispered in primitive areas of the Koronus Expanse; almost as if these beings were daemons. Their capture and flee tactics have left many worlds stripped of large populations of inhabitants. When a Stryxis Slave Master is in the vicinity, one can almost be guaranteed that some form of slave exchange is attempted, either by trade or by force.

These foul and unforgiving beings seem to universally carry Æther whips; which, those that have encountered them and survived to tell the tale—or escaped the bitter slavery of these unforgiving beings—speculate is a symbol of their station. These fearsome weapons are said to rend one's very soul when they strike, moving through armour, flesh, and bone with impossible ease.

Skills: Add Awareness +10 (Per), Evaluate +10 (Int), Commerce (Int), Command +10 (Fel), Trade (Slaver) +20.

Talents: Add Air of Authority, Infused Knowledge, Whispers, Talented (Command).

Weapons and Gear: Add Xeno Mesh Combat Cloak (All 4), Æther Whip, Obedience Device trigger consoles, large amount of exotic and obscure trinkets.

VAT-LABOURER

The Stryxis are some of the Expanse's best gene manipulators and are well known as growers of biological labour that they refer to as "meat." Although this term is often applied to any non-Stryxis inhabitants of Stryxis Pacts, it is most frequently used when referring to these genetically grown beings.

The creatures that Stryxis manufacture are grown in large vats under the arcane directions of Vat Masters, and are more commonly known as Vat-Born. The Vat-Born come in all manner of shapes and sizes filling many roles for their Stryxis masters. Some are created for the sole purpose of combat, while others are specifically designed for very specialised labour.

Although they come in many forms, the Vat-Born almost always follow the basic template of four appendages, with a head and torso. In some rare cases, creations move on all fours, or have multiple heads or extra appendages. It is unclear if these deviations in design are purposeful or if they are merely experiments gone horribly awry. These constructs are also known to be augmented with implants and tools for the tasks they are specifically built to undertake.

These unnatural servants often account for the vast majority of the population on board Stryxis ships or asteroid hives. It is rare for a Stryxis Pact to have fewer than four times their population consist of these Vat-Born constructs.

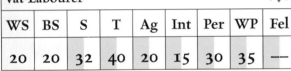

Vat-Labourer

WS	BS	S	T	Ag	Int	Per	WP	Fel
20	20	32	40	20	15	30	35	—

Movement: 3/6/9/18 **Wounds**: 12
Armour: Dense Augmentics (All 1). **Total TB**: 4
Skills: Awareness (Per), Trade (Vat-Labour) (Int).
Talents: None.
Traits: Machine (1), Dark Sight, Size (Hulking).
Weapons: Fists (1d10+3 I; Pen 0).
Gear: Practical but worn clothing.

STRYXIS SLAVES

The Stryxis are said to possess massive quantities of slaves that are taken from the ranks of any race that they can manage to dominate. The most common of these races are humans, Gretchin, and Kroot; however, they are not the only races that serve under the Æther whips of Stryxis Slave Masters.

Slaves perform a variety of roles on Stryxis ships and hives ranging from simple labour to more reputable work as soldiers and even, under special circumstances, as the personal bodyguards of important Stryxis Masters. It is said that some of these slaves are even given a chance at freedom if they fulfil the roles they have been enslaved to perform. These are very special cases and one is more likely to die than be released from servitude.

The Stryxis perceive value in their own unfathomable way, and a Slave Master never simply sacrifices a slave unless the benefits gained by doing so far outweigh the losses. Slaves are kept in relatively clean quarters and in fact some say their living conditions are significantly better than those found in many underhives. When dealing with outsiders and attempting to trade slaves, the Stryxis refer to these unfortunates by the demeaning moniker of "meat."

A slave's willpower is sapped as they are tortured and subjected to many conditioning procedures. Although the Stryxis value their slaves highly, they never run the risk of having an unruly slave population due to the massive discrepancy between the number of slaves and the number of Stryxis. Slaves outnumber Stryxis on a three to one basis within most Pacts, a number that is much higher in Pacts controlled by Slave Masters. However, slaves are aware that if they do not comply with their controllers they face death as a consequence.

COMBAT SLAVES

The more martially proficient a slave is before capture, the more likely they are employed as combatants in the sparse instances of Stryxis warfare. Stryxis see the utility of using Slaves to perform dangerous boarding actions along with other combat manoeuvrers, and are always more likely to risk the potential loss of slaves over the loss of one of their own kind.

Imperial soldiers, Kroot mercenaries, and those unfortunates found on lost worlds who possess a strong arm and resilient constitution are most commonly used in the role of combat slaves. The Stryxis see these beings' previous training as a quality to be utilised, not wasted on the labour decks of Stryxis vessels. Some of the most well-known battles involving the Stryxis were won or lost on the backs of combat slaves.

Combat slaves are often administered drugs to increase their ferocity and strength; Slave Masters are careful not to overuse this technique, though, not wanting to unnecessarily damage their "goods." Legends tell of combat slaves who were finally released after exceptional service, though the Stryxis could be propagating these myths themselves for obvious reasons.

A combat slave is treated in all respects as a standard Stryxis slave save for the single weapon they are equipped with during battles and the drugs that are used to increase their strength, speed, and toughness. These weapons tend to be basic laspistols and primitive melee weapons such as knives or clubs, though depending on the nature of the combat they might be given almost any weapon from the Armoury section from Chapter V of the ROGUE TRADER Core Rulebook. The drugs used on Combat Slaves act like Slaught and Stimm (see pages 142–143 of the ROGUE TRADER Core Rulebook).

STRYXIS ADVENTURE SEEDS

When using the Stryxis in their games, GMs should strive to impart a completely alien experience onto their players. The peculiar trading habits of the Stryxis and their penchant for turning on those they once held as allies make them ideal double-crossers or potential dealers of extremely rare items and information.

Stryxis are not a common sight but can be found in relatively large numbers around the God-Emperor's Scourge, the Cauldron, and the Cinerus Maleficum. They rarely destroy a ship or colony outright, always preferring to loot and take slaves. The Stryxis also make every effort to conduct trade with almost every race they encounter. The only known exceptions are the Eldar or Rak'Gol; these xenos are always treated with hostility and never used as trading parties.

GMs are encouraged to play up the odd nature of the Stryxis, especially when it comes to barter and trade. Their very strange sense of worth can add an interesting element to any encounter. This race is very protective of its personal secrets and go out of their way to ensure that detailed information concerning Stryxis origins or technology of Stryxis design does not fall into the wrong hands.

Below are several Adventure Seeds to help GMs add the Stryxis to their games of ROGUE TRADER.

SKELETAL SEEKER

Rumours have surfaced within the Cold Trade's communication channels that tell of Mordechai Sebastor, an infamous xenographer, and his search for a captain with an unscrupulous mind and a penchant for silence. These whispers expound many fanciful tales, but one thing underpins them all, the involvement of the ever-elusive Stryxis. Mordechai Sebastor has studied the sparse accounts of the nomadic Stryxis since his banishment from the Collegus Xenorum on Archaos in the Calixis Sector for his heretical research on xenos physiologies. He is currently in the market for the skeletons of Stryxis; he'll have them by any means necessary. However, the Stryxis are viciously defensive of their secrets and more than capable of keeping them.

THE LOST NOBILITE

The rumour mills of Footfall are abuzz with talk concerning the fate of Navigator Jarvis Benetek. It is said that this member of the highly regarded Navigator House of Benetek was accompanying an Imperial expeditionary force on a voyage of conquest deep into the heart of the Koronus Expanse. However, communication was lost with the fleet several weeks ago and it is rumoured that the Stryxis may have played a part in this. The Agents of House Benetek on Footfall are offering a great reward for any information pertaining to Jarvis, with a hefty bonus to be awarded if he is returned alive.

CONFLICT OF THE WANDERERS

The Stryxis Pact Houri has been locked in a struggle with the Eldar known as the Children of Thorns for several decades. It seems as though the vicious Eldar Corsairs are following Pact Houri throughout the Expanse and every battle between the two has ended with great losses to the Stryxis. Pact Master Mobri Gethi has requested the assistance of any Rouge Trader willing to risk open conflict with the treacherous Eldar, and has offered an incredible reward to any who take up arms in defence of Pact Houri.

THE YU'VATH

"Beware the dead, even as you fear death. For the God-Emperor protects us after death, but that which slumbers eternal may rise again."

–From the journal of Kobras Aquairre

W e landed on the planet under the auspice of Inquisitorial dictate. For long forgotten reasons, the planet had been interdicted during the Angevin Crusade. Some member of the Ordo Xenos—I know Alberses dropped the name, but it meant nothing to me—asked that he take a look at it. There was obviously some benefit to the dynasty as well, but it clearly was not going to affect my bottom line.

When we arrived, it seemed safe enough. The atmosphere was foggy and rank, but breathable. The Inquisition had provided some advance equipment, so the crew had gleaming carapace armour that perfectly matched the dynasty's colours. If I could have seen clearly through the fog, I'm sure they would have looked glamorous. As things went, we were forced to rely on auspex and visual enhancers in order to attempt to navigate at all.

In spite of all that, there weren't any initial signs of why the planet was forsaken. Alberse had been given a map, though, and we were tasked to follow up on it. It turned out to be several hours from the landing site and, given the poor atmospheric conditions, we were told not to move the lander. As we travelled on foot through the marshy swamps, we all knew that we were being watched. The squad was getting jumpy from the tension. Harrigan even fired off a full magazine at a tree that he insisted "leaped out" at him. Even the servo-skulls were acting oddly, floating in patterns as if they were catching images of things that none of us could see.

When we reached the site, we knew it wasn't a mountain. It was a Yu'Vath ruin. We took the lead to explore the complex, and things went well for the first few hours. Then one of the troopers decided to place his hand upon a control panel. Within moments, the complex's structures began to shift and change. Walls moved and energy arced. Our weapons were useless against the crushing forces of the structure and the unleashed dark energies that lashed throughout the walls. Of the platoon, only three survived the encounter. I expect that two of those will spend the next month in surgery while the third's mind is shattered beyond recovery. We saw things within the energy flow. I cannot let myself think of them, but they haunt my mind whenever I close my eyes.

Over the decades that I have travelled the Koronus Expanse, I had never before seen a Yu'Vath site. But I saw a gleam in Alberse's eye. I think he wants to find more so that he might leave a legacy to his dynasty. It would certainly be an impressive one; even though the blessed Crusade wiped them out they left behind enough things that still bedevil the living. Being known as the Rogue Trader who finally ended their menace would certainly be enough, even for his massive ego. Right now I can only let his luck play out. If he falls, I only hope to have greater influence on his successor.

LONG DEAD BUT STILL DEADLY

During the time of Angevin Crusade, in the 39th millennium, the Yu'Vath were eliminated from the portion of the galaxy that would later become the Calixis Sector. In spite of this, their wretched taint remains present within the Koronus Expanse. The technology of these ancient creatures and the terrors that they spawned remain a blight and a constant danger. Much of it lays dormant beneath the surface of seemingly serene worlds and scattered among ancient space hulks adrift through the ages. All of these silently wait for some ancient sign or foolish sentient to trigger their activation. Many of these devices seem innocuous as they subtly influence their wielders towards the ways of the Ruinous Powers. Others are blatantly hideous in the way they directly expose victims to the raw power of the warp. Yu'Vath technology represents one of the most blasphemous threats to the strictures of the Adeptus Mechanicus, and those who dare to trifle with it risk destruction and utter damnation.

HISTORY

"From the moment of their first defeat, their will for battle was overcome. When the xenos wretches faced their betters, they knew that their warp-tainted souls would soon face damnation."

–Attributed to Saint Drusus, at the conclusion of the Angevin Crusade

At the dawn of the 39th millennium, the Imperium returned to the Calyx Expanse. The Yu'Vath and their client races represented the most potent xenos opposition active within the region. Their blasphemous technology in concert with their inherent psychic abilities presented a substantial challenge to Imperial efforts to seize control of the region. The Yu'Vath had maintained control of this section of the galaxy for untold millennia, and during this time they had established countless colonies and created or subsumed dozens of other xenos species into their empire. Untold planets already bore the abandoned ruins of ancient Yu'Vath civilisations, even as their expansion continued in every direction throughout the Calyx Expanse. Throughout the region, mankind found evidence of Yu'Vath activity on the vast majority of inhabitable worlds they encountered in the Expanse.

From the first contact, there was little chance of peaceful relations. Yu'Vath technology clearly embraced the warp in ways that were anathema to the Adeptus Mechanicus and the Ecclesiarchy. In place of traditional void shields, many of the xenos vessels incorporated foul devices that functioned by directly interacting with the Immaterium. Loyal servants of the Imperium lost their minds when simply viewing these vessels in combat without a single salvo fired. The histories recount countless unnatural creatures emerging from these devices to spread terror and destruction upon those who opposed them. The Yu'Vath's man-portable weapons and even the architectural designs posed comparable threats to the minds and souls of all who interacted with them. The leaders of the Angevin Crusade wisely chose to take swift and decisive action to eliminate this threat from the galaxy.

THE CRUSADE'S TRIUMPH

To this day, it remains unclear just how many of the Yu'Vath were active within the region when the Crusade arrived. The wretched species had attained a high level of decadence as they ruled over their servant races from their blasphemous towers and installations. Reports suggest that every Yu'Vath may have had in excess of a million slaves bound to see to its every need, and some of the corrupt beings clearly had entire worlds devoted to fulfilling their every whim. Their urges were as diverse as their imaginations, but almost all involved harnessing the unstable nature of the warp to incur perversion on a planetary scale.

Reports of their physiology and psychology are fragmentary. Inquisitorial edicts certainly eradicated some of these records, while others were lost to the vagaries of time and the eccentricities of local archival systems. There are no extant reports indicating that any of these wretched xenos were captured alive. There are numerous references to reports compiled by members of the Adeptus Mechanicus Magos Biologis, but none of the actual analyses are known to have survived intact. Fragmentary records indicate that at least three autopsies were performed, but the available data is remarkably inconsistent and uninformative. It may be that none of these studies had access to a complete Yu'Vath corpse or it could be that the available samples were markedly divergent in their anatomy. It is clear that the combination of warp influence and their advanced technology resulted in significant degrees of morphological variance between members of the species. If the available data is any indication, then the Yu'Vath were not necessarily humanoid in structure, but this may have been a direct result of extensive bodily modifications or accidental mutations.

Some members of the Ordo Xenos suspect that the Yu'Vath culture may have been in decline prior to the arrival of humanity in the region. It could be that the ancient race had achieved such a height of decadence that they were no longer capable of sustaining it, even with the assistance of the races they had enslaved. A few members of the Magos Biologis have even gone so far as to suggest that the common genetic markers shared by their client races might actually indicate a commonality of origin. If this were true, then those species might actually be the synthetically engineered descendants of the Yu'Vath rather than unique xenos in their own right.

This logical path begins with the notion that the Yu'Vath must have had a total population that was immeasurably large in order to have established colonies upon so many worlds within the Expanse. However, when the Angevin Crusade overcame their war machines, the number of opposition forces was modest at best. It might also suggest that somewhere beyond the explored reaches of the galaxy, a massive Yu'Vath civilisation yet remains. Given their abilities to manipulate the energies of the warp, they might even have developed facilities within the daemonic realms beyond the borders of reality. If such survivors remain, they might lie in wait to re-establish their empire at the expense of any humans who dare to stand in their path.

The countless Yu'Vath ruins spread throughout the Koronus Expanse also cause concern. The vast majority of these are little more than broken cities buried beneath tonnes of rubble, characterised in part by the Yu'Vath's architectural preferences. While the styles varied substantially, most of their

buildings were constructed of raw stone, crystal, or bone-like ceramics. In the majority of cases, these structures were encapsulated with complex polymeric layers that preserved the construction and may have also played a decorative role. In many instances, these unusual coatings were applied to the structures such that they inscribed complex geometric structures, arcane formulae, or complex and blasphemous pictographs of inhuman iconography. Further, many of these structures seem capable of some degree of self-repair, a feature that makes dating their origins extremely challenging.

The iconography of these sites represents another common reference point to identify their origins. The symbols inscribed are often uneven and asymmetric in their style. Though no known literature has survived the passing of the species, many of their ancient devices also bear such iconography. Rumours suggest that some agents among the Ordo Xenos may be capable of translating these ancient markings. However, the rumours also hold that any who attempt such a translation could lose all semblance of sanity in the process of deciphering the hideous glyphs.

The overall preservation of the complexes varies substantially between various sites and planets. In some instances the structures often seem habitable, while others are little more than buried rubble. The inconsistencies between various discoveries also pose their own mysteries. In some systems with multiple habitable worlds, only a single planet shows signs of Yu'Vath inhabitation. In others, Yu'Vath structures are densely packed upon airless rocks too small to ever have maintained an atmosphere. Due to the unusual technology, dating their creation by traditional methods is seldom accurate. Fortunately, in some cases, the surrounding rock and soil offers a better clue to their age than the basic structures. Of course, this is only true for the oldest of structures, where the underlying planetary elements have shifted due to the passage of time that can only be measured in a geological sense. For those sites that were active up until the arrival of the Angevin Crusade, such reference points are far less common.

RUINS OF AN EMPIRE

A few of the ruins seem to still have some remaining functionality, but the nature of their precise function is uncertain. Some analysts have concluded that they are little more than ancient mines, but others wildly theorise that the arcane devices might be designed to trigger the death of local suns or unravel the materium. It is clear that they draw energy from whatever power is available; the stars, geothermal sources, or even the warp are tapped to keep these complex machines active long after their creators have ceased to live. However, their ultimate purposes remain an unknowable mystery. Legends tell that some of these machines may be haunted—driven to carry their blasphemous xenos message to any who would approach them. Others seem devoted to defend a location against any threat that might appear. Every active port circulates dozens of legends that recount the disasters faced by those who delved too far into an ancient Yu'Vath site.

Beyond planetary surfaces, a handful of ancient Yu'Vath voidstations appear active within the Koronus Expanse. Some are located on rogue asteroids, while others travel adrift in the vast empty spaces between the stars. Legends even hint of stable constructs within the warp far from any mortal civilisation. Through their sophisticated and blasphemous technology, these stations seem to continue to actively pursue the tasks commanded by their long dead masters. Those who dare to intrude face defences engineered by these potent xenos and risk becoming a part of such a station's debris field.

Xenoarchaeologists that have studied these ruins disagree about their age. This is, in part, due to the unusual materials, but also is due to the lack of any cultural progression throughout the various structures. There are few signs of cultural diversity among a population that clearly spanned an enormous region of the void. Similarly, the technology involved in even the most worn of ruins seems consistent with that found among samples that were inhabited during the time of the Angevin Crusade. Best estimates suggest that the Yu'Vath civilisation may have reached its peak more than a hundred thousand years ago, but it may have been stable for countless ages prior to when the Imperium exterminated the race. Even those samples believed to be the oldest show signs of warp contamination and devoted servant races; it is very possible that far more ancient ruins remain to be discovered.

TECHNOLOGY

"There is a corrupt logic present within these artefacts, but to understand it would be to risk corruption of the soul and the mind. The Machine-God has no tolerance for such blasphemies."

–Magos Mortigen Hale, Disciple of Thule

Scattered among the Yu'Vath ruins are artefacts that incorporate their unholy science. To some individuals, these ancient devices are of tremendous value simply due to their rarity and age. Many less-than-scrupulous Explorers willingly exploit this fact by selling the artefacts through the Cold Trade for an enormous profit. Some who engage in this practice have been caught and punished by agents of the Inquisition or the Adeptus Arbites. Others have retired to sedentary lifestyles of peace and wealth within the Calixis Sector. However, the vast majority of those who dared to dabble with these devices have paid for their hubris with damage to their minds, bodies, or lives.

Yu'Vath artefacts are most easily identified based upon their material composition and their iconography. Almost all of these devices are constructed of a crystalline or ceramic material that resembles natural or fossilised bone. These devices often bear twisted and asymmetric symbols that seem to distort and shift under most lighting conditions. The precise reason for this is unclear; some hold it is simply a holographic effect inherently designed into the construction materials. Beyond these basic points of commonality, little more information is available about these devices through legitimate Imperial resources.

The core problem with the authorised study of Yu'Vath technology is that it is inherently anathema to the Adeptus Mechanicus. Only the bravest, most foolhardy, or heretical Tech-Priests dare to trifle with these artefacts. More conservative members of the order choose to keep their distance and advocate that any Yu'Vath creations be contained and buried or destroyed (preferably all three). In instances where such objects are found in the void, their advice typically favours launching the artefacts into the nearest available star.

ARTEFACTS OF DOOM

There are two primary reasons for this attitude. The first is that many of these devices are capable of direct interaction with the warp. Virtually all of the surviving artefacts rely upon a constant connection to the unnatural realm as their primary source of power; some go a step further and utilise this unholy association in their core function. A few might serve a relatively useful and minor role, such as warning of a presence within the warp or monitoring the nearby warp for any anomalies that might cause difficulties in travel and communications. Others, however, have far more dangerous interactions such as unleashing vast quantities of warp energy in unpredictable patterns, presenting a beacon to warp entities, or even opening a portal to the warp.

The second major blasphemy of Yu'Vath technology is that much of it incorporates synthetically constructed spirits. Unlike the blessed machine spirits that dwell within all sanctified Imperial technology, these entities are unliving creations of the extinct xenos. Those few Tech-Priests who willingly speak of these devices mention that the spirits may be daemonic essences captured from the warp or simply unholy creations that have grown more malicious over the millennia since their creation. The fools who dare to tamper with these artefacts are often influenced by the dark spirits to perform actions that could damn their minds and souls. Some may unwillingly establish a close relationship with the Ruinous Powers, while others might simply destroy themselves and all they hold dear as the devices subsume their minds for their own dark purposes.

These two combined dangers represent a significant threat to even the best-trained members of the Adeptus Mechanicus. For those without such a background, these objects pose an even greater danger. Many of the Yu'Vath artefacts become active the moment that a sentient being approaches. More than one Inquisitorial report begins when a single undisciplined individual acquired and activated such a device without even realising that his mind had already fallen under its influence. In many cases, such artefacts pose an even greater threat aboard a vessel that travels through the warp. It is for this reason that so many Rogue Traders who dabble in the Cold Trade have become lost. These xenotech creations already interact with the warp directly, and some create a portal through a vessel's protective Gellar Field. In the presence of a warp storm, this pinhole can sometimes offer hostile entities access to the vessel's interior with predictable results.

Of course, for some individuals, the rewards offered by these potent artefacts more than offset any risks associated with them. Legends tell of Yu'Vath devices that could transport planets through the warp, provide limitless energy, or even extinguish stars. More modest examples are clearly capable of reading and controlling minds or slaying a sentient in countless subtle ways. A single device, if used effectively, could make a person unimaginably rich or save a planet from the brink of starvation or ecological destruction. These blasphemous constructs harness unbelievably potent forces in efficient and effective manners. It is not the devices that pay the price for their use however, it is instead the users who dare to work with the artefacts knowing that it may cost them their souls.

A few Rogue Traders have discovered Yu'Vath vessel components among the space hulks that drift within the Koronus Expanse. While rare, these devices often enhance vessels in ways that are not in keeping with the Imperium's understanding of science. Voidsmens' tales include Yu'Vath engines that can allow a vessel to complete a warp transit at shocking speed, travelling from one end of the Expanse to the other in moments. Other stories recount shields that are utterly impenetrable and weapons capable of shearing through a battleship in a single salvo. Yet virtually all of these stories tell of the dark price that the vessels paid for their use. Those craft which were not lost during a warp transit were inevitably soon populated by crews driven mad by the components that had once seemed their salvation. When Imperium technology breaks down it is typically only inconvenient or deadly. When a Yu'Vath component fails, the ship and her crew may suffer fates far worse than mortal death.

A few known Yu'Vath artefacts pose a substantial individual risk in that they graft onto the owner when used. Such devices clearly represent a xenos analogue to cybernetic devices. Imperial cybernetic replacements are typically only installed at the patient's discretion; most often after a loss of a limb. These unholy creations are capable of completely subsuming a user's organs when first activated. Astropathic observers have even

suggested that just as the artefact merges with the individual's body, so too does its mind and soul fuse with the wielder's. Most immediately die during the process, as the devices attempt to interact with neurophysiology that is clearly at odds with their original design. Those who survive the process may be changed as the unholy synthetic spirit attempts to seize control of their body. At least three anecdotal reports indicate cases where what started off as a handheld device eventually completely replaced the user's body with a bony exoskeleton, devouring the body and the mind to drive it towards a task that had been pre-programmed millennia in the past.

Interestingly, some of these devices seem to physically grow in size and capacity as they are used. Ancient tales suggest that such expansion in capacity comes as they devour the wielder's soul. Better-documented reports from the Angevin Crusade indicate that this may actually be an inherent part of Yu'Vath manufacturing. Some reports from the time of the Crusade suggest that with sufficient use, some of these artefacts actually produce functionally identical devices. In this way, a critical ship's component might grow its own replacement part or a device that served a frequent need might be duplicated and spread throughout the Yu'Vath Empire. In spite of these tales, it remains rare to find identical Yu'Vath artefacts. It may be that these duplicates are not as capable of preservation or it may be that over the millennia the original device somehow absorbs them once again. Without confirmation and analysis by Adeptus Mechanicus agents, the Ordo Xenos retains only a limited understanding of those unknowable creations it has seized and destroyed.

TIES TO THE WARP

A less common hallmark of Yu'Vath technology is that some of their artefacts blatantly display the unholy energies that they wield. While some can channel the warp into a weapon, many radiate its foul essence wildly as they function. Vulgar plumes and arcs of darkly coloured and poorly focused light often form baleful shapes as the devices convert energy into function. This light can play tricks on the eyes and the minds of all who observe it. Some see decay and depravity in all things illuminated by the dark energy. Others simply crave the power that the artefacts represent—and may be driven to attempt to seize such items for their own purposes. None who have seen this power in action can forget it, as merely the sight of such a flow leaves its mark upon the viewer's soul.

Some of the Yu'Vath devices exhibit their sentience in a more direct fashion. A few artefacts are actually independently mobile, travelling across worlds to feed upon minds and souls. Those that encounter these unholy terrors are often utterly devoured. The combination of a spirit propelled by the warp merged with the miracle of Yu'Vath technology poses a threat that is nigh unstoppable for even the bravest of Imperial warriors.

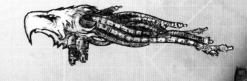

BONE CONQUEROR

"These xenos know true power when they find it, for they dare to desecrate humanity so that they might share in our grand destiny. This blasphemy must further fuel our hatred and devotion!"

–Missionary Jacobus, during the Angevin Crusade

Today went badly, but in an odd way it did make me feel better about the way things have been going. Alberse set up a meeting with a merchant with whom he had dealt in the past. The ship was to meet us in an uninhabited system to complete a trade of goods, and I deliberately chose not to learn the fine details. In spite of the fact that this was supposed to be a routine operation, Alberse asked me to come along with him to seal the deal—I think he wanted a show of force, and on another party's ship there would be no way he could simply take his trading partner on an extended tour through his own treasury of digi-weapons, explaining the finer points of each specialized killing instrument in gory detail.

The other captain was an obsequious, drooling fool. He had some notion of courtesy, but I think that was the full extent of his repertoire. After proper introductions were completed, an officer led us to their cargo bay so that we could view the goods prior to formal acceptance. That was where the problem began. Just before we reached the bay, the ship shuddered and we heard a sharp thud. The sounds of battle were in the air.

Just as we opened the door to the cargo bay, a corpse missing several limbs flew through the portal. After recovering from this shocking display, we cautiously moved inside. In the bay, we saw the remains of a dozen dead armsmen littered about the floor, and what I recognised from tavern tales as a Yu'Vath construct composed of the bodies of other corpses. Like many things in the Expanse, it was no longer just a story but now a deadly threat. Several of the ship's crew were blindly firing lasguns at the thing, but their efforts seemed to have little impact, even when they actually managed to hit the enormous target. Others cowered behind the packing crates that filled the cargo bay praying for salvation.

I didn't even think about what to do. My bolter, trusty as it usually was for me, was clearly inadequate for this fight and there were no other proper weapons to be found. Instead, I hit the emergency release to evacuate the cargo bay into the void, disposing of the creature, the vessel's cargo, and any surviving armsmen unfortunate enough to be within. The captain was in such a state of shock and so glad to be alive that he didn't even raise a fuss about losing his crew and cargo—until Alberse sent him the bill for my consulting services.

GUARDIAN OF THE DEAD

There are clear signs that the Yu'Vath engaged in some form of ancestor worship. Within their towers and their catacombs there are massive shrines devoted to the dead. Though all of the identified remains belong to known slave races, analysts believe that similar unidentified locations must house the remains of the Yu'Vath. Those who search for and investigate such sites, however, and tread upon the forbidden ground of the Yu'Vath, often discover such ruins attended by the most horrifying of guardians.

Many such investigators are unlearned hirelings worried only about the spirits of the entombed dead and other superstitions. Explorers more experienced in the nature of Yu'Vath ruins, however, know to fear more corporal hazards, such as the dreaded Bone Conqueror. Indeed, to those seeing it for the first time, the Bone Conqueror might well seem to be the spirits of the ancient dead rising up from the grave to strike down the interlopers treading carelessly on their hallowed ground. This is not the truth of the matter, but the reality of Bone Conquerors is just as terrifying.

These constructs seem to be created for the sole purpose of guarding the remains of the dead, or perhaps using the dead to provide one last service to their ancient masters. The Ordo Xenos have no confirmed reports indicating the origins or causes for activation of a Bone Conqueror. It is clear that they are only found within locations that resemble Yu'Vath mausoleums unless moved to a new location by ambitious, careless, or ignorant outsiders. However, some analysts suggest that these supposed Yu'Vath graveyards only appear at mausoleums due to the Bone Conqueror's instinctive desire to maintain a supply of corpses. It is also possible that, far more often than one would like to assume, Bone Conquerors that cannot get enough corpses to form bodies have simply gone unnoticed by treasure-hunters, and have been filed away as mere baubles, waiting dormant in the hands of some unsuspecting unfortunate for the right conditions to awaken them to their dark purpose and set about their terrible work.

The physical basis for a Bone Conqueror is a small artefact, typically less than fifty centimetres in length. The precise shape and mass of its makeup reportedly varies substantially, though all appear to be composed of a bone-like ceramic material. When inactive, these components are often mistaken for a tool crafted from a bone, as they are heavily inscribed with many indecipherable characters suggesting perhaps the Yu'Vath language. Typically, this gives them an innocuous and primitive appearance that give the uninitiated no reason for fear.

If one of these artefacts is brought within roughly twenty metres of one or more corpses, they immediately begin to assemble an oversized humanoid body from the remains. Generally, the Bone Conqueror is able to use its inherent warp-based technology to reanimate these body parts and keep them active for an extremely long period of time. So long, in fact, that the majority of confirmed Bone Conqueror encounters began when individuals discovered an active example rather than the isolated artefact. It is also believed that these artefacts have some inherent capacity to preserve the remains they are actively using. In this way, a Bone Conqueror's component bodies typically decompose at a rate much, much slower than is normally observed.

Bone Conquerors typically vary in size based upon their access to available corpses. The largest confirmed sightings were in excess of six metres tall, while less well-preserved specimens are typically much smaller. In some instances, Bone Conquerors utilise non-humanoid corpses in order to assemble their forms. Such variants may be distinctively different constructs, or they might just be an instance of the entity working within the context of available resources. The constructs clearly demonstrate environmental variation as well. In instances where a mausoleum is located within a room with a lower ceiling, Bone Conquerors reform their physical structures so that the reduced height is not an inconvenience.

The bodies that comprise the Bone Conqueror are linked together with an ever-flowing and rippling series of energy arcs. The exact type of energy involved is unclear. Tech-Priests of the Adeptus Mechanicus typically identify it as "dark energy" and refuse to offer any additional insights, and those seeking further information regularly find it unavailable through standard Imperial channels. These entities often use this same energy to launch attacks against those that intrude upon their domains. Those who survive Bone Conqueror attacks often complain that they are haunted by the experience ever after. At least two known victims deliberately returned to their attacker once more so their bodies might continue in its service. This suggests that there may be a telepathic element present within the constructs energy reserves, but there is limited data available to confirm this theory.

It remains unclear if these constructs were put into place to guard remains for sentimental reason or if there were a more pragmatic basis. It is clear that they represent a substantial threat to anyone that encounters them. It is also apparent that they are capable of using human remains to create their "bodies" as effectively as they can work with the remains of Yu'Vath client races. At the same time, there are no reports of them using non-sentient remains within their structures. The reason for such a requirement is unclear, and Ordo Xenos agents have repeatedly requested members of the Adeptus Mechanicus to investigate this phenomenon.

One unusual characteristic of the Bone Conqueror is that, because of its organic components, they seem to be far less stable than most other Yu'Vath constructs. When these terrors are left in isolation from any available corpses, they eventually revert to an inactive state. However, if they are later moved into a region where bodies become available, they swiftly reactivate. Anecdotal reports suggest that in such cases their capacity is proportionate to the number of bodies available, but no upper limit to its capacity has been identified. In at least one incident, a ship's crew discovered an active Bone Conqueror in their hold after human remains awaiting processing to corpse starch were temporarily stored near a cache of unknown xenos artefacts.

Bone Conqueror								
WS	BS	S	T	Ag	Int	Per	WP	Fel
59	37	(10) 54	48	36	43	38	44	––

Movement: 3/6/9/18   **Wounds**: 62
Armour: Ablative Corpses (Body 4).   **Total TB**: 4
Skills: Psyniscience (Per) +10.
Talents: Lightning Reflexes, Psy Rating 6, Swift Attack.
Traits: Cloud of Corpses†, Fear (2), Size (Enormous), Strange Physiology, The Stuff of Nightmares, Unnatural Strength (x2), Warp-Shard Crown††.
†Cloud of Corpses: Because the Bone Conqueror is a collection of dead animated flesh and bone, it can spread itself across a large area by sending bodies spinning and writhing through the air. Typically, a Conqueror is comprised of more than a dozen bodies spread over an area of up to a fifteen-metre radius from its crown. Anyone in or next to this area may be attacked by the Conqueror. As a Full Action, the Conqueror can make a single melee attack against every target in this area. A flamer or similar area-effect weapon inflicts double Damage upon the Bone Conqueror.
††Warp-Shard Crown: At any time, a Bone Conqueror can spend a Full Action to regenerate 1d5 wounds for every corpse within twenty metres as its shards burrow into their dead flesh and they are dragged into to the creature's mass. Once a corpse is used in this way, it becomes part of the Bone Conqueror and cannot be used again. The Warp-Shard Crown also has a secondary power to disrupt energy attacks and fields in its presence as the crystals sap their power. Power weapons thus only do half Damage against the Conqueror.
Disciplines: Telekinesis.
Psychic Techniques: Force Shards, Storm of Force.
Weapons: Claws and Fists (2d10+10 I, Pen 4), Warp Blast††† (10m; S/–/–; 2d10+8 R; Pen 12; Clip –; Reload: –).
Gear: None.
†††Warp Blast: The Bone Conqueror draws the power for its Warp Blast from the warp and so its ammunition is functionally limitless. These attacks also count as having the Warp Weapon Trait.

CRYSTALWISP

"When we saw the lights coming towards us, we thought it was a search party come to save us. We were so very wrong."

–Ensign Gordon Horne, upon his return to the destroyer *Legacy of Truth*

The crew was surprised when we detected another Imperial craft already in orbit around the isolated rock we knew as DN-382. The frigate, which bore the name *Honour's Shield*, did not respond to our vox hails. Augers showed that all of her systems appeared fully functional and active, but not even Senior Astropath Quarling could provoke a response from the craft. Alberse decided that I should take a team over to investigate. If the frigate were abandoned, she represented a valuable prize, and we certainly had the crew to at least safely return her to the scrappers.

Upon arrival, I discovered the voidship's passages were littered with bodies desiccated by the vessel's air purifiers. There were no signs of any struggle, sorcery, or disease. The corpses were simply seated against the walls, as though they had chosen to contentedly wait for death.

Within hours, we had seen hundreds of bodies, but things soon turned even uglier. The tedium of searching the vast craft had set in when a wisp of bright light shot from around a corner and fastened onto Sergeant Tarbin's head. There didn't seem to be any physical substance to the light. We opened fire, but the blasts passed through the energy with no effect. By the time we rounded the corner, there was no sign of anything that unleashed the strange light. When Tarbin came to, he did not recognise any of us, or even remember the *Aureus*. The tendril of energy had somehow reached into his mind and spirited away his memories of his time aboard the ship. After breaking him out of his stupor, and then making no small effort to calm the now panicked Sergeant, I sent him back to the *Aureus* with an escort and set out to deal with the creature.

I eventually found and eliminated the spherical floating creature that had taken Tarbin's memories, leaving shards of ruptured crystals on the deck plating along with my spent bolter casings. Though the wisps of energy were unaffected by my bolter, the crystalline body proved vulnerable to sufficient concentrated fire, and once the explosive rounds had torn that apart, it expired. Before we left, one of my party attempted to harvest part of the creature as a trophy, but I intervened to caution him about letting such abominations lie, and we left the dead creature aboard *Honour's Shield*.

Unfortunately, when we returned to the ship, I discovered that three others had no recollection of the incident or of the ship's standard engagement protocols. Further, Tarbin's memories did not return upon the creature's termination. I believe that this thing is what slew the crew of *Honour's Shield*, draining their minds and leaving their bodies to die a slow death of apathy. Given the three others who lost their memories during the expedition, I fear that more like the creature may dwell upon *Honour's Shield*. I have counselled Alberse to eliminate the ship rather than to try and salvage it, and with any luck he will listen instead of racing off to kill one and mount it on his wall. Whatever these things are, we cannot risk suffering the same fate as *Honour's* crew.

STEALERS OF THOUGHTS

The tools of the xenos do not always depend upon darkness. Some present the false light of salvation, only to drown those who view it with its blasphemous nature. The Crystalwisp—believed to be a creation of the Yu'Vath—is one such being. These terrors have been found on worlds that contain the ruins of that ancient civilisation, often in the presence of other artefacts. Legends suggest that the ancients created these beings as angelic guardians of their treasures. If that is the case, then these creatures are supremely capable of fulfilling their duties.

Physically, the Crystalwisp resembles a cluster of floating crystals interwoven with crackling energy. Typically one of these crystals is much larger than the others. The largest reported specimen was estimated to have a central crystal that was more than two metres in diameter. The smaller crystals are typically less than half the size of the central one. These move in eccentric orbits around the largest crystal, constantly arcing tendrils of energy back towards it. This constant arcing of energy creates characteristic flashes of light that illuminate the creature and all around it in a strobing, unnatural manner.

All of the crystals seem to be made of a partially translucent, milky-white substance. Most show extensive patterns of cracks and chips that cover their surface. Observer reports—at least from those who remember their encounter—indicate that the patterns change constantly. This may be a function of its unusual lighting effects or rotation, or the patterns might actually be changing to new shapes. Legends suggest that the construct records all of its memories upon its surface, and these changes in appearance hallmark the constant fluctuations in its latest memories.

These legends also touch upon the dangers of encountering a Crystalwisp. As the monstrosity moves, it constantly extends additional tendrils of its unholy light outwards from its crystalline structures. Whenever one of these luminous tendrils comes into contact with an object storing information, the data is gradually erased through unknown means. This effect works on electronic, mechanical, and living storage mediums; scrolls and murals may be absorbed just as easily as the information stored within a vessel's cogitators or a human mind.

The motives of these creatures, on the other hand, are far less obvious than their methods of operation. Most xenobiologists believe their behaviour is instinctive, like a beast's need to hunt and feed, but others claim that their predations are part of some dark purpose.

While a brief contact is generally insufficient to completely destroy all of an individual's memories, extended contact can be devastating. Further, the creature always begins by eliminating the most recently stored memories. Those who survive an initial Crystalwisp attack have no memory of the encounter and are momentarily disoriented as they attempt to get their bearings. This often allows the creature to surprise them with another strike before they realise what is happening. After a series of such attacks, an individual's mind may be wiped completely clean, leaving them with no memory of language or how to control their bodies. Once such a point has been reached, the Crystalwisp typically moves on to new prey, as the data storage has been completely emptied.

Because of this unusual attack mechanism, members of the Adeptus Mechanicus who dare to study Yu'Vath artefacts believe that these constructs may be fairly common within the Koronus Expanse. They posit that most encounters go unrecorded, as the Crystalwisp devours the memories of individuals and any recording devices they might carry. Those who were injured but survived the encounter with some memories intact might not be able to find the way back to their vessel—or even know where they were and how they had travelled to that point. These factors suggest that undocumented Crystalwisp encounters could constitute a substantial portion of the individuals lost within the Expanse each year due to unknown causes. The Adeptus Mechanicus, in particular, finds this possibility—that precious and irreplaceable knowledge can be so casually devoured—to be a horrifying anathema to their creed, and an affront to the Omnissiah. More fanatical and martially-minded Explorers in the Expanse sometimes go out of their way to hunt down Crystalwisps, or more often, pay others with more expendable and less sacred memories to slay the abominations.

Legends also suggest that the only way the creature can perceive its surroundings is through its energy tendrils. There are certainly no visible sense organs upon the creature's surface. As the crystals float through the air, they constantly avoid making contact with solid objects, their only interaction through these lashes of energy and unholy light. These factors make it unclear how the creature perceives the world around it; while they display an uncanny ability to sense the presence of devices containing record information, little else is known of their sensory mechanisms.

As these constructs travel through the dark passages of Yu'Vath worlds, the arcs of energy that they emit often give off a characteristic crackling sound. Many of those who have seen them and lived (and remembered) to tell of their encounters warn to flee when they hear the noise that they describe as "zzt-tk-tk-tk." Strangely, all who have heard the sound say and record it with the same vocalisation and letters, and it may be that those who hear it become psychically imprinted with the unique noise.

While a Crystalwisp is hardy, it is not indestructible. There are several confirmed reports of individuals that have successfully eliminated one of these specimens. In all known cases, encounters concluded when the largest crystal shattered and its energetic aura faded. In some of these reports, the remaining crystalline components broke down into fine dust-like granules within moments. In others, the crystals remained intact, but darkly clouded. At least two analysts have used cogitators and auspex systems to attempt to recover data from these crystals, but no such attempts have met with success. If the information that the Crystalwisp steals is contained within its crystalline form, recovering it may be beyond Imperial technology. Even so, members of certain groups within the Adeptus Mechanicus pay hefty prices for the crystalline shards from a slain Crystalwisp, in the hopes that they might recover stolen knowledge from eons past. And this is to say nothing of the dark whispers occasionally heard of Heretek sects that claim the key to prying out the knowledge is to take one of these horrifying specimens alive.

Crystalwisp								
WS	BS	S	T	Ag	Int	Per	WP	Fel
—	64	20	35 (6)	25	42	41	55	—

Movement: 4/8/12/24 **Wounds:** 25
Armour: Crystalline Shell (4 Body). **Total TB:** 6
Skills: Awareness (Per), Dodge (Ag) +10.
Talents: Combat Sense, Marksman.
Traits: Datavore†, Fear (2), Hoverer (4), Size (Hulking), Strange Physiology, The Stuff of Nightmares, Unnatural Toughness (x2).
Weapons: Energy Lash†† (5m; S/–/5; 2d10+4 R; Pen 5; Clip –; Reload: –).
Gear: None.

†**Datavore:** The Crystalwisp's Energy Lash allows it to interface with any data storage material—mechanical, electronic, or organic—and devour the information. Devices and inanimate storage materials are incapable of resisting the attack. Sapient beings that sustain Damage from the attack must make a **Challenging (+0) Willpower Test** with a –10 Penalty for each Degree of Success that the Crystalwisp received on the attack. For each Degree of Failure, the victim loses their most recent day's worth of memories, including the memory of the current conflict.

††**Energy Lash:** The Crystalwisp draws the power for its Energy Lash from the warp. Its ammunition is functionally limitless.

FOSSIL HORROR

"The Yu'Vath may have engineered planets as easily as they created vessels. Beware the worlds that they inhabited, for arcane horrors may stretch to the very core of those places."

–From the journal of Xenographer Kobras Aquaire

Alberse was ecstatic this morning as the first load of ore was successfully extracted from the mine. I had scouted the asteroid's interior myself on our earlier visit, and even to my untrained eyes it was incredible. The rocky core was absolutely littered with tunnels as well, making it easier than normal to delve deep enough to see first hand the riches inside. I still do not understand why whoever created those passages chose to leave the ore and crystals behind, but that would hardly be the most bizarre thing I've seen in the Expanse. The asteroid absolutely represented a valuable find though. For once, I was sure that Alberse had made the right decision when he chose to follow the tenuous lead to this asteroid and to invest the time and energy to extract its contents. It certainly promised to be one of few endeavours where safety and profitability were equally high. I should have known better, of course.

Two hours later, the tides of fate had turned against us. First, we lost contact with the mining team. Alberse tasked me with a team of armsmen to discover the cause of it. At first I thought there must have just been some sort of vox interference, natural or otherwise. All of the power systems were running properly though and our deep auspex scans matched up with previous ones. The rock was still nothing but a barren wasteland, with no signs of life or even anything resembling a breathable atmosphere. I then sadly realised that I should have been able to detect the mining team on the scans, even if they were unable to communicate with us.

We pressed on through the interior and, as I dreaded, we found the bodies of our crewmates deep inside the dense rock. They had been torn to shreds, their voidsuits and remains littered about the mine's dimly lit tunnel.

As we absorbed the devastation, I caught movement from the corner of my eye. I raised my bolter to shout a warning to Corben, but it was already too late. Rocky tentacles quickly emerged from one of the darkened side passages. Each one was more than five metres long and nearly a metre in diameter. I fired and saw my first burst of bolter rounds skid off of the tentacle even as I heard Corben's scream over the vox and the sound of his bones being crushed through his voidsuit. Then the seals gave and blood sprayed everywhere. Continued fire from our group had the same effect, and the tentacles kept coming.

I didn't like it, but we had no choice. We ran, bounding in the low gravity, but only four of us made it back to the *Aureus*. The creature, or creatures, kept attacking out of the dark as if they permeated the entire area. Once we were safely back on the *Aureus* I demanded that Alberse destroy the asteroid—if he wants, we can always mine later the rubble. At least that way, we would have a chance to see the thing coming. I fear that even the blast might not destroy it, but at least it won't have terrain to hide in anymore.

ROCKY TENDRILS

Explorers unlucky enough to encounter them have reported one type of construct far more often than any other known Yu'Vath creation. Known as the Fossil Horror, it is a massive tentacled worm that has been observed far beneath planetary surfaces and even upon isolated asteroids. More is known of the creature's habitat and its ability to wreak destruction than of its inherent nature or impulses. What information exists has been compiled from anecdotal reports of survivors as no specimens have been captured nor have any confirmed remains been recovered.

The creations are thought to be more than twenty metres in length and at least four in diameter, though very few reports indicate encounters where a specimen has been observed in its entirety. Rather, survivors generally report that they observed the creature's massive tentacles extend from smoothly tunnelled openings, likely made by the creature itself. In all cases, observers reported that the tunnels seemed devoid of life when initially examined. The attacks were generally preceded by an unusual grinding sound, like that of rock moving across rock. After that noise, the tentacles emerged and began to rend their companions. The attacks are usually devastating, striking targets unerringly despite the lack of any obvious sensory organs.

Members of the Magos Biologis have expressed an interest in capturing an active specimen for further study (though there is debate over if the term "alive" would be applicable). This is because a core part of the legends associated with Fossil Horrors is that life sign monitors do not detect them. This may be an indication that these creatures are constructs made entirely of inorganic materials; some legends support this, stating that the creatures are composed entirely of rock-like materials. At the same time, standard monitoring systems should be capable of detecting movement and warning the operator of activities not fitting in with normal, natural occurrences. That they do not seem to notice the movement of these huge creatures may mean that calibrations set to tune out normal changes in the local environment are too broad for creatures such as the Fossil Horror. This inconsistency is a significant concern for those working in areas where these creatures have been observed. Explorers learn quickly to rely entirely upon their physical senses for security rather than counting on the once-trusted mechanical assistance. Often extra guards are hired purely to stand ready in the tunnels, eating into profits but helping ensure faster and more effective response should an attack occur.

A few of the verifiable incidents indicate that Fossil Horrors were capable of summoning more of their kind. These accounts include reports of the creatures emitting an ear-shatteringly loud wailing sound, which oscillated among several low tones in an irregular and dissonant fashion. As many times this was mixed in with the screaming of assaulted victims, it was only recognised as from the creature when a lone miner recorded an encounter. Several minutes after such cries, tentacles from additional Fossil Horrors often emerge into the same region. There are few such reports, though, either indicating these were isolated incidents or the decreased survival rate associated with multiple Fossil Horrors. Another unusual facet of such legends is that they indicate these constructs may function in a co-operative fashion, a level of co-ordination unexpected among Yu'Vath artefacts. A few xenographers speculate that this hallmark behaviour could even indicate that Fossil Horrors were once a slave race that perhaps had undergone additional modifications to become more mindless and brutal.

KILLING MACHINES

There is no knowledge regarding what motivates these constructs. They are capable of burrowing through any known strata, including at least one incident where a Fossil Horror burrowed through the armourplas shell of a mercenary drop-base to reach the unwary fighters asleep inside. This suggests that they may be driven to seek out specific items and are unconcerned with intervening terrain. As the Yu'Vath were known for their ability to undertake complex engineering projects, as witnessed by the cyclopean ruins littering the Expanse, it could be that these constructs are constantly involved in some sort of planetary construction or maintenance. Alternatively, the Fossil Horrors may engage in an unfathomable mining process or serve as an additional line of defence to guard Yu'Vath resources.

To date, there are no records of successful communication with one of these constructs. Legends indicate that they are nothing more than unstoppable killing machines. This is inconsistent with some of the attack patterns and degree of co-operation seen in some of the reported incidents. There are at least two reported instances where multiple Fossil Hunters worked together to systematically collapse a facility's power grid prior to attacking the humans located within. This suggests an unexpected degree of intelligence and social interaction.

GUARDIANS OF THE TUNNELS

While they readily eliminate sentient life when they encounter it, there is no evidence that Fossil Horrors feed upon the remaining bodies. As constructs, it is believed that these creations do not need to eat, relying instead upon some unholy Yu'Vath power source. Their victims' remains are typically displayed in a gruesome fashion, perhaps as some sort of warning. Further, some believe that the patterns utilised in these horrific displays of blood and tissue may be consistent with the xenos iconography observed at some ancient Yu'Vath sites. This suggests that the constructs might have a malicious intelligence, but this could also be an isolated function that their creators deliberately provided to these constructs. While this activity provides an effective deterrent to additional intruders, it seems an exceptionally complex solution. If they eliminate all life forms they encounter merely to fulfil a biological imperative, then that inherent nature has not yet been determined.

Legends among voidsmen in the Expanse claim that Fossil Horrors exist to protect valuable treasures of precious ores and valuable crystals, left behind by the Yu'Vath for reasons unknown. Such deadly and powerful guardians must, as the logic goes, be guarding only the finest of riches. These tales invariably include countless deaths and the rich triumph of a sole survivor who recovers a portion of the treasures. However, there are no confirmed reports that directly support these stories. Most of these constructs have been discovered through the course of mining operations or massive archeological expeditions, but there has never been any indication that what was found within were anything but regular naturally occurring ores or other unremarkable materials. If Fossil Horrors were assigned by their long-dead masters to protect refined or constructed assets, it seems more likely that those assets may have succumbed to the vagaries of time far faster than their unholy guardians.

Fossil Horror								
WS	BS	S	T	Ag	Int	Per	WP	Fel
48	—	(12) 43	(12) 42	35	24	39	15	––

Movement: 4/8/12/24   **Wounds:** 40
Armour: Stone-like Hide (All 6).   **Total TB:** 12
Skills: Awareness (Per) +10.
Talents: None.
Traits: Burrower, Crawler, Fear (3), Improved Natural Weapons, Multiple Arms†, Size (Enormous), The Stuff of Nightmares, Unnatural Physiology††, Unnatural Senses (100 metres), Unnatural Strength (x3), Unnatural Toughness (x3).
Weapons: Fossilised Tentacles (1d10 +15 R; Pen 2).
†**Multiple Arms:** When the Fossil Horror makes a Multiple Attack Action, it attacks with 2d5 independent tentacles.
††**Unnatural Physiology:** Explorers using scanners such as an Auspex can only detect a Fossil Horror by passing a **Very Hard (–30) Tech-Use Test.**

SANDSLIME

"Mankind must fear the darkness, for there are things that dwell within it that can shatter the body and the mind."

–Inquisitor Tellemain

Alberse must be cursed. There is no other reasonable explanation. The Astropath directed us to a barren rock after insisting that the God-Emperor commanded it. I'm hardly in a place to question that authority, but I was not looking forward to putting on a bulky voidsuit and crawling through unstable tunnels in search of some desperate quest.

To my surprise, not long after we landed, one of the squads identified an inactive promethium well. It was old, but appeared abandoned. There were lasburns and other clear signs of a conflict, but we all assumed that was due to piracy. Alberse directed the Tech-Priests to examine the facilities to see what state they were in. If the reserves were decent, the mine might turn Alberse a decent profit in short order. I had a squad with me in case this was some sort of trap set by whoever had won the earlier conflict.

Tech-Priest Ovis thought it could be made functional quickly, and started fiddling with dials and switches, anointing it with oils, chanting all the while. In no time, lights came on within the control room and I could feel the pumps working through my heavy magboots. As it became active, something emerged from the vats—a mass that flowed like liquid plascrete but glowed with unholy light. Within moments, the monstrosity struck three of my trained armsmen with massive limbs made of rock-like sludge. They should have been tossed like parchment in the wind against the fall walls, but none moved from the brutal impacts.

They all howled in agony though, and I witnessed their screams of agony transform into terror. Inexplicably, we could see their suits and then their very flesh began to transform into the same sludge that made up the creature. As I tried to rally our forces to counter-attack, I watched several more of my men die. As they changed, I saw their voidsuits and everything else they touched absorbed into more of the unholy sludge. We fired all we had at the thing, with little discernible impact. It slid away, but if that was the result of our weapons or if it was simply tired of our company, I could not tell. We tried to follow it with no success; worse yet when we returned what was left of our crewmates was gone as well.

We evacuated, leaving more than a dozen somewhere behind us, hopefully blessedly dead. Alberse directed the ship's lance fire at the refinery. We needed to be certain, and nothing less than the power of the shipboard batteries tearing the refinery off the face of the asteroid would be enough to make sure that this abomination was purged. The lance strikes left little doubt that the job had been done, reducing the refinery and anything within to ash in a single blinding stab of light.

Most chilling of all, perhaps, I swear I heard a chorus of voices shriek in pain through the void as we left the asteroid. I pity those who fell. But with the God-Emperor's blessing, I hope it was the last noise the thing ever made.

WAVES OF DEATH

Those who dare to search through Yu'Vath ruins seeking ancient treasures seldom find what they seek. Worse yet, some find exactly what they sought, but are unprepared for the consequences of their discoveries. For those who discover a Sandslime, it most often falls into the latter category. These creatures dwell in the darkest depths of abandoned voidstations, subterranean chasms, and other places far from the purifying light of the stars.

Physically, these constructs typically occupy a volume of more than seventy-five kilolitres. However, they are capable of shifting their mass and volume substantially to create sheets less than three centimetres thick or limbs more than a metre in diameter. As they flow across a surface, they may absorb portions of virtually any material to increase their size and mass—destroying the matter in the process. In spite of their soft nature, they are also capable of securely grasping objects and anchoring their forms to surfaces with a powerful grip. The mechanism behind this shift in tensile strength is unclear, but may be an inherent factor in their chemical composition.

At times, when a Sandslime flows through a region, it emits flares and arcs of plasma-like energy typical of Yu'Vath constructs. These blasts illuminate the area around it with a purple light that legends say tears at the minds of all who view it. None know the reasons for these emissions. Some who have viewed it suggest that these are a manifestation of the creature's fury. Others believe that the energy occurs as the construct transforms physical matter into some warp-charged energy.

Regardless of the cause, the light that accompanies these flares is a signature of the construct's presence. Those who have previously confronted a Sandslime immediately know to flee the area when they see the irregular lighting approach.

No humans know why the Yu'Vath might have created these terrors, unless they were to serve as guardians or destroyers. There seems to be little logic to where they are encountered. The records associated with confirmed sightings seldom associate them with any items of great value. In fact, many of the reported incidents involving these horrors occurred in places where there was no known Yu'Vath activity. It might be that the Sandslimes have destroyed any other Yu'Vath artefacts or converted them into more of their own type. Alternatively, it might be that the infectious nature of these creatures permitted them to spread to locations where the Yu'Vath had never travelled.

This infectious reproduction is their greatest threat. Those exposed to the substance of a Sandslime are virtually always transformed into another of these creatures. Mere contact with the surface of one of these foul creations can result in its victim creating more of the spawn. For most, this is an agonising process that takes place over the course of two days. However, some undergo the transformation within moments of their exposure to its unholy touch. While Imperial medical treatments can halt a progression that has begun, there is no known way to reverse it. Most of those who have survived such exposure lose a limb in order to preserve their lives.

These entities seem to be able to selectively apply their destructive nature as they travel. In some locations where Sandslimes are known to be active, the structures bear substantial wear marks that are consistent with its activities. However, in other locations, the characteristic markings are not present. Similarly, while Sandslime reports typically indicate that the constructs destroy everything with which they interact, others report finding intact xenos artefacts within the remains of a destroyed Sandslime. The basis for these variations is unclear. It may be that there is more than one Yu'Vath construct that shares this appearance and nature.

A few anecdotal reports within Ordo Xenos records suggest that a Sandslime may have a vicious cunning. These indicated that Explorers fell prey to one of these specimens when they unknowingly walked into it. In one instance, the construct had spread itself thinly across a floor, then simply folded itself over upon its prey, consuming their gear and transforming all who had stepped upon it into more of its kind. In another unconfirmed incident, three Sandslimes were said to have infiltrated a vessel planetside by entering through its waste disposal chutes. The terrors soon spread through the voidship, transforming crew and destroying the craft as they travelled. The survivors insisted that they were only able to tell their stories after a desperate escape aboard a saviour pod and years in cryosleep awaiting recovery. Neither of these reports mentions the Sandslime's energetic flares. It may be that the construct is capable of suppressing them or it could be that there are specimens that do not exhibit this characteristic trait.

The Sandslime appears to be one of the more successful of the Yu'Vath creations. Legends of these creatures now extend throughout the Koronus Expanse. Agents of the Ordo Xenos have confirmed sightings on more than a dozen worlds, though many Explorers believe that this estimate is dramatically lower than could possibly be accurate. Few groups that encounter such a construct survive, so they could be responsible for dozens of expeditions that have been lost for unknown reasons. On at least two occasions, Rogue Traders have reported discoveries of these constructs aboard space hulks discovered far from any inhabited planets. Analysts suggest that these may be due to cases where an infected survivor transformed into another Sandslime and devoured its vessel's crew.

Because of their deadly and infectious nature, there are stories that circulate on Footfall of a pirate who attempted to capture and control a Sandslime. The tales recount how the captain recovered a portion of one of these creatures and loaded it into a boarding torpedo. However, the legends also tell how the construct escaped its containment before the pirate was able to launch the torpedo at an enemy vessel, and so it devoured the pirate's crew and vessel instead. This legend could of course be a simple morality tale of one's reach exceeding one's grasp and the dangers of contact with xenos, but those who know the terrifying power and cunning of the Sandslime firsthand are less willing to dismiss such stories out of hand.

Sandslime								
WS	BS	S	T	Ag	Int	Per	WP	Fel
58	–	(10) 53	(15) 57	25	15	25	30	––

Movement: 3/6/9/18 **Wounds**: 54
Armour: Crystalline Structure (8 All). **Total TB**: 15
Skills: Awareness (Per), Climb (S) +10, Shadowing (Ag) +10.
Talents: Combat Master, Frenzy, Resistance (Cold, Heat, Psychic Techniques), Strong Minded, Swift Attack.
Traits: Amorphous†, Fear (2), Improved Natural Weapons, Size (Enormous), Strange Physiology, The Stuff of Nightmares, Sandslime Toxins††, Unnatural Strength (x2), Unnatural Toughness (x3).
†Amorphous: The creature exists as a foul, ooze-like mass. It can alter its Size one step in either direction as a Free Action, although it cannot change more than one step from the base, and doing so does not change its Movement.
††Sandslime Toxins: Any individual struck by the Sandslime must make an immediate **Difficult (–10) Toughness Test**. Those who fail suffer an immediate 1d10 Wounds, ignoring Armour and Toughness Bonus. Characters who suffer wounds from the toxin must then pass a **Challenging (+0) Willpower Test**. Characters who fail this Test begin to transform into a Sandslime over the course of the next forty-eight hours. This can be averted with a dose of De-Tox or similar medical attention, but for every nine hours that passes before it is administered, the character loses a limb as it transforms into a Sandslime. If the character suffers more than four Degrees of Failure on the Willpower Test, the transformation is immediate; there is no opportunity for treatment. The character may burn a Fate Point to avoid this "death" in the usual manner.
Weapons: Pseudopods (1d10 + 12 I; Pen 3).
Gear: None.

YU'VATH ADVENTURE SEEDS

A truly ancient and extinct race, these foul xenos have strewn countless artefacts and ruins throughout the entirety of the Koronus Expanse, leaving behind a tremendous temptation of power and reward that could be all but irresistible to the greed of a Rogue Trader. However, this greed and the associated Yu'Vath ruins need not be the only way to involve these creations. This section introduces a few alternative approaches.

DEADLY DEFENCES

The Explorers receive a distress call from a mining world claiming attack by native fauna. The planet begs for military assets and offers generous payment in valuable ores in exchange for any assistance. The offer even includes a generous stake in ownership of the colony. When the Explorers arrive, they discover that the intruding fauna are Yu'Vath constructs—Fossil Horrors. The characters are challenged to both defend the colonists but also discover what precious treasures the Yu'Vath might have left the Fossil Horrors to guard. Of course, confronting an unknown number of Yu'Vath constructs in their native environment also means the risk is substantial.

DEAD COLONY

The Explorers arrive at an isolated frontier world, having already made a substantial investment to bring supplies a long distance, and expecting to be well compensated for their efforts. However, the colony does not respond to their hails and seems abandoned. Searching reveals that the small colony's inhabitants are now Sandslimes. Damaged property, abandoned meals, and worn tracks through the colony might serve as an early warning. The Explorers must decide if they wish to eliminate the infestation, try to salvage their investment, or simply flee with their lives. The Sandslime infestation might be a sign that there are Yu'Vath ruins on the planet, or it could simply be a coincidental disaster.

HAUNTED TECHNOLOGY

The Explorers stop part way through a warp journey at the Navigator's request—he sensed something out of the ordinary. Far from any known systems, they discover an isolated voidstation, which bears all the hallmarks of Yu'Vath technology. The apparently abandoned station is a veritable treasure trove of archeotech and xenostech! However, as the Explorers begin to scavenge the station, they notice anomalies. At first, items are lost and crew members go missing. Soon, they discover that the station is attempting to seize control of their vessel's cogitators. The station is charged with identifying new "client" races, and turning them to its own inscrutable ends. The Explorers must overcome its defences and escape, or their vessel and all its crew might be tested and modified to serve the long-dead Yu'Vath.

UNWANTED CARGO

A few hours after the Explorers enter the warp, they find several crew members passed out near the cargo bay entrance. Over the next few days, they find more and more crew members functionally disabled, as they have completely lost all of their memories. An inert Crystalwisp was amongst their cargo and became active when the ship entered the warp. Now, they must find and defeat it before the dread construct can devour the memories of the entire crew, along with all of the ship's records and charts. Alternatively, some Game Masters might choose to begin the scenario with characters who have already lost their recent memories. In this case, the Explorers first challenge is to discover how they lost their memories, as the now-active xenos continues to wreak havoc on their vessel.

CLIENT RACES

While knowledge of the Yu'Vath remains limited, information about the races bound to their empire in the Expanse is more readily available. It is unclear how many different Yu'Vath client races once existed however. Throughout the Angevin Crusade, countless specimens were defeated, many of which may have been heavily modified experiments or completely separate species. A few of the better-known examples follow, but many more were defeated and some others may yet remain active within the lesser known portions of the Koronus Expanse.

The mercenary Byavoor were once slaves, sacrificed to feed the Yu'Vath's dark hunger. The few that remain are little more than sentient cattle scattered throughout the Calixis Sector. At the height of their sponsor's power, the Byavoor were constantly incorporated into the dark rituals that the ancient xenos performed. Historical reports suggest that the Yu'Vath might have worked to limit the race's capacity for independent thought, causing them to be much more docile. This seemingly passive nature may also have saved them from extermination at the hands of the Angevin Crusade, for the Inquisition designated them as a minor threat and not a concern at that time.

In contrast, the aquatic Djarlik represented a threat that the Crusade overcame at the same time as their sponsor race. The Djarlik spent countless generations developing three dimensional combat techniques. Transitioning these techniques from an underwater environment to that of the void represented a relatively simple intuitive leap for the Djarlik. This inherent edge made them extremely expert void pilots and tacticians. Inquisitorial agencies thusly sponsored a purge of the species. There are no known surviving Djarlik; their extermination is celebrated as one of the Crusade's many such successes.

The near-microscopic colony beings of the Strinx survive on many barren asteroids throughout the Expanse. Today, these entities possess little that would resemble a civilisation by human standards, but during the height of the Crusade tens of thousands of these crystalline colonies formed key parts of the Yu'Vath fleet. With the collapse of their dark masters, the individual groups separated and became isolated. The Ordo Xenos no longer even classifies these isolated groups as sentient. However, some archaic records suggest that in the presence of specific xenos tech, the isolated colonies could once more represent a substantial threat.

III

DENIZENS OF THE WARP

CHAPTER III: DENIZENS OF THE WARP

"There were no bodies to gather, just bits and pieces of meat scattered across decks awash with blood. The ship itself seemed... infected. Like whatever had done this never really left."

–Boarding Officer Lt. Cheshal Saso, aboard *The Burning Maw*

A dimension parallel to the one inhabited by mortals, the warp is a universe of psychic energy, where normal physical and temporal laws do not apply. It is virtually unknowable by human minds and can only be traversed with any degree of safety by ships equipped with Gellar Fields. To do otherwise attracts the attention of the beings that live within the warp, beings who gladly peel even the most powerful vessel apart to devour the succulent souls inside. Worse yet, the warp and the Chaos Gods are tied together intimately. The gods are formed out of the very same unnatural energies, and as a particular god rises in power, the warp tends to respond in kind. Daemons are fragments of the Chaos Gods given form and animation, created to carry out their unfathomable objectives throughout both the warp and in the material realm of mortals. For Explorers accustomed to the material threats of hostile xenos races, alien creatures, and the treacherous dealings of their fellow men, daemons represent a unique danger for which they are often be quite unprepared.

THE NATURE OF DAEMONS

A daemon is a being of the warp, spawned by the Ruinous Powers to serve them. Thus, daemons cannot be said to be truly alive; they are the raw energies of the warp given physical form, as opposed to the flesh and blood of an organic being. That said, a daemon encountered in real space can be "killed," although in most cases this only serves to sever the daemon's tenuous link to the mortal realm and send them back into the warp, where they eventually reform. This is why daemons seem to shrug off so much of man's ordnance, and only those weapons made specially to combat the daemonic threat can truly destroy them.

As minions of the Chaos Gods, most daemons lack self-will, at least as humanity understands it. Instead, they serve only to spread the aims of their masters. For example, a daemon of Khorne seeks only battle, and wages war upon other daemons with the same fervour as it does upon mortals. Daemons seemingly spend much of their existence in conflict with other daemons, as each of the Chaos Gods seeks to expand its power and influence as part of the Great Game. It is only when the mortal world is involved that daemons tend to band together and cooperate, and even then, such alliances are short-lived, as each of the four Chaos lords seeks to prevent the other from gaining any sort of advantage.

DAEMONIC PERILS WITHIN THE WARP…

The difference between life and death in the warp lies in the strength of a vessel's Gellar Field, which serves as a barrier between the localized real space of a ship and the roiling energies of the warp. If these fields were to ever fail, if just for an instant, the entire ship would be laid bare for invasion. For Explorers who spend much of their lives travelling across the Expanse via the warp, this represents a constant threat that is often beyond their direct control. Explorers can expect and even predict the attacks of the foul xenos, but are often unprepared for deadly threats that materialize out of nowhere in the very heart of their ship.

Considering the scale of the warp, a single ship would seem to be too insignificant to draw attention, but human minds and souls burn brightly to the senses of the warp-born. Those with psychic abilities shine even brighter, and the mere presence of a psyker such as a Navigator, or worse yet a nascent psyker unaware of his powers, often draws daemons as moths are drawn to a flame. Even the best protected vessel entering the Immaterium is soon surrounded by hordes of daemons and other beings of the warp, all seeking entrance in order to glut their desire for souls.

For all the danger the warp represents, there are those ignorant (or foolish) enough to consider the warnings mere "traveller's tales." Rich and powerful passengers, used to controlling their surroundings to their desires, often slough off such risks as beneath their notice. Many who travel in the warp, however, take the stories to heart and spend the entire voyage in fear, certain the fields can fail at any moment. Many a passenger spends the entire time in the warp praying to the Emperor, asking only for a safe voyage and for the Gellar Fields to remain sure and stable, a practice encouraged through regularly scheduled chapel gatherings on many ships.

…AND IN REAL SPACE

Even those who remain in the mortal realm are not fully safe from the threat of daemons. The Koronus Expanse, with its roiling warp storms, is rife with daemonic incursions. The storms often cause great rifts to open between the dimensions, fissures the daemons are more than willing to exploit. These rifts are also known to form around areas of intense emotion. Battlefields, torture chambers, execution grounds—all can be the cause of a breach in the dimensional barriers. Worse yet, psykers who lose control of their powers may inadvertently (or by design) release the energy of the warp into real space. And perversely, a large enough daemonic incursion may be sufficient to open further rifts, often resulting in different factions appearing in the same area, each wishing to be the dominant force.

Depending on the size of the dimensional breach, the assault may range from a single possessed mortal to vast armies of daemons engaging in open warfare. Some also enter through dreams and visions, slowly gaining dominion over their victim until they have enough of a hold to infuse their mortal host with a measure of their power. Others wait for foolish mortals to study, experiment with, and try to master ancient arcane relics. Finally, Chaos worshippers, xenos psykers, and others may attempt to summon a daemon directly, pulling it from the warp to the mortal realm. Depending on the summoner's power, he has either acquires a mighty (albeit temporary) servant, or—more likely—his presumed slave brutally tears him asunder soon after the summoning is complete.

ROGUE TRADERS AND DAEMONS

Of all the dangers a Rogue Trader must face in pursuit of his profession, daemons are perhaps the most insidious. They appear in a myriad of forms, and a naive Trader may fatally think them to be some bizarre form of xenos to be easily dispatched with a few well-placed lasgun shots. A Trader might even be arrogant enough to think they can "deal" with daemons, believing that he can arrive at a bargain with any being. But daemons are not Eldar or Orks, or any number of other xenos races, to be bribed, hoodwinked, or bought off. Daemons deal in one currency and one currency only: souls, and gladly take that of a Rogue Trader as they will the lowliest hive-worker (in fact, the Rogue Trader's might be more delectable).

Worse yet, daemons are utterly unknowable to the human mind and many violate what man considers the natural laws. A Rogue Trader seeing an Eldar in action believes the speed displayed is presumably due to accelerated xenos biology, and most assume an Ork's size and strength stems from its origins as a fungal life form. But nothing he knows allows him to explain (or comprehend) a tiny being of supposed flesh and blood vomiting forth huge gouts of maggots and flies or slashing through the thickest armour with glass claws. Daemons, like the warp itself, are unknowable—and those who dare to try and understand them run the risk of becoming utterly damned themselves.

BEAST OF NURGLE

The essence of mindless decay and horrid rot given flesh, Beasts of Nurgle exemplify the Plaguelord's endless enthusiasm and excitement for forces of life and death. Thus, a Beast delights in discovering new things and making (to its very simple mind) new friends. When brought into real space they act almost akin to a curious and inquisitive pet, investigating anything and everything in sight, and spreading illness and rot wherever they go.

Immense slug-like monstrosities, Beasts of Nurgle crawl across the ground on their bellies, weakly propelled by clawed flippers, leaving a layer of stinking slime in their wake. While slow, the Beast is implacable in its advance, undeterred by all but the most fearsome of weapons, as relentless as the decay it embodies. Each is a nightmarish conglomeration of parts, with a lengthy neck holding a wide-eyed face of almost blissful idiocy. The gaping tooth-filled mouth houses a lolling tongue dripping with putrid saliva. Clusters of writhing tubes sprout from the Beast's neck and back, each one spewing forth swarms of buzzing flies, clouds of vomit-inducing gases, flesh-eating fluids capable of finding gaps in even the most secure of armour, or other foul gifts.

Unlike most daemons, a Beast kills not with rending claws and ripping teeth, but with a strange form of kindness. Victims are caressed, petted, and stroked with the daemon's multiple tentacles, while the long tongue delivers slobbery and slimy licks. In very short order, the victim is sickened, infected, dissolved, and then crushed, ground under the Beast's vast bulk. The Beast, for its part, feels a touch of sadness at the inability of its now-dead friend to join in on the merriment, but quickly forgets about him as something (or someone) new attracts its attention.

A prime example of the destructive power of a Beast of Nurgle can be found on the agri-world of Gabali III in Winterscale's Realm. There the province of Gevaudan suffered hundreds of

casualties as a Beast wandered about the farm fields, destroying crops, herd animals, and buildings. Seemingly unstoppable, it took the combined efforts of Enforcers and local planetary militia units to finally destroy the daemon. Even after death, however, its presence lingered, as crops grew sickly and many fields had to be torched to the bedrock to remove the diseased corruption.

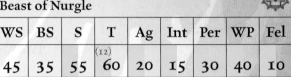

Beast of Nurgle								
WS	BS	S	T	Ag	Int	Per	WP	Fel
45	35	55	(12) 60	20	15	30	40	10

Movement: 2/4/6/12   **Wounds:** 25
Armour: None.   **Total TB:** 12
Skills: Awareness (Per), Climb (S).
Talents: None.
Traits: Crawler, Daemonic (TB 12), Daemonic Presence†, Dark Sight, Fear (3), From Beyond, Improved Natural Weapon, Regeneration, Size (Enormous), Spewing Tentacles††, Sturdy, Trail Of Slime†††, Warp Instability.

†**Daemonic Presence:** Living things with 20 metres of a Beast feel ill and nauseous. Plants wither, turn black, and die. All creatures take a –10 penalty to Willpower Tests.

††**Spewing Tentacles:** The mass of tentacles and tubes on a Beast's back can emit different substances each Round. The substances have a range of 10 metres and the Beast must succeed on a Ballistic Skill Test to hit its target. The options are:

- *Clouds Of Flies:* Effects equal to a smoke grenade for 1d5 Rounds.
- *Foul Gases:* All targets within 10 metres of the Beast must make a **Difficult (–10) Toughness Test** or become Stunned for 1d5 Rounds.
- *Noxious Fluids:* The target may Dodge the jet of fluid, but cannot Parry it. Targets struck must make a **Difficult (–10) Toughness Test** or take 1d10 I points of Damage, ignoring Armour Points.

†††**Trail of Slime:** Creatures who come in contact with the Beast's slimy trail must make a **Difficult (–10) Toughness Test** or any current wounds become infected as they had been caused by a Toxic weapon.

Weapons: Claws, Teeth (1d10+5 R; Pen 0; Toxic).

FLESH HOUND OF KHORNE

ound by the hundreds and thousands on the bone-littered plains surrounding Khorne's realm, Flesh Hounds are great wolf-like beasts that hunt down and destroy the enemies of the Blood God. They are often unleashed into real space to pursue those who have earned Khorne's wrath. Flesh Hounds are implacable when on the hunt and pursue their target across vast—even interstellar—distances. Constantly closing in, their howling often drives their target to madness before the Hound's own razor sharp teeth sink into flesh. What remains of their victims, especially their skulls, are brought back to their master, to add to the uncountable others that make up his massive throne.

Navigators have even reported hearing the cry of Hounds on the hunt while guiding ships through the warp, such as the possibly apocryphal tale of *The Ready Brace* and Rogue Trader Meical Rede. Rede was unlucky enough to have a Hound manifest on board his ship, apparently seeking one of his passengers. The Hound raged through the vessel and slaughtered hundreds before finally being brought down by the ship's Arch-Militant and masses of gun servitors.

Though vaguely canine in form, Flesh Hounds are more a horrific cross between dog and reptile. Covered with thick scales, Hounds mount large horns and usually feature a series of spikes down the spine. Frills grow from various locations, such as the back of the skull, on the throat, or the rear of the jaws. Coloration ranges from dark red to greyish-black, and all Hounds wear the spiked brass Collar of Khorne, granting them protection from the psychic energies so despised by their master.

While patient enough as trackers, Hounds tend to give in to their inherent bloodlust when prey is finally sighted. With bone-chilling howls, they rush forward, crossing open ground with astonishing speed. Leaping at the last moment, the Hounds attempt to physically overpower their targets, savaging them with teeth and claws. Large or particularly well-armed foes (such as armoured vehicles) are encircled, with individual Hounds darting in from different directions, worrying at their target until it finally falls from exhaustion (or, in the case of a vehicle, is disabled and unable to move.) Once the foe is down, the Hounds rush in en masse for the final kill. Hounds normally hunt in packs, and only the most well-armed and disciplined of groups can hope to face such an assault and survive.

Flesh Hound of Khorne

WS	BS	S	T	Ag	Int	Per	WP	Fel
49	–	(8) 45	(8) 40	(6) 30	15	60	40	10

Movement: 8/16/24/48 **Wounds:** 15
Armour: None (all 4). **Total TB:** 8
Skills: Awareness (Per), Dodge (Ag), Tracking (Int).
Talents: Berserk Charge, Crushing Blow, Double Team, Frenzy, Furious Assault, Hard Target, Heightened Senses (All).
Traits: Bestial, Blood for the Blood God†, Collar Of Khorne††, Daemonic (TB 8), Daemonic Presence†††, Dark Sight, Fear (3), From Beyond, Improved Natural Weapons, Natural Armour 4, Improved Natural Weapons, Quadruped, Size (Hulking), Unnatural Senses (30 metres), Unnatural Strength (x2), Warp Instability.
†Blood for the Blood God: Creatures of Khorne suffer no penalties from physical damage. Combat effects such as Blood Loss, falling down due to damage, or penalties to Weapon Skill Tests do not apply to creatures of Khorne.
††Collar Of Khorne: The Flesh Hound does not suffer extra damage from the Psy Rating of a wielder of a force weapon. In addition, any Psychic Powers used against the Flesh Hound have their Psy Rating reduced by 3. The Flesh Hound's Daemonic Trait is not ignored by Force Weapons unless the welder succeeds at a **Difficult (–10) Willpower Test**.
†††Daemonic Presence: All creatures within 20 metres take a –10 penalty to Willpower Tests.
Weapons: Teeth and claws (1d10+10 R; Pen 2; Razor Sharp, Tearing).

FURY OF CHAOS

Unlike many of the daemons studied by the Ordo Malleus, Furies do not belong to the hosts of the four unholy powers that dominate the warp. Reputedly formed from the souls of mortals who tried to draw on the power of Chaos without swearing allegiance to one of the Ruinous Powers, these unclaimed daemons are doomed to endlessly wander the Immaterium in a state of endless, meaningless existence. Furies are barred from entering any of the Realms and must contend with the tumultuous storms of the Immaterium on their own. Weaker than most other daemons, which often enslave them for their own uses, they are nearly-mindless manifestations of Chaos in its purest form.

As Furies constantly seek a respite for their eternal torment, they are especially watchful for weakness in the walls between the worlds. Thus, Furies are often one of the first daemons to appear near an open warp gate or when Gellar Fields begin to flicker and fail. When they appear in real space, Furies are quick to find mortals to vent their rage upon. Gathering in large packs, they slaughter all they can find in a vain attempt to appease their inner hunger for a sense of purpose amid the roiling and uncaring waves of the warp.

Somewhat larger than a man, with a hunched posture, Furies are hideous winged creatures. They have bestial, long-jawed faces and mouths full of jutting teeth and fangs. A bristly mane of black hair runs from their short horns to the base of the spine, while two broad batwings sprout from the shoulders. Their colouration varies with the flow of the warp or the daemonic powers currently ascendant, but black and red tones seem most common.

When on the hunt, Furies keep to the air, looking to ambush their target by attacking from above. Cowardly by nature, due to their status at the bottom of the daemonic hierarchy, Furies prefer those who have ventured out alone, are wounded or injured, or otherwise look to be unable to fully defend themselves. Dropping down on outspread wings, uttering bone-chilling howls, the Furies attack in swarms, seeking to rend their target limb from limb.

While individual Furies can be defeated by a man who holds to his faith in the Emperor and stands his ground (and is well-armed), and hunting flocks may be repelled by sufficient firepower, Furies found in the service of greater daemons are a different matter. Driven by a combination of fear and awe, these Furies attack with enthusiastic viciousness, looking to gain favour in the eyes of their daemonic betters. It is also rumoured that in these cases they often have a purpose beyond simple death and destruction, and may even seek to capture specific individuals or items in order to present them to their daemonic commanders.

Mortal servants of Chaos also attempt to summon and enslave Furies. Their great mobility, horrifying visage, and relative weakness make them a popular summoning choice for heretical worshippers seeking power. Various cults in the Koronus Expanse are known to have used Furies for a variety of purposes, the most common being simply sending the daemon out to cause death and destruction, be that on a planet or inside a vessel. Most of these sad practitioners find, to their dismay, that even the weakest of daemons is more than a match for a deluded mortal.

Fury of Chaos

WS	BS	S	T	Ag	Int	Per	WP	Fel
45	–	45	(8) 40	40	25	45	40	10

Movement: 4/8/12/24 **Wounds:** 15
Armour: None (All 1). **Total TB:** 8
Skills: Awareness (Per), Dodge (Ag), Psyniscience (Per), Speak Language (any one) (Per).
Talents: Heightened Senses (Touch), Sprint, Swift Attack.
Traits: Daemonic (TB 8), Daemonic Presence†, Dark Sight, Fear (3), Flyer 10, From Beyond, Natural Armour (1), Improved Natural Weapons, Size (Hulking), Warp Instability.
†**Daemonic Presence:** All creatures within 20 metres take a −10 penalty to Willpower Tests.
Weapons: Claws and Teeth (1d10+4 R; Pen 0; Tearing).

SCREAMER OF TZEENTCH

Also known as sky sharks, Screamers normally dwell in the Immaterium, where they seek the souls of those foolish enough to enter the warp unprotected. They also gather in immense flocks wherever the walls between real space and the warp have grown thin, such as amid the warp storms that bracket the Maw. Void ships traversing such sections of space are often shadowed by vast numbers of Screamers, as the daemons probe for weak spots in the Gellar Fields. If a gap is found, the always-ravenous sky sharks swarm through, ripping apart the ship's outer hull with their powerful jaws. Once inside, the Screamers race from deck to deck, slaughtering all they encounter as an offering to the Great Schemer. Attacks such as this are thought to be but one explanation for the occasional appearance of empty ghost ships within the Expanse.

Screamers are strangely shaped creatures, appearing more akin to ocean life than any other mortal being. They swim through the air on broad, fleshy wings and flattened bodies, and their long tails end in clusters of thick blades. Huge tusks bracket the mouth, while short spikes run along the spine. As creatures of Tzeentch, though, no two are ever alike, and many even change shape multiple times whilst manifested. Lacking limbs, Screamers arc though the sky with unnatural speed. They emit constant series of piercing, shrieking cries, thus giving them their name. Often the daemons are heard long before they appear.

When manifesting in the Materium, Screamers hunt with a cunning that belies their rather base intellect. Streaking across the sky, leaving sparkling multi-coloured trails behind them, Screamers generally keep to a lofty altitude. From this vantage point they search the ground below for worthy sacrifices to their master. Once they have located suitable prey, the Screamers dive down from on high, emitting unnatural arcs of warp lightning. Anything left standing after their initial slashing attack is snatched up in the Screamer's jaws, to be either devoured on the wing or dropped from great heights to smash into the ground far below.

As they possess only a modicum of intelligence, Screamers are often used as scouts and skirmishers by other, more powerful daemons or ambitious sorcerers. However, if control ever lapses, the Screamers return to their more instinctive behaviour and are likely to turn on their former master.

At times, the Lord of Change sees fit to grant one of his favoured daemonic heralds—or a mortal champion—the use of a Screamer as a steed. Binding the Screamer with bands of metal and blades of gold and silver, the Screamer is transformed into a Disk of Tzeentch. In even rarer instances, a herald or champion is given a flying chariot pulled by two Screamers. In either case, the steed is capable of carrying its rider not only across real space, but into the warp as well. Such creations are usually seen at the head of vast hosts of daemons and have announced the doom of several planets in the Expanse.

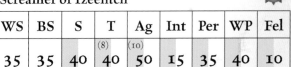

Screamer of Tzeentch

WS	BS	S	T	Ag	Int	Per	WP	Fel
35	35	40	(8) 40	(10) 50	15	35	40	10

Movement: 8/16/24/48   **Wounds**: 15
Armour: None.   **Total TB**: 8
Skills: Acrobatics (Ag), Awareness (Per) +20, Dodge (Ag), Psyniscience (Per).
Talents: Improved Warp Sense.
Psychic Powers (Psy Rating 3): Force Bolt.
Traits: Creature of the Warp†, Daemonic (TB 8), Daemonic Presence††, Fear (3), Flyer 8, From Beyond, Improved Natural Weapon (Warp Jaws), Size (Hulking), Strange Physiology, Unnatural Agility (x2) Warp Instability.
†**Creature of the Warp**: Screamers of Tzeentch never invoke Psychic Phenomena.
††**Daemonic Presence**: All creatures within 20 metres take a –10 penalty to Willpower Tests.
Weapons: Warp Jaws (1d10+4 R; Pen 10; Razor Sharp, Tearing).

VEILED DECEIT

"The shadows... they whisper to me and tell me secrets. Terrible secrets."

—Ensign Matte Steen, *Drusus' Vengeance*

It started while most of us were asleep. Kavor Jennick, one of the junior bridge officers and seemingly a promising lad, calmly stood up during the last dog watch, drew his sidearm, and destroyed several key auspex cogitators and their servitors before losing himself in the depths of the *Aureus*. We were now blind except for our own eyes peering through the ports, dangerous stuff while as close into the system as we were. We had to halt for repairs. This all seemed designed to set us up for reavers or pirates, and we readied ourselves for the worst while the Tech-Priests were pressed to hurry their ministrations. Normally, when a crewman goes bad like this, they explode in a fury of shells until either we fill them with metal or they eat their gun themselves. Other than the bridge assault, though, Jennick was quiet, and search teams had no luck finding him. We were hunting through the decks near his berthing quarters when we got lucky.

Lieutenant Pharres noticed the ice first, thin layers on the walls that got thicker as we moved farther along the level. It was getting colder, worse than I'd felt on the ship in many a day. The doorway to the berthing hall was frosted over. We readied our weapons and ourselves as I pushed it open. Jennick was there, but he wasn't alone. There were dead men scattered across the floor. Pistol fire had taken some, but others were ripped apart and missing limbs. The madman himself seemed to be rigging together demolition charges, and was somehow casting a huge jagged shadow on the far wall, void-black despite the weak light. The room itself was freezing. Alberse wanted him alive for interrogation, so my Locke put an end to Jennick's kneecaps but not his life. His odd shadow fell with him, settling, seemingly, a touch more slowly than his body.

We got nothing from him, though, other than a madman's rant about shadows with too many eyes and teeth, and voices commanding him to cripple the *Aureus* and keep her in the system. He insisted it spoke to him of ancient secrets, of armies of dead men brought to life through strange technologies, worlds where the sun and stars ran on tracks, and the need to appease the voices with offerings of blood. He also managed to whisper something to Alberse, who turned pale but had dealt with these things more often than I. My master drew himself together and declared Jennick warp-tainted. We gave him to the void and, for all I know, he is still babbling into the dark.

We returned to the berthing hall to gather what remains we could for a proper ceremony. The cold was now gone and our shadows were stark and black against the walls. I could have sworn I heard screaming as we burned the hall with a heavy flamer, but then again, it had been a long time since I'd slept well. I kept wondering what Jennick whispered to Alberse. We found out later that the system was attacked by a massive xenos fleet mere days after we left. I've started to watch the shadows more carefully since then.

WHISPERS IN THE DARK

My platoon had been in the warp for untold time; our chronos meaningless except to track the artificial passage of time in the ship's perpetual dim lighting. It had been a rough journey, and even grounders like myself could tell the Gellar Field was having troubles dealing with the storms that pounded the ship. Things got calmer after a while, though, until we were wracked by hard shudders that I recognised as internal explosions; no mistaking that if you've been inside a Baneblade that's fouled a shell.

I ordered my men to ready themselves just in case as we felt that indescribable sensation of dropping into real space. I only heard later in scuttlebutt that some stupid ensign had gone mad, raving about the walls coming to life long ago and constantly talking to him, convincing him he had to destroy the ship in order to fulfil his true duty to the Emperor. He had tried to disrupt the plasma feeds vital to the drive engines, but being only a Navy man he didn't even know enough to do that properly. Still, he did enough to delay the planned assault. We still got paid, but all that was left when we arrived were the foul symbols blood-painted across the palace to show the rebels had been there.

—Sgt. Pol Jannis, 3rd Platoon, of the mercenary brigade Blooded Iron, aboard *Drusus' Vengeance*

It appeared on a wall in my penance cell one night, an inky stain on the barren rockcrete. Shadowy yet not a shadow, it was darker even than the unlit fields here on Naduesh. Its shape was a disturbing evolution of blackness, the edges like the unravelling of woven cloth, with filaments of reality and the Accursed Dominions drifting through the air. The very air was also affected, seeping into this foul void in chill mists as the chamber became colder. Within this blackness existed numerous cruel eyes, scattered about with no perceivable pattern. They all fixed their gaze on me, though they blinked individually, as if each pair actually belonged to a different unseen face. Then appeared several great sets of teeth, with fangs of many lengths, that moved in unison as they began to speak to me. I tried to denounce this unholy abomination with prayer and exhortations for His Succour, but I could still hear its silken words, compelling me in soft choruses using the gutter-speak of Hive Asperg's lower depths, something I had not heard since childhood.

It whispered to me of things I must do, awful things to holy personages, terrible things to those I did not know were soon to arrive here. I would not even have the skills to perform such elegant sabotages and dreadful murders it insisted I accomplish. My Lord Inquisitor, I know not why the others did not hear my professions of faith or this abomination's insidious temptations. I only know the Ruinous Powers called to me and yet I resisted their honeyed words, pure to this, my end.

–Final Testimony of Novice Ellese Bo of
The Chapel of His Eternal Light

We had just entered the warp, lumens and arc-candles momentarily dimming across the bridge as usual, when my orderly noticed one of the shadows remained dark. In fact, it seemed to grow darker and larger even as the bridge grew brighter. I can only describe it now, upon later reflection—it was as if a great clawed hand had simply reached out and snatched a section of reality away to expose the deep blackness of the endless void. The edges were rough fractures of ebony that dissolved away as even new ones were pushed out from the interior, like some awful wellspring of night constantly spewing itself into day. The darkness also brought cold, as the air rapidly grew frigid and hard rime began to form along the surrounding brasswork.

Our thoughts were immediately of a breach, and Yanto ran from his port batteries station to seal the growing tear. When the seal-plate hit the shade though, the blackness suddenly grew larger, and rows of bleached teeth forming along the inside, enough to engulf the plate and most of Yanto's arm. Somehow the shadow was now a hole, deep enough to swallow his arm to the shoulder, and with a terrible bite it closed down on him. He fell back to the deck, bleeding out, and the shadow now formed additional mouths, all full of teeth and laughing, a horrible, low sound that still echoes in my nightmares. We moved to staunch his wound but it was too late, and the poor lad died never knowing his true lineage. I could only watch as the shadow slowly faded away, and by the Emperor I swear the mouths were grinning all the while. You call it a Veiled Deceit? I call it daemon, and that is enough for me.

–Rogue Trader Grellin Knox, *The Golden Star*,
under berth at Port Wander

Veiled Deceit

WS	BS	S	T	Ag	Int	Per	WP	Fel
25	—	20	35 (6)	25	50 (10)	45	50	35

Movement: N/A **Wounds**: 10
Armour: None. **Total TB**: 6
Skills: Awareness (Per), Charm (Fel), Deceive (Fel), Psyniscience (Per).
Talents: Heightened Senses (all).
Psychic Powers (Psy Rating 6): Delude, Dominate, Mental Bond, Mind Probe, Mind Scan.
Traits: Creature Of The Warp†, Daemonic (TB 6), Daemonic Presence††, Dark Sight, Fear (3), From Beyond, Glossolalia†††, Hoverer (3), Size (Hulking), Strange Physiology, The Stuff Of Nightmares, Unnatural Intelligence (x2), Warp Instability, Warp Weapon.
†**Creature of the Warp**: Veiled Deceits never invoke Psychic Phenomena.
††**Daemonic Presence**: When a Veiled Deceit manifests, the local temperature drops to near freezing as frigid winds blow into the rift formed by the Veiled Deceit's presence. All creatures within 20 metres take a –10 penalty to Willpower Tests and those without appropriate thermal protection within 10 metres must take a **Difficult (–10) Toughness Test** or suffer one point of Fatigue.
†††**Glossolalia:** When a Veiled Deceit speaks, each individual listener hears it talking in their native tongue.
Weapons: Endless Teeth (1d10+2 R; Pen 0, Tearing, Warp Weapon).

USING CREATURES OF CHAOS IN GAMES

Game Masters of ROGUE TRADER have an advantage (of sorts) over their players when using creatures of Chaos. While the average Explorer has seen a great many strange things, he probably has had little direct contact with such forces. Thus, a GM can present agents of the Ruinous Powers without the Player Characters necessarily grasping the true threats they face. Explorers can become almost blasé in their encounters with xenos races and creations, given the nature of their professions. When encountering daemons, however, they should typically be as ignorant and unprepared as normal Imperial servants would be when encountering a xenos being. Daemons are in many ways the "xenos" for Explorers—bizarre, unpredictable, and terrifying. Here the GM can insert threats beyond those of a mere financial or moral nature; he can introduce foes that present a danger not just to the Explorers' lives but to their very souls.

WHAT YOU DON'T KNOW CAN KILL YOU

Possibly the greatest fear is that of the unknown, and nothing is more unknowable than the warp. It changes constantly to such an extent no one, not even a Navigator, can look upon it and make absolute sense of what he sees. The creatures of the warp are much the same. While many daemons share a certain resemblance, no two truly look alike and some may look like nothing the Explorers have ever seen before. GMs can capitalise on this by describing a daemon in only the most general terms; later, when the daemon has been destroyed or driven off, the players may not be sure they actually encountered a creature of Chaos. They may even develop false impressions of whatever it is they fought, and a wise GM can use this against them in later adventures.

By the same token, the unknowable nature of the warp and its denizens makes it easy for GMs to develop new creatures to confound players. Adding such Traits as Daemonic, From Beyond, and Warp Instability to any of the beasts found in this or other books allow a GM to instantly create a new resident of the Immaterium. The most important aspect of this plan is to never use the same creature twice. No character in a ROGUE TRADER campaign can ever understand all there is to know about the warp and the players should be no different.

Some daemons are blatantly obvious as to their unnatural origins and there is little a GM can do to hide it. Instead, the GM should emphasize the effect such daemons have on real space, using audio, olfactory, and visual clues to slowly build tension before ever actually introducing the daemon into the scenario.

Khornate daemons, for example, are often heralded by the sound of clashing blades, a metallic taste in the air, and the presence of newly-spilled blood seeping from walls. The presence of such daemons may also affect people's emotions, heightening feelings of anger and causing them to fight among themselves, possibly to murderous levels.

Nurgle's creations announce themselves with the buzzing of vast swarms of flies, the smell of mildew and rot, and growths of stubborn fungi and moulds. Crewmembers may become ill and suffer from any number of diseases.

Slaaneshi beings are far more subtle. They may be preceded by beguiling sounds, tempting smells, and flickering images of material riches, pleasures of the flesh, or power in all its forms. Those overcome may fall into reckless scenes of debauchery.

Tzeentch's minions are perhaps the most unnerving, as they tend to alter reality to suit their desire for constant change. As a servant of Tzeentch draws near, people may hear whispered secrets or fragments of conversations and speeches occurring elsewhere in the Expanse. Worse yet, the world around the individual changes into new and ever more bizarre forms.

These effects are potent enough that the GM may call for a Fear Test long before the daemon itself has actually arrived, especially for less stalwart NPCs accompanying the Explorers. Nothing highlights the dangers of the warp more than having a loyal crewmember descend into madness by the mere presence of an as-yet-unseen daemon. When the daemon finally arrives, the impact can be even more terrifying.

CHAOS DOES NOT MEAN RANDOM

When daemons manifest in real space, they often appear little more than killing machines. However, this doesn't mean a daemonic incursion is without real meaning. Individual daemons may run rampant, but often the attack has a greater purpose. Game Masters can use this to present any number of challenges to players. Naturally, as they become more familiar with these perils of the warp, the GM should occasionally up the ante with a larger or more numerous daemonic threats. Below are some adventure seeds to offer suggestions for daemonic introductions:

- The Explorers arrive at a long-forgotten Imperial planet, but find the inhabitants have become Chaos worshippers in the many centuries that have passed. Game Masters can be as subtle or blatant as they want in presenting these changes, ranging from mere cultural curiosities to full-blown representation of obvious Chaos iconography, sacrifices, preaching, and prayers. Now the Explorers must not only get off of the planet with lives and souls intact, but also ensure the ship is kept safe and secure, lest this heresy spread across the sector.
- Whilst travelling through real space (perhaps on the fringes of a remote system), the Explorers encounter a derelict voidship. When they investigate, they may either find an eerily empty ship or an abattoir. Ravaged by daemons when the Gellar Fields failed, the ship managed to drop out of the Immaterium, carrying some of its attackers with it. Now the Explorers find themselves stalking (and being stalked by) soul-hungry beings of the warp through the bowels of the ship—and even if they decide to abandon the derelict to its fate, they must still find a way to get safely back to their own vessel.
- A Rogue Trader NPC sells or gives a strange xenos relic to the Player Characters. While most may see it as just another curiosity, what the Player Characters don't know is that the relic contains a daemon trapped within it or acts as a daemonic lure. A variant of this scenario puts the relic (or a similar object) in the hands of passengers on the Player Characters' vessel, who then release the daemon once the ship enters the warp to disrupt the crew. Now the Explorers must not only deal with a rampaging daemon, they must also deal with an attempt to hijack their ship!

XENOS
GENERATOR

- FLORA
  GENERATION
  •
- FAUNA
  GENERATION
  •
- PRIMITIVE SPECIES
  GENERATION
  •
- NEW SPECIES
  TRAITS

CHAPTER
IV: XENOS
GENERATOR

"Know the alien, kill the alien."

—Imperial Proverb

Innumerable alien species crowd the galaxy, races and creatures so varied and strange they could not be fully catalogued even in all the data-vaults of the Administratum. Some are benign or even useful to the Imperium, such as the humble Grox—a staple of countless worlds' diets. Others are vast, galaxy-spanning threats, like the green tide of Orks or the Tyranid Hive Fleets. Most lie somewhere in-between— the unsurpassed apex predator of a single world or a minor xenos empire not yet crushed by an Imperial Crusade.

This chapter is intended to help GMs populate the worlds of the Koronus Expanse with new alien creatures for their bold Explorers to discover. Whether filling the woodlands of a possible colony world with deadly plant life or creating monstrous combatants suitable for use in Calixian Beast Trade, the tables within should provide a GM all the resources needed for the task. This chapter also includes a generator for primitive xenos cultures and civilisations with which to populate the Expanse, suitable for Explorers to trade with or crusade against.

GMs may find they create very odd, even bizarre creatures using this generator. While they may not feel these creatures fit or are appropriate, the GM should give a particularly odd creation a second thought before discarding it. After all, the worlds of the Koronus Expanse are wildly varied, and a phasing, 20 metre tall pinecone with poison spores may not be as strange as it first appears!

RANDOM FLORA GENERATOR

The Explorers aboard a Rogue Trader vessel frequently travel to worlds devoid of life; some unable to sustain it through a lack of atmosphere or water, while others are simply too harsh for any known organism to survive. Tectonic upheaval, massive radiation, or atmospheres so toxic a single breath can kill are just some of the hazards of the various worlds in the Koronus Expanse. But even on the so-called "habitable" worlds the more fortunate Explorers might locate, life does not always fit into familiar forms. For every strain of edible vegetation and for each exotic bloom safe to sell to the hothouses of a noble's estate, there are dozens of varieties of choking vines, toxic plants, and fungal mounds filled with soporific spores.

This generator assists GMs in developing plants with which the Explorers can interact, usually as hazards or obstacles to be overcome. It is capable of generating a wide variety of plants and fungi suitable to populate whatever world the Explorers encounter. However, it is only intended to provide game Traits for the flora generated, not provide a comprehensive list of all possible plants on a planet. GMs seeking to emphasise the alien ecosystems of the Expanse are encouraged to come up with their own details about more minor local plants and grasses.

TRAPS

Most plants likely to present a danger to the Explorers do so passively, through subtle toxins and spores, or slowly-constricting foliage. These plants, referred to in game terms as Trap Flora, are common to many worlds in the Expanse, and positively abundant on the many of the more hazardous ones. They take on many forms and present a variety of different threats.

Most seek some variety of nourishment from the poisoned or strangled corpses of passing fauna, a category that even the noblest of Rogue Traders fall into according to a plant's limited senses. Others show more unusual interest in their prey, such as the Wanderer Vine which lulls its prey to sleep with a heady musk, so they may be implanted with seedlings for distribution to distant glades. Some voidsmen even tell tales of sentient plants which kill simply to warn more mobile life not to disturb their sedate existence, leaving rotting corpses hanging from countless vines as a macabre boundary marker.

Trap Flora is never mobile in any meaningful sense, usually relying upon contact poisons or inhaled toxins, though some can lash out as a reflex against sensory stimuli.

COMBATANTS

The most dangerous plants of the Expanse are frequently mobile, or very nearly so, exhibiting a degree of awareness and activity quite unlike other flora. They are fully capable of defending themselves, or even making unprovoked attacks against incautious Explorers, and are referred to in game terms as Combatant Flora.

PROFIT MOTIVES

The xenos flora and fauna generated in this chapter can be more than adversaries to be overcome—they can be sources of profit. As such, any creature has a 25% chance of gaining the Valuable Trait, with the details of how it will apply varying with the actual creation.

Like Trap Flora, most such plants use the flesh of corpses or captive lifeforms to nourish themselves, but they tend to be much more aggressive in their acquisition of nutrients. Sprays of blinding pollen, whipping vines, and grasping thorns are all common tools for Combatant Flora, while some variants use virulent toxins or even launch their own branches as projectiles.

Some of the most fearsome varieties are capable of uprooting themselves and pursuing particularly desirable prey, leading to superstitious voidfarers' tales of virgin forests on colony worlds taking vengeance on the first loggers to approach them. Most Xenos Savants dismiss these tales, citing the impossibility of nourishing enough neural development for sentience alongside such fearsome combat capabilities. Whole colonies would need to be devoured to feed such creatures, surely making their sustained existence impossible—or so most Explorers would hope.

FLORA GENERATION TABLES

To generate the basic characteristics of a strain of xenos flora, roll once on **Table 4–1: Flora Base Profile**, and once on **Table 4–2: Flora Type**.

The Base Profile provides the flora strain's Characteristics and Size, as well as certain other Traits. Sizes can range from large swaths of small plants such as grassy areas to huge megaflora which can sustain entire ecosystems.

The Flora Type describes the way the plant gathers sustenance and may modify certain aspects of the Base Profile, and determines which Species Traits it is likely to have (see page 139). Trap flora are generally static, attracting food to them in a variety of ways, while combatant plants actively seek out prey much like animals. Each of the different Flora Types have different qualities:

- Passive Trap Flora lack any characteristics other than Toughness and lose whatever Weapons are listed on their Base Profile.
- Active Trap Flora reduce the Weapon Skill characteristic listed on the Base Profile by 10, and automatically have a Perception characteristic of 5, regardless of Base Profile.
- Combatant Trap Flora have a 30% chance to gain the Snare Quality for their weapons.

FLORA BASE PROFILES

Xenos flora follows all the rules for normal creatures, except where noted here and elsewhere in this chapter. All flora has the Strange Physiology and From Beyond Traits (as shown in the Base Profiles below), and cannot use the Dodge Skill. Flora may ignore environmental effects or be affected differently at the GM's discretion.

Diffuse Flora

This Base Profile represents a large field of tiny plants, grasses, or fungal aggregations, covering an area of at least twenty metres by twenty metres. GMs should feel free to adjust the Size and Wounds of a field of Diffuse Flora to match a different arrangement.

Diffuse Flora Profile								
WS	BS	S	T	Ag	Int	Per	WP	Fel
30	—	10	20	25	—	15	—	—

Movement: N/A — **Wounds:** 24
Armour: None. — **Total TB:** 2
Skills: None.
Talents: None.
Traits: Diffuse†, From Beyond, Natural Weapons, Size (Enormous), Strange Physiology.
Weapons: Thorns, Barbs, or Tendrils (1d10+1 R or I; Pen 0).
†**Diffuse:** Any attack that does not have the Blast, Flame, or Scatter Quality only inflict half damage on a Diffuse target. A Diffuse target cannot be Knocked Down, Grappled or Pinned, and counts as destroyed once all its Wounds are lost.

TABLE 4-1: FLORA BASE PROFILE	
Dice Roll (1d10)	**Base Profile**
1	Diffuse Flora
2-4	Small Flora
5-8	Large Flora
9-10	Massive Flora

TABLE 4-2: FLORA TYPE	
Dice Roll (1d10)	**Base Profile**
1-3	Trap, Passive
4-6	Trap, Active
7-10	Combatant

Small Flora

This Base Profile represents shrubs, bushes, and large mushrooms or fungi. It could also represent a young example of a larger strain of xenos flora.

| Small Flora Profile | | | | | | | | |
WS	BS	S	T	Ag	Int	Per	WP	Fel
40	—	35	35	35	—	25	—	—

Movement: N/A   **Wounds:** 8
Armour: None.   **Total TB:** 3
Skills: None.
Talents: Sturdy.
Traits: From Beyond, Natural Weapons, Size (Scrawny), Strange Physiology.
Weapons: Thorns, Barbs, or Tendrils (1d10+2 R or I; Pen 0).

Large Flora

This Base Profile represents most trees, or particularly impressive aggregations of vines or fungal mounds. It could also stand in for a partially mature specimen of a strain of Massive Flora.

| Large Flora Profile | | | | | | | | |
WS	BS	S	T	Ag	Int	Per	WP	Fel
50	—	50	50	20	—	35	—	—

Movement: N/A   **Wounds:** 20
Armour: Bark or Rind (Body 2).   **Total TB:** 5
Skills: None.
Talents: Sturdy.
Traits: From Beyond, Natural Weapons, Size (Enormous), Strange Physiology.
Weapons: Oversized Thorns, Barbs, or Tendrils (1d10+6 R or I; Pen 0).

Massive Flora

This Base Profile represents the largest and most ancient of plants, from trees that predate Imperial entry into the Expanse to huge mushrooms whose caps block out sunlight across a vast area. Many flora specimens reaching this size become riddled with parasites, but their tremendous vitality remains undiminished.

| Massive Flora Profile | | | | | | | | |
WS	BS	S	T	Ag	Int	Per	WP	Fel
45	—	65	75	15	—	20	—	—

Movement: N/A   **Wounds:** 40
Armour: Thick Bark or Rind (Body 4).   **Total TB:** 7
Skills: None.
Talents: Sturdy.

Traits: From Beyond, Improved Natural Weapons, Size (Massive), Strange Physiology, Swift Attack.
Weapons: Fearsome Thorns, Barbs, or Tendrils (1d10+9 R or I; Pen 1; Tearing).

SPECIES TRAITS

The unnatural forms of the alien are numerous beyond counting, but among the myriad variations there are often certain broad patterns that the most successful species adopt. These are referred to as Species Traits.

A typical strain of flora possesses three Species Traits. All of these Traits are generated by rolls on the appropriate sections of **Table 4–3: Flora Species Traits.** The GM makes two rolls on the appropriate section for the Flora Type (Passive, Active, or Combatant), and one roll on the section that matches the type of world the flora exists on (Death, Jungle, Ocean, or Temperate). If the world or environment to which the flora strain is native does not correspond to any of the tables, roll on the Temperate World Species Traits section. Species from Death Worlds roll twice on the Death World Traits section and apply the results of both rolls.

At the GM discretion, a highly evolved or unusual specimen may be granted a free roll on the Exotic Species section.

Passive Trap Flora generally are immobile, and attract prey with perfumed scents, visual cues, and even auditory lures to draw them into digestion pits. They often have specific defences against attack including strong smells which can repel most animals. Active Trap Flora use vines and other stalks to grasp their prey and draw them in to feed. Combatant Flora are as ferocious as many predatory animals and should be faced only with extreme caution.

EXAMPLE: CORPSE SNARE

Robin is the GM for a group of Explorers who are planning an expedition to a little-known Death World in the Expanse. He needs some local lifeforms to keep the Explorers on their toes, and elects to start with a xenos flora strain.

First, he needs to generate the Base Profile and Flora Type, and rolls on the appropriate tables. The dice tell him to use the Large Flora Base Profile—but the creature is an Active Trap, and thus does not use those Characteristics exactly as they are. Robin could narrow down some details about what the flora looks like or how it behaves at this point, and so he decides the flora is a vast conglomeration of vines that lash out at nearby creatures. He modifies the Weapon Skill and Perception to the appropriate levels, and notes the relevant details about the flora's attacks, resulting in the following Base Profile:

| Corpse Snare Base Profile | | | | | | | | |
WS	BS	S	T	Ag	Int	Per	WP	Fel
40	—	50	50	10	—	05	—	—

Movement: *N/A*   **Wounds:** *20*
Armour: *Bark (Body 2).*   **Total TB:** *5*
Skills: *None.*
Talents: *Sturdy.*
Traits: *Natural Weapons, Size (Enormous).*
Weapons: *Lashing Vines (1d10+6 I; Pen 0).*

TABLE 4-3: FLORA SPECIES TRAITS

Passive Trap Species Traits

Dice Roll (1d10)	Species Trait
1	Armoured
2	Deterrent
3	Frictionless
4	Sticky
5-6	Foul Aura (Soporific)
7-8	Foul Aura (Toxic)
9	Resilient
10	Roll on the Exotic Species Traits section of this table.

Active Trap Species Traits

Dice Roll (1d10)	Species Trait
1	Armoured
2	Deadly
3	Flexible
4	Mighty
5	Sticky
5	Paralytic
7	Resilient
8-9	Venomous
10	Roll on the Exotic Species Traits section of this table.

Combatant Species Traits

Dice Roll (1d10)	Species Trait
1	Armoured
2	Deadly
3	Venomous
4	Deterrent
5	Mighty
6	Projectile Attack
7-8	Resilient
9	Uprooted Movement
10	Roll on the Exotic Species Traits section of this table.

Death World Species Traits

Dice Roll (1d10)	Species Trait
1-2	Armoured
3	Deadly (re-roll for Passive Trap Flora)
4	Deterrent
5	Disturbing
6	Mighty (re-roll for Passive Trap Flora)
7	Resilient
8	Unkillable
9	Lethal Defenses
10	Uprooted Movement (re-roll for all Trap Flora)

Jungle World Species Traits

Dice Roll (1d10)	Species Trait
1	Deterrent
2	Stealthy
3-4	Flexible
5-6	Foul Aura (Soporific)
7-8	Foul Aura (Toxic)
9	Paralytic (re-roll for Passive Trap Flora)
10	Venomous (re-roll for Passive Trap Flora)

Ocean World Species Traits

Dice Roll (1d10	Species Trait
1-2	Deterrent
3	Disturbing
4	Paralytic (re-roll for Passive Trap Flora)
5-6	Projectile Attack
7-9	Uprooted Movement (re-roll for all Trap Flora)
10	Venomous (re-roll for Passive Trap Flora)

Temperate World Species Traits

Dice Roll (1d10)	Species Trait
1	Armoured
2	Venomous
3	Stealthy
4-5	Deterrent
6	Foul Aura (Soporific)
7	Foul Aura (Toxic)
8	Projectile Attack
9-10	Resilient

Exotic Species Traits

Dice Roll (1d10)	Species Trait
1-2	Disturbing
3	Lethal Defenses
4-5	Silicate
6-7	Fade-kind
7-8	Unkillable
10	Warped

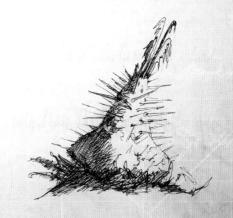

EXAMPLE: CORPSE SNARE (CONTINUED)

*Now Robin needs to generate the Species Traits for his vines. He rolls on **Table 4–3: Flora Species Traits** twice for Active Trap Species Traits to generate the Traits it uses to hunt, and twice for Death World Species Traits to show how the strain evolved to meet the pressures of a Death World ecosystem. The first two rolls come out with the Mighty and Deadly Traits, granting increased Weapon Skill and Strength, as well as the Improved Natural Weapons Trait. The first roll on the Death World table shows that these vines keep predators away by being Disturbing, granting a Fear Rating of 1. Being from a Death World means the creature gains two rolls appropriate to its environment, instead of the normal one, and so the creature is also Armoured, adding two to the Natural Armour value of the vines. Robin could choose to roll one or more times additionally, but he decides his new flora strain is fine as it is. He decides one of the few previous visitors to the Death World called the vines "Corpse-Snare," after the way in which the vine incorporates elements of devoured creatures into its thick rubbery frame as a warning (also accounting for the Fear Rating). The final creature's Profile is as follows:*

Corpse Snare Modified Profile

WS	BS	S	T	Ag	Int	Per	WP	Fel
50	—	60	50	10	—	05	—	—

Movement: N/A
Wounds: 20
Armour: Thick rubbery coating (Body 4).
Total TB: 5
Skills: None.
Talents: Sturdy.
Traits: Fear 1 (Disturbing), Improved Natural Weapons, Size (Enormous).
Weapons: Lashing Vines (1d10+9 I; Pen 0).

RANDOM FAUNA GENERATOR

Just as the flora of a life-sustaining world may vary considerably from the established and comfortable forms known to the Imperium's citizens, the fauna of the Expanse's untamed worlds possesses a staggering diversity far beyond what is familiar. With effort, xeno-arcanists and the Magos Biologis savants of the Priesthood of Martian have managed to fit most encountered species into broad categories, but there is always ambiguity in such tidy classifications. More than one Tech-Priest devoted to such studies has lamented life's unregulated nature compared to the precision of the machine.

Fauna in a ROGUE TRADER game is likely to fall into one of the roles below; these broadly describe the general ways a creature operates in its environment. The fauna generated using the tables below usually fit into one of these types; if it does not fit, the GM may want to consider such a beast to be local flavour, rather than a game element. Such species can still be valuable tools in establishing a scene or setting the tone of a session.

DOMESTICABLE

This category covers a wide variety of species, from the ubiquitous Grox found across the Imperium to the legendary "thunder horse" of the Halo Stars alluded to in the writings of certain long-dead Rogue Traders. A domesticable beast is one that is relatively safe for humanity to deal with, and which can be trained or utilised in a way that serves the Imperium of Man. These are generally herbivorous, though some may be omnivores. Native herd beasts with palatable flesh are a primary staple of new colonies, and many xenos species can be harnessed as steeds or beasts of burden if the need is sufficient. More adventurous Explorers might even try taming xenos hunting beasts or training deadly predators for battle.

Endeavours can be based around domesticable species of xenos fauna, whether forming colonies to utilise them, or exporting them to other worlds. Acquiring specialised ark-ships is advisable for transporting herds of Grox, but the holds of any vessel can suffice for at least a short trip. Sometimes beasts do not take well to void travel, and much less to warp translation, leading to possible Misfortunes as they run amok.

PARASITICAL

Predation is not confined to the cycles of hunter and hunted—it also includes species adapted to make hosts and victims of other creatures. Many xenos creatures have unique methods of infection, such as the Genestealer's implantation attack. Such strange beasts cannot be covered here in adequate depth, but a GM may consider adding details to physically weak creatures with appropriate Species Traits. A Gestalt xenos could release some of its component life forms with each attack to burrow into the target, for example, or a Paralytic beast might lay eggs in unconscious foes. The game effects of such reproduction are left to the imagination of the GM, although it is advised that putting too much focus on such an element can alter the tone of a game.

FLORA AND FAUNA: DIFFERENCES IN GENERATION

Both flora and fauna generated by the tables in this chapter are classified into Types based on their behaviours, as well as the function this places them into within the context of a ROGUE TRADER game. However, Type is only used as a mechanical designation in the flora generation system, and is applied after generation for fauna.

The ROGUE TRADER system is built around representing creatures and characters that display Traits quite different than even the most exotic xenos flora. The behaviours of a wild beast can easily be adjudicated by the GM, but a plant requires special handling. The Flora Type strain provides the additional detail a GM needs to represent this.

Similarly, the Size of a flora strain is implicit in its Base Profile, while it is generated randomly for species of fauna. The primary mechanical difference between a large tree and a small fungal mound is that of durability and lethality, with the various ecological roles each fills having little to do with the strain's use in a ROGUE TRADER game. The ROGUE TRADER system's creature-focused Profiles allow more diversity in beasts, and so Size for them is more appropriate as a factor in their overall Profile, rather than as a defining Trait.

SCAVENGING

Scavenging creatures tend towards cautious, stealthy behaviour, and are unlikely to expose themselves to a group of hale and hearty Explorers. However, when the Explorers make a kill, they may find previously unknown beasts slinking out of the shadows after they move on. Similarly, bolder or more desperate scavengers may be driven to attack wounded Explorers after a fierce battle to try to finish them off, particularly those foolish enough to separate from the group while in such a state.

Scavengers can come from almost any Base Profile, with the Profile of the same name representing only the most archetypal varieties. If a GM has generated several predatory creatures, it is likely that the weakest of these creatures is forced into a scavenging role.

PREDATORY

Tales abound in Footfall and Port Wander of the deadly hunting beasts of the Expanse. The world of Burnscour is particularly notorious for the abundance of such beasts, but is far from the only planet to house them. While not every

TABLE 4-4: FAUNA BASE PROFILE

Roll 1d10	Base Profile
1-2	Avian Beast
3-5	Herd Beast
6-7	Predator
8-9	Scavenger
10	Verminous Swarm

TABLE 4-5: FAUNA SIZE

Roll 1d10	Size	Profile Modifiers
1	Miniscule	−25 to Strength and Toughness, −10 Wounds (minimum of 3) before Species Traits
2	Puny	−20 to Strength and Toughness, −10 Wounds
3-4	Scrawny	−10 to Strength and Toughness, −5 Wounds
5-6	Average	No modifiers
7-8	Hulking	+5 to Strength and Toughness, −5 to Agility, +5 Wounds
9	Enormous	+10 to Strength and Toughness, −10 to Agility, +10 Wounds
10	Massive	+20 to Strength and Toughness, −20 to Agility, +20 Wounds

predator in the Expanse is a hyper-evolved killing machine, Rogue Traders tend to take the most interest in the ones that match such descriptions. These are the creatures most likely to threaten their interests—or provide for them.

The Beast Houses of the Calixis Sector is always looking for new and deadly predators for their fighting pits, and the fiercer the specimen, the better. For truly monstrous beasts, they offer sums that make even the heads of thriving Dynasties take notice. Beyond this, having a reputation as a hunter of the most dangerous beasts of the Expanse can impress jaded nobles and cow timorous officials, providing useful leverage and influence to the canny Rogue Trader.

FAUNA GENERATION TABLES

To generate the basic characteristics of a species of xenos fauna, roll once on **Table 4–4: Fauna Base Profile**, and once on **Table 4–5: Fauna Size**. The Base Profile provides the species' Characteristics and certain other Traits, as well as determining the Species Traits the species possesses (see page 139). The Size of the fauna may modify certain aspects of the Base Profile.

Note that fauna using the Verminous Swarm Base Profile do not use the Profile Modifiers on **Table 4–5: Fauna Size**, instead using the special Traits described in the relevant Base Profile. Furthermore, Verminous Swarms re-roll all results on **Table 4–5: Fauna Size** of 4 or lower (meaning a Verminous Swarm cannot be smaller than Average Size).

FAUNA BASE PROFILES

The following Base Profiles describe broad categories of creatures, and are named after what a typical example of a creature with that Base Profile is likely to resemble. A fully detailed creature may end up being something quite unfit to classify as a member of the category the Base Profile initially indicates. Such examples might include a Scavenger receiving Species Traits making it deadly enough to hunt its own prey with ease, or a Herd Beast large and formidable enough to live a solitary existence without fear.

Any species of xenos fauna not using the Verminous Swarm Base Profile has a 20% chance of possessing the Multiple Arms and/or Quadruped Traits (roll once for each). If the creature already possesses the Quadruped Trait, increase its Speed multiplier by 1 as described on page 367 of the ROGUE TRADER CORE Rulebook.

Avian Beast

This Base Profile can represent birds and airborne creatures of all types. It can also serve for flying mammals such as bats and ptera-squirrels, or even winged reptiles and insects.

Avian Beast Profile

WS	BS	S	T	Ag	Int	Per	WP	Fel
36	—	30	30	45	16	44	30	—

Movement: 4/8/12/24   **Wounds**: 9
Armour: None.   **Total TB**: 3
Skills: Awareness (Per).
Talents: None.
Traits: Bestial, Flyer (AB x2), Natural Weapons.
Weapons: Beak or Talons (1d10+3 R; Pen 0).

Herd Beast

This Base Profile covers a wide variety of animal life, from placid, cud-chewing bovines and skittish grazers to lumbering behemoths whose solitary tread is heavy enough to scare off predators. It is typical for creatures using this Base Profile to band together for mutual defence, but not a universal rule. Advantageous Species Traits or great Size may make a creature strong enough to withstand the predators of its world.

Herd Beast Profile

WS	BS	S	T	Ag	Int	Per	WP	Fel
24	—	40	45	25	16	30	40	—

Movement: 4/8/12/24   **Wounds**: 14
Armour: None.   **Total TB**: 4
Skills: Awareness (Per).
Talents: None.
Traits: Bestial, Natural Weapons, Quadruped, Sturdy.
Weapons: Hooves, horns, or paws (1d10+4 I; Pen 0).

Predator

Although typical of creatures that hunt and kill other fauna for sustenance, this Base Profile can represent any creature evolved to fight. Many herd-dwelling herbivores on Death Worlds might use this Base Profile to represent their aggressive defences evolved to protect against such environments.

Predator Profile

WS	BS	S	T	Ag	Int	Per	WP	Fel
48	—	45	40	40	16	40	45	—

Movement: 4/8/12/24   **Wounds**: 15
Armour: None.   **Total TB**: 4
Skills: Awareness (Per), Tracking (Int).
Talents: Swift Attack.
Traits: Bestial, Brutal Charge, Natural Weapons.
Weapons: Claws or Fangs (1d10+4 R; Pen 0).

Scavenger

This Base Profile could represent a weaker predatory beast, as well as a carrion eater capable of holding its own against its peers once the true hunters have abandoned their kill, or even a foraging omnivore. It could also represent any fierce or dangerous creature less mighty than the Predator Base Profile.

Scavenger Profile

WS	BS	S	T	Ag	Int	Per	WP	Fel
40	—	36	36	40	16	40	35	—

Movement: 4/8/12/24   **Wounds**: 12
Armour: None.   **Total TB**: 3
Skills: Awareness (Per), Tracking (Int).
Talents: None.
Traits: Bestial, Natural Weapons.
Weapons: Claws or Fangs (1d10+3 R; Pen 0).

Verminous Swarm

Many small creatures that would be individually inconsequential to face have a tendency to band together in a roiling tide of bodies that forms a threat to even a well-armed group of Explorers. This Base Profile represents such an aggregated threat, as appropriate for a hive or colony of insects as a squirming carpet of rodents or a darting school of fish.

Verminous Swarm Profile

WS	BS	S	T	Ag	Int	Per	WP	Fel
30	—	05	10	35	05	40	10	—

Movement: 3/6/9/18
Wounds: 10+ (See Size (Swarm) Trait below)
Armour: None.   **Total TB**: 1
Skills: Awareness (Per).
Talents: None.
Traits: Bestial, Fear 1, Natural Weapons, Overwhelming†, Size (Swarm)††, Swarm Creature†††, 30% chance of Flyer (6).
Weapons: Abundance of tiny Fangs, Claws, or Stingers (1d10 R; Pen 1d5; Tearing).
†Overwhelming: A Verminous Swarm is made up of many

Table 4-6: Fauna Species Traits

Avian Beast Species Traits

Roll 1d10	Species Trait
1-3	Deadly
4	Flexible
5-6	Projectile Attack
7	Stealthy
8	Sustained Life
9	Swift
10	Roll on **Table 4–7: Exotic Species Traits.**

Herd Beast Species Traits

Roll 1d10	Species Trait
1-2	Armoured
3	Deterrent
4	Lethal Defences
5	Mighty
6-7	Resilient
8-9	Swift
10	Roll on **Table 4–7: Exotic Species Traits.**

Predator Species Traits

Roll 1d10	Species Trait
1	Apex
2	Armoured
3-4	Deadly
5	Mighty
6	Paralytic OR Venomous (GM's choice)
7	Projectile Attack
8	Stealthy
9	Swift
10	Roll on **Table 4–7: Exotic Species Traits.**

Scavenger Species Traits

Roll 1d10	Species Trait
1	Crawler
2	Darkling
3-4	Deadly
5	Deathdweller
6	Disturbing
7	Flexible
8	Stealthy
9	Swift
10	Roll on **Table 4–7: Exotic Species Traits.**

Verminous Swarm Species Traits

Roll 1d10	Species Trait
1	Crawler
2	Darkling
3-4	Deadly
5	Deathdweller
6-7	Deterrent
8-9	Disturbing
10	Roll on **Table 4–7: Exotic Species Traits.**

Death World Species Traits

Roll 1d10	Species Trait
1	Apex
2	Armoured
3	Deadly
4	Deathdweller
5	Disturbing
6	Lethal Defences
7	Mighty
8	Resilient
9	Swift
10	Unkillable

Desert World Species Traits

Roll 1d10	Species Trait
1	Crawler
2	Thermal Adaptation (Cold)
3-4	Deathdweller
5-6	Tunneller
7-10	Thermal Adaptation (Heat)

Ice World Species Traits

Roll 1d10	Species Trait
1	Darkling
2-3	Deathdweller
4	Silicate
5-9	Thermal Adaptation (Cold)
10	Tunneller

Jungle World Species Traits

Roll 1d10	Species Trait
1-2	Amphibious
3-5	Arboreal
6-7	Crawler
8	Paralytic
9	Stealthy
10	Venomous

Ocean World Species Traits

Roll 1d10	Species Trait
1-4	Amphibious
6-10	Aquatic

Temperate World Species Traits

Roll 1d10	Species Trait
1	Amphibious
2	Aquatic
3	Arboreal
4	Armoured
5	Crawler
6	Mighty
7	Resilient
8	Stealthy
9	Swift
10	Roll on **Table 4–7: Exotic Species Traits.**

Volcanic World Species Traits

Roll 1d10	Species Trait
1	Armoured
2-3	Deathdweller
4	Sustained Life
5-9	Thermal Adaptation (Heat)
10	Tunneller

TABLE 4-7: EXOTIC SPECIES TRAITS

Dice Roll (1d10)	Species Trait
1	Amorphous
2	Darkling
3	Disturbing
4	Fade-Kind
5	Gestalt
6	Silicate
7	Sustained Life
8	Lethal Defenses
9	Unkillable
10	Warped

hundreds of creatures at least, and is capable of attacking many things at once. For every 10 Wounds the Swarm has remaining, it may make one additional melee attack as part of a Standard Attack Action. These attacks may never be against the same target.

††**Size:** By definition, a Verminous Swarm is made up of the smallest of lifeforms, creatures too tiny to fit on the scale typically used. However, when gathered into a Verminous Swarm, such creatures gain an effective Size Trait similar to other Fauna. The rolled result on **Table 4–5: Fauna Size** represents the typical size of a fully active swarm, hive, colony, or other group of the species. A Swarm receives 20 additional Wounds for every Size category past Average on the chart (so a Hulking Swarm would have 30 Wounds). This also works in reverse, meaning as a swarm takes Wounds, it shrinks in Size, representing the component creatures dying or fleeing. In addition, swarms may fill rooms, cover fields, and generally take up large amounts of space at the GM's discretion.

†††**Swarm Creature:** Any attack that does not have the Blast, Flame, or Scatter Quality only inflicts half damage on a Swarm Creature. In most circumstances, a Swarm cannot be Knocked Down, Grappled, or Pinned; the Swarm may "pour" through suitable small openings such as ducts, vents and the like, but cannot Jump. The Swarm counts as destroyed once all its Wounds are lost. Its attacks have a variable penetration value (roll each time an attack lands), representing its ability to engulf its victims and attack vulnerable areas.

SPECIES TRAITS

Like flora, species of xenos fauna have distinguishing characteristics in the form of Species Traits, representing unusual qualities, make-ups, behaviours, and defence mechanisms.

A typical species possesses three Species Traits. All of these traits are generated by rolls on the appropriate sections of **Table 4-6: Fauna Species Traits.** The GM makes two rolls on the appropriate section for the type of fauna (Avian, Herd, Predator, Scavenger, or Verminous Swarm), and one roll on the section that matches the type of world the fauna

exists on (Death, Jungle, Ocean, or Temperate). If the world or environment to which the species is native to does not correspond to any of the tables, roll on the Temperate World Species Traits section. Species from Death Worlds roll twice on the Death World Traits section and apply the results of both rolls. Desert Worlds may possibly have extremes of both hot and cold temperatures, with denizens adapted for perhaps only one variety (and thus Thermal Adaptation occurring for both extremes in the Desert World section).

At the GM discretion, a highly evolved or unusual specimen may be granted additional rolls in the appropriate sections or a free roll on **Table 4–7: Exotic Species Traits.** The GM may also assign one or more pre-chosen Species Traits to a creature in order to better adapt the results to the needs of the game, although it is advisable to do this sparingly (a creature intended to be present in a lightless tunnel system would almost certainly have the Darkling Species Trait, for example).

EXAMPLE: CASMIRRE'S BEHEMOTH

Robin's game has progressed beyond the Death World where Corpse-Snare blooms and onto a world covered in arid desert. The players are there for business, but Robin wants to include a memorable local creature or two. He starts by rolling for Base Profile and Size. The results give him a Massive Herd Beast. He adjusts the Base Profile with the modifiers for Size, and notes that the creature, while using the Herd Beast Base Profile, is most likely to be encountered alone. It's already tough enough to resist a concerted assault by a group of well-armed Explorers, much less other, lesser wild beasts—not to mention that a herd of such creatures couldn't feed themselves off a desert's fare. He records the adjusted Base Profile as follows:

Casmirre's Behemoth Base Profile

WS	BS	S	T	Ag	Int	Per	WP	Fel
24	—	60	65	05	16	30	40	––

Movement: *6/12/18/36*   **Wounds:** *34*
Armour: *None.*   **Total TB:** *6*
Skills: *Awareness (Per).*
Talents: *None.*
Traits: *Bestial, Natural Weapons, Quadruped, Size (Massive), Sturdy.*
Weapons: *Hooves, horns, or heavy paws (1d10+6 I; Pen 0).*

EXAMPLE: CASMIRRE'S BEHEMOTH (CONTINUED)

Now, Robin needs Species Traits to define what exactly this huge creature is. He rolls twice on the Herd Beast Species Traits section of **Table 4–6: Fauna Species Traits**, *and once on the Desert World Species Traits section. His first two rolls are both instances of the Armoured Trait, which, after a quick follow-up roll, yields a whopping 7 Armour, leading to an extremely durable creature. The roll on the environmental table yields the Species Trait of Thermal Adaptation (Cold).*

Robin decides the creature likely waits out the blazing heat of the day under its thick carapace before becoming active in the much colder night-time, as the Thermal Adaptation would indicate. At first he pictures it as something resembling an enormous armadillo, before deciding to add some additional details to the description to make it more intimidating, such as a scaly hide to cover the weak points in its shell, and vicious claws so large they crush rather than tear.

The only thing left for him to do is name the beast, and he decides it was discovered by an established Rogue Trader NPC from his campaign, Regias Casmirre, who brought down several of the creatures during a hunting expedition. This gives the players plenty of motivation to seek out the beast—now known as Casmirre's Behemoth—and one-up their rival with a trophy of their own. Robin then makes note of the final profile for what they face:

Casmirre's Behemoth Modified Profile

WS	BS	S	T	Ag	Int	Per	WP	Fel
24	—	60	70	05	16	30	40	––

Movement: 6/12/18/36   **Wounds**: 34
Armour: *Heavy Plated Carapace (All 7).*   **Total TB**: 7
Skills: *Awareness (Per).*
Talents: *Resistance (Cold)†.*
Traits: *Bestial, Natural Weapons, Quadruped, Size (Massive), Sturdy.*
Weapons: *Enormous crushing claws (1d10+6 I; Pen 0).*
†*Casmirre's Behemoth also suffers −20 on Tests to resist the effects of extreme heat.*

PRIMITIVE XENOS GENERATOR

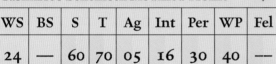

Amongst the glorious peerage of the Rogue Trader dynasties, legends are told of Warrant-holders who drove away the warfleets of an Ork Waaagh! or who visited Eldar Craftworlds as honoured guests. But these powerful voidfaring races are not the only aliens in the Expanse, and many cunning Rogue Traders know to seek their Cold Trade profits from other sources.

PRIMITIVE CIVILISATIONS

The xenos races in this section are not typical fare for the **ROGUE TRADER** setting. They possess no advanced technology and pose no threat to other worlds, much less to the Koronus Expanse. While some groups might find this disappointing, it would take far more time and space than could be included in this book to give a generator for advanced xenos civilisations its proper due.

However, this focus on fledgling cultures does not mean that stories of danger and hazard cannot occur. While simple warclubs may not penetrate carapace armour as easily as Eldar lasblasters, a tribe of savages angered by the patronising attitude of a haughty Rogue Trader is not a threat to be discounted, especially when their mastery of local terrain can cut off escape routes or ground assaults. No alien race is to be assumed non-threatening, as the Imperial Creed will readily assert.

Throughout this area of wilderness space, countless xenos races still thrive. Some hold regional pocket empires, employing starships and small warp-capable fleets. Far more commonly they exist on but a single world, often as a pre-industrial civilisation with only rudiments of the technology that others have mastered. These races are ostensibly rivals to mankind's rightful dominance, and—according to Imperial doctrine—are to be viewed as a threat as great as that posed by the ravening Tyranid or rampaging Ork. Some Rogue Traders in the Expanse rigidly adhere to this philosophy and have purged many a race from existence. Other Rogue Traders adopt a more flexible view, believing there are greater profits to be made through trade and conquest, as they can often deal with these lesser species from a position of strength and control. As a result, many dynasties reap huge fortunes from alien artefacts of a considerably less hazardous provenance than Egarian geodes or the glass knives of the Fra'al.

While dealing with such races is usually less perilous than braving the guardianship of Eldar Maiden Worlds or the corpse-choked ruins of the Yu'vath, it is still not altogether safe. These primitive cultures are often as proud and vicious as starfaring races, and trade deadly weaponry for a ruthless will to survive, often coupled with a perfect knowledge of the local flora and fauna that makes them unmatched in their native environment.

The only reliable way to deal with such a culture is to engage it with cautious diplomacy, preferably from a position of great strength. Intimidation from orbit rarely works, as the xenos typically have no conception of the threat they face until everything that could have been of value has been scorched to glass or shattered under macrocannon barrages. Some Rogue Traders prefer to engage in raids from guncutters and shuttles, seizing what they can before fleeing beyond retaliation, but the cunning and spite of primitive races has led to more than one Warrant being passed to the next in succession.

TABLE 4-8: PRIMITIVE XENOS SPECIES TRAITS

Roll 1d5	Species Trait
1	Deadly
2	Mighty
3	Resilient
4	Stealthy
5	Swift

TABLE 4-9: XENOS MORPHOLOGY

Dice Roll (1d10)	Trait
1	Crawler
2	Flyer (6)
3	Hoverer (4)
4	Multiple Arms
5	Quadruped
6	Size (Hulking)
7	Size (Scrawny)
8-10	Humanoid, Size (Average)

XENOS BASE PROFILE

The following profile represents the baseline for most species that have mastered basic tool-use and social organisation. However, such species have begun the trend towards individual specialisation, and so GMs are encouraged to grant modest bonuses (no greater than 10 to 15 Characteristic points in total) to individuals based on their role in the society. A hunter might receive +5 to Ballistic Skill, Agility, and Perception, while a chieftain's personal bodyguard might have +10 Weapons Skill or Toughness.

Primitive Xenos Profile

WS	BS	S	T	Ag	Int	Per	WP	Fel
35	25	30	35	30	30	35	30	25

Movement: 3/6/9/18   **Wounds**: 10
Armour: Hides (Body 2, Arms 1, Legs 1).   **Total TB**: 3
Skills: Awareness (Per), Survival (Int) +10, Wrangling (Int).
Talents: None.
Traits: None.
Weapons: Hunting Spear (Melee/Thrown; 5m; 1d10+3 R; Pen 0) or Heavy Club (1d10+4 I; Pen 0).

SPECIES TRAITS

Those species clever enough to master tool use tend to be driven to overcome a natural deficiency or weakness, and are rarely as well adapted to their environment as their feral counterparts. As such, most Primitive Xenos races receive one roll on **Table 4–8: Primitive Xenos Species Traits**, and receive no special benefit based on the world they evolved upon. At the GM's discretion, a Primitive Xenos race may receive one additional roll for Species Traits, or be granted a single Species Trait that assists them in dealing with their home environment.

PHYSIOLOGY

Most primitive species tend to have a humanoid form with the expected number of arms and legs. This may be because the zealous individuals who found more unusual species burned settlements from orbit rather than deal with such a deviant race. The truth of the matter is that sentience does not discriminate between the bipedal or the many-limbed. Roll once on **Table 4–9: Xenos Morphology** to determine the race's morphology. The new race thus has a 25% chance of unsettling or bizarre characteristics; if this happens, roll once on **Table 4–10: Exotic Xenos Physiology** to determine any oddity beyond their overall shape.

PRIMITIVE XENOS COMMUNICATIONS

When contact is made with a new race, there is usually a significant barrier to trade and exchange in the form of the xenos' language. While most non-Imperial human civilisations share enough of a common origin to make use of Low Gothic as a common medium, the same cannot be said of alien races.

Typically, a xenos race has its own language, which must be learned as an Elite Advance for 200xp (though the cost may vary at the GM's discretion) to facilitate proper communication. Qualifying for this advance typically takes at least two weeks of interaction, although at the GM's discretion characters with the Polyglot Talent may acquire it after a few days of interaction.

Until one or more Explorers can communicate with the xenos, all Interaction Skills are treated as untrained Basic Skills, regardless of training level, and the difficulty of Interaction Tests is increased by one step. A character with the Polyglot Talent may avoid these penalties and use the Talent as normal.

There is a 25% chance that a given race encountered by the Explorers may vary from these guidelines, whether through an unusual language structure or medium of communication. In such cases, roll on **Table 4–11 Unusual Xenos Communication**.

PRIMITIVE XENOS SOCIAL STRUCTURES

While a xenos civilisation of sufficient age and power might achieve a form of governance beyond basic tribal structures, there are thousands of xenos races that possess considerably less advancement. Without the millennia of history or infrastructure to shape their cultures, it is possible for an experienced eye to view the various xenos cultures as fitting certain patterns. The xenos themselves would likely disagree, but if they know so much, ask xenographers, then why haven't they mastered void travel yet?

TABLE 4-10: EXOTIC XENOS PHYSIOLOGY

Dice Roll (1d10)	Trait
1	Armoured
2	Disturbing
3	Deathdweller
4	Lethal Defences
5	Disturbing
6	Warped
7	Darkling
8	Unkillable
9	Projectile Attack
10	Deterrent

TABLE 4-11: UNUSUAL XENOS COMMUNICATION

Roll 1d5	Method of Communication
1	**Intuitive Communicators:** The xenos race possesses the ability to understand and communicate with the Explorers without prior contact, whether through low-level telepathy, an uncanny ability to intuit body language, or other unusual means. Interaction Skills suffer no penalty, unless the Explorers take issue with this clearly unnatural power.
2	**Previous Contact:** Certain members of the xenos culture have adequate fluency in Low Gothic to allow use of Interaction Skills without penalties. The question of where they learned the language is likely to be an issue—the only Imperial contact such beings are likely to have had would be a rival Rogue Trader dynasty.
3	**Relic Civilisation:** The entire race speaks a debased form of Low Gothic, not unlike what a long-separated fragment of pre-Imperial civilisation might use. Mastering the idiosyncrasies of their variant might take a week or two, but unravelling the mystery of their language's origin could be much more challenging...
4	**Simplistic:** The language of the xenos is simplicity itself—largely because their civilisation has little use for advanced concepts, and their communication has barely progressed beyond grunting. The language is learned for free after a week of interaction. Communication without fluency in the language treats Interaction Skills as Basic, but does not penalise them. However, even a trained speaker must pass a Speak Language test to get across advanced concepts and metaphors.
5	**Exotic:** The xenos communicate via elaborate mechanisms impossible to fully duplicate without their unique biology. Pheromones, pigmentation shifts, or body language beyond human physiology to replicate may play a part. Interaction Skills suffer an additional –10 penalty, whether the user trained in the language or not. Characters with the Polyglot Talent also suffer from this penalty, despite their unique abilities.

TABLE 4-12: PRIMITIVE XENOS SOCIAL STRUCTURES

Roll 1d10	Social Structure
1-2	**Agriculturalist:** The xenos have based their lifestyle around farming crops and herding local fauna. Such societies tend to be stable, if not outright peaceful. While many primitive xenos cultures have the tools to farm, this represents a culture where the herd or crop is the central cultural value. In some xenos cultures, the herd may even be a related species, or degenerate members of their own race.
3	**Hunter:** This race lives by their prowess in the hunt, supplementing lean seasons with foraging. They may know of agriculture and scorn it as weakness, or even have a physiology not far divorced from the predators they compete with for food. Explorers must take care not to present themselves as potential prey animals when dealing with such a culture.
4	**Feudal:** The xenos live in a society rigidly defined by oaths of loyalty. This could as easily refer to blood-bonds between feral chieftains as the vows made by vassals of an alien lord aping true Imperial nobility. Such societies are tight-knit, but often divided along multiple lines that can be exploited to gain influence over one lord or another.
5	**Raiders:** While some section of the xenos culture is devoted to the production or acquisition of food and other necessities, true status in this society belongs to the warriors. Crops grown are valued less than those seized from others, and only strength is respected. A Rogue Trader can easily impress such aliens with his military might, but must be careful not to let himself seem too dependent on his tools or servants.
6	**Nomadic:** The race is constantly on the move, travelling along with migratory herds, moving from area to area as they exhaust local food supplies or deplete the land, driven to keep roaming perhaps due to local weather conditions. Explorers may find it impossible to deal with them unless they are willing to also move with the tribes.
7	**Hivemind:** Linked together in a network of pheromones, neurological energies, or some other mechanism, the xenos think and speak with one mind. There are no actual individuals in the race, and their "representative" might change daily as a new member is chosen to interact with the Explorers. This race views the death of a member as nothing more than a mild nuisance, but will also view a slight against one as a slight against them all.
8	**Scavengers:** The xenos make their living by picking through the ruins of an older civilisation. Whether they dwell amidst a fallen human colony, archeotech ruins, or the remains of a xenos race such as the Egarian Dominion, the end result is that these supposed primitives have access to advanced tools, although they may understand little to nothing about these items. They may trade priceless relics for new kinds of "magic," for example, or view the intrusion of other advanced races as a sign of an impending apocalypse.
9	**Xenophobic:** It is possible this race was previously exploited by less benign Explorers, or they may have simply evolved to treat anything but themselves as a deadly threat. They will aggressively attack anyone outside their race or tribe, and it will take extensive patience and peace offerings to even begin attempts at communication.
10	**Tradition-bound:** Unlike most primitive xenos, the lack of advancement for this culture is not based on youth, but an ancient and established tradition. The hallowed ancestors or ancient edicts of this race forbid diverging from their long-held path. Anything new—like the Explorers—is to be mistrusted.

The basic foundation of a given primitive xenos race can be determined by rolling on **Table 4–12: Primitive Xenos Social Structures**. Some of the results assume a certain level of technological or societal development, but this can be altered or tweaked at the GM's discretion.

EXAMPLE: KOETH BONE-PICKERS

A group of Explorers are approaching a world deep within the Unbeholden Reaches where they have heard a primitive xenos race dwells. Their GM, Robin, laid this plot hook down a while back, but hasn't had time to detail the culture yet, so he decides to generate it randomly. He notes there is only one Base Profile the xenos can use, and moves immediately on to the Species Traits that might modify it. His roll indicates the new race is Stealthy, and he records the bonuses onto the Base Profile.

*Xenos races are humanoid by default, but have a chance of an unusual physiology, which Robin rolls for. This race turns out to be one of the outliers, and so Robin rolls on **Table 4–9: Xenos Morphology**. The result grants the race the Multiple Arms Trait. At this point, the physical details of the race have been determined, so Robin sets about figuring out what the species looks like. He envisions tall creatures with pale, hairless skin and four long, graceful arms, used for climbing and swimming through difficult terrain. The Base Profile doesn't include the Climb or Swim Skills, but Robin decides that many of the xenos have let their natural advantages degrade in favour of mastering more advanced and complicated tools. He notes that individual members of the species should be trained in Climb and Swim where appropriate. He does not roll to allow any Exotic Physiology, thus keeping his new race relatively normal.*

*Most xenos race have their own unique tongue, sophisticated enough to communicate complex concepts, but not something impossible for an interested Explorer to learn. Robin rolls to see if his new species varies from this pattern, and the dice indicate that they seem standard in the respect. However, looking at **Table 4–11: Unusual Xenos Communication**, he notes the option for a small number of individuals to speak Low Gothic, and he decides to use this element, as the race has had previous Imperial contact.*

Robin notes he is nearly done and makes his last roll, this time for the social structure the race tends towards. His result is Scavengers—these xenos live amidst the ruins of an older civilisation. The previous details Robin had given to his players about this race said nothing on this topic, and he briefly considers re-rolling—but decides against it. Not all information learned about the Expanse is good, and everyone has their reasons for keeping secrets, after all. He decides the xenos live amidst an old archeotech necropolis, plundering tomb-structures for the grave goods of a long-dead pre-Imperial culture. He decides the race has two names, one which they call themselves (Koeth), and one given to them by the previous Imperial representative who contacted them (Bone-Pickers). Now, all that remains is to add modifiers to the Base Profile for key NPCs, and see how the players react to the new aliens.

REPORTS FROM THE EXPANSE

The most typical goal of Rogue Traders dealing with primitive xenos civilisations is to secure artefacts for the Cold Trade, typically art and other trinkets reflecting the bizarre sensibilities of the race that created it. There are countless tales circulating the obscura dens and voidsmen's taverns of Footfall regarding Traders who found something else entirely in this quest, often more than they bargained for. A small selection of such tales can be found below, which can serve as seeds for new adventures. Their veracity is unknown, and voidsmen are notorious tellers of tall tales and weavers of fiction. But behind many outlandish yarns lie kernels of truth, and a chance of great profits...

- A race of relic scavengers dwells on a barren planet in a system plagued by fierce gravity riptides. When the system's hazards cause a ship to founder on their planet, the xenos attack the vessel in search of new technologies (which they can understand only poorly, at best).

- Huge monoliths capable of fabricating advanced mechanical components dot the surface of a planet amidst the Foundling Worlds cluster. The xenos there worship the monoliths, constantly mining so they can feed in the minerals they believe nourish their "gods." When these automated foundries produce a new piece of alien technology, the xenos add it to their pantheon, believing it to be a divinely born scion of the monolith that produced it. They also likely view any attempts to trade for or steal these items as a deadly blasphemy.

- Deep in the Unbeholden Reaches, there exists a world where both humans and xenos dwell—not side by side, but in alternating shifts. When the local star shines its light on the surface, the human colonists control the planet and strive to build up their civilisation. But when night falls, the humans disappear into protective barracks, and the native xenos emerge to tear down everything their counterparts have raised up, and to create their own blasphemous works.

- Several worlds across Winterscale's Realm have small enclaves of the same primitive race. They have no industry, let alone starships, and deny having ever travelled from world to world when questioned by explorers. But the enclaves are there, and some even swear that the same xenos have been spotted on further worlds across the Expanse. Either they do possess voidships, or some other race is transporting them for reasons unknown...

- One of the primitive races near the Undred-Undred Teef has had remarkable successes in repelling the marauding Orks who occasionally land on their world. Some claim they have a natural witch-talent that repels the Orks, while others say their flesh emits a fume toxic to Greenskins. If this race could be examined, perhaps even hired on as mercenaries, the Ork threat to the Expanse might be greatly lessened.

- It is the opinion of many among the Magos Xenobiologis that intelligent species tend to be those who must overcome great disadvantages on their native worlds—after all, a species already high on the food chain has little need to evolve further. But some voidsmen tell of a mighty hunting beast deep in the Expanse that thinks, crafts tools and traps, and even speaks. It is the apex predator of an entire world, although no two tales agree on its exact form. Some speculate that each differing encounter represents an entirely different species of an equally deadly nature.

- A curious tale, told by a reputable Rogue Trader, is making the rounds. Apparently, he was hosted and entertained by a species he never saw. Words and even goods were exchanged, but no sign of the xenos' shape or nature could be discerned. Even their footprints and signs of passage were hidden from the eyes of his crew. When he had an auspex brought from his ship to try and solve the mystery, the whole settlement rose up in anger against him. Some whisper his ship hosts a small contingent of these enraged phantoms to this day, hunting and killing his crew to avenge the slight.

- One of the cursed worlds of the far Corpse Stars is said to be unusually blooming with life, a Trait credited to the nurturing xenos that dwell there. However, the life sustained by the xenos race is all plant life, as are the xenos themselves. Those of flesh who step onto this world are said to take their lives into their own hands, for these sentient flora do not welcome creatures that are not of their own kind.

SPECIES TRAIT LISTING

This section contains the full listing of Species Traits used in the random generation system above. GMs can find full rules for all the results they have generated using the random tables in this chapter.

Most Species Traits "stack" if rolled multiple times, providing increased versions of the normal effects. When a Species Trait is listed as having no additional effects, re-roll any further results of that Trait. Similarly, some Species Traits can only stack a certain number of times, and so should be re-rolled for all instances past that point. Some Species Traits interact in unusual ways, and the following rules apply:

- No combination of Traits can take a creature's Characteristics above 99. Ignore all further modifiers to that characteristic.
- A creature that already has the Swift Attack Talent from its Base Profile or another Species Trait instead gains the Lightning Attack Talent, or +10 WS if it already has that Talent.
- A creature that already has an Unnatural multiplier to a Characteristic that gains the Unnatural Trait to the same Characteristic instead increases its multiplier by 1.
- A creature that gains the Improved Natural Weapons Trait multiple times increases the damage of its Natural Weapons by 2 instead. This may only occur once.
- It is possible for a creature to have both Foul Aura (Soporific) and Foul Aura (Toxic). However, they count as separate Traits, and so only multiple instances of a specific Foul Aura "stack."
- The Thermal Adaptation (Cold) and Thermal Adaptation (Heat) Species Traits are incompatible. Re-roll all such results.

APEX

This creature is the top predator of its environment. More than one or two such species on a planet may result in its classification as a Death World. The big game hunters of the Imperial nobility would pay well to hunt this creature from a safe distance, and the Beast Traders of the Calixis Sector yearn to see it in their fighting pits. The creature gains +10 to Weapon Skill, Strength, Toughness, Agility, and Perception, as well as the Swift Attack Talent and the Improved Natural Weapons Trait. A second instance of this Trait instead grants the Unnatural Strength (x2) and Unnatural Toughness (x2) Traits, while further instances have no effect.

AMORPHOUS

Creatures with this Trait have no defined body structure, instead existing as a foul, ooze-like mass. They can alter their Size one step in either direction as a Free Action, although they cannot change more than one step from the base, and doing so does not change their Movement. Due to the difficulty of propulsion without muscles, the Movement of an Amorphous creature is calculated with half their Agility Bonus, rounded up. They gain +10 Toughness, as well as the Strange

Physiology and Unnatural Senses Traits, and receive a Fear Rating of 2 (or increase their existing Rating by 1 if it is already equal or higher). Amorphous species have a 50% chance of gaining a level of training in the Climb and Swim Skills. Multiple instances of this Trait have no effect.

AMPHIBIOUS

This Trait allows a creature to survive equally well on water or land, although most Amphibious creatures are terrestrial by nature, using bodies of water as concealment or a hunting ground. An Amphibious creature can swim at their full Speed even under hazardous conditions, and gains a +20 bonus to Swim Tests (rules for Swimming are found on page 267 of the ROGUE TRADER Core Rulebook). There is a 25% chance that an Amphibious species is also able to breathe water for a number of hours equal to its Toughness Bonus. Multiple instances of this Trait have no effect.

AQUATIC

Aquatic species dwell exclusively in the water (or whatever liquid the native oceans and rivers of the species are made from), and cannot survive for any significant length of time outside of it. Use the rules for Suffocation on page 261 of the ROGUE TRADER Core Rulebook if an Aquatic species leaves the water. Most Aquatic species are also unable to move when removed from the water, suffering −20 to Agility Tests and treating their Agility Bonus as 1. While immersed, they automatically pass all Swim Tests and may move as if their Agility bonus was 1 higher than normal. Aquatic species can breathe water indefinitely. Multiple instances of this Trait have no effect.

ARBOREAL

The treetop canopy of vast forests and jungles is home for Arboreal creatures. Such species are native to an environment far above the ground, and seem at times to have as much kinship with flying beasts as those lumbering along on the ground below. Such creatures are automatically trained in Acrobatics, Climb, and Dodge, and gain +20 to Tests with those Skills. They also receive the Catfall Talent. Arboreal creatures double their climbing speed on any Simple Climb, as described on page 266 of the ROGUE TRADER Core Rulebook. Multiple instances of this Trait have no effect.

ARMOURED

Tough, resilient protection encases creatures with this Trait. Whether this armour is simply a rough hide, a layer of bark, scales, bony plates, or even the result of sub-dermal metal deposits, the effect is the same. The creature gains the Natural Armour (1d5) Trait, or, if it already possesses Natural Armour, increases that value by 2 (to a maximum of 8 Armour). Multiple instances of this Trait add Armour as described above.

CRAWLER

This Trait is common both to legless beasts such as serpents and worms, as well as those with far too many legs for the comfort of onlookers, such as the occasionally-domesticated Cerapede of the Calixis Sector. Such creatures gain the Crawler Trait, and have a 25% chance of being trained in the Climb Skill. Multiple instances of this Trait increase the likelihood of possessing the Climb Skill by +5% to a maximum of +20%.

DARKLING

These are creatures native to lightless worlds or environs far from illumination by a sun. They are universally blind in terms of conventional sight (and thus have the Blind Trait), but gain acute Unnatural Senses, with a range of 30 metres or more. Darkling Creatures have a 50% chance of gaining the Sonar Sense Trait instead of Unnatural Senses. All receive the Awareness and Silent Move Skills, with species native to caverns or other subterranean environments also gaining the Climb and Swim Skills. Some Darkling creatures are hideous to gaze upon, granting 10% of species with this Trait a Fear Rating of 1. Multiple instances of this Trait have no effect.

DEADLY

The attacks of this creature bite through carapace and ceramite as easily as they rend flesh and crush bone. Explorers facing such a creature should do so from a distance, and pray to the Emperor it does not close. The creature gains +10 Weapon Skill and the Improved Natural Weapons Trait. A second instance of this Trait grants the Razor Sharp Quality to its natural weapons, and any further instances grant only an additional +10 Weapon Skill.

DEATHDWELLER

Not all worlds are well suited to life's development, but life frequently finds expression on these worlds nonetheless. The species that survive the ravages of a hostile environment often have this Trait. Such lifeforms are immune to Toxic attacks not native to their homeworld or not specifically tailored to their biology, and gain the Resistance (Radiation) Talent. They also receive +3 Wounds. Additional instances of this Trait grant +5 Toughness and an additional +2 Wounds.

DETERRENT

A foul stench, chemical haze, unconscious psychic field, or similar defence imposes penalties to attacks against any creature with this Trait. Blows are sapped of striking power and shots are thrown astray. Attacks against creatures with this Trait suffer –20 to the attack roll. Further instances of this Trait reduce the Damage of attacks that land by 1 per additional application.

DISTURBING

Something about this creature feels unnatural and innately wrong to human senses. Whether its body aligns with unnatural geometries or its hunting cry pierces through sound-filters to chill the heart of listeners, merely being in its presence is a nerve-wracking experience. The creature gains a Fear Rating of 1. Each further instance of this Trait increases the Fear Rating by 1, to the normal maximum of Fear Rating 4.

FADE-KIND

Creatures with this Trait are ghostly and out of touch with normal physical existence, dwelling in an unnatural half-life between the layers of reality. They possess the Incorporeal or Phase Trait (with a 50% chance of each). At the GM's discretion, certain conditions or materials may prevent them from using these abilities, such as an Incorporeal creature that cannot pass through the stones of the world to which it is native. Given the unnatural and possibly warp-touched nature of such abilities, there is a 25% chance for a creature with this Trait to possess a Fear Rating of 1. Multiple instances of this Trait have no effect.

FLEXIBLE

The bone structure of a creature with this Trait is unusually malleable, or perhaps it does not even possess a skeleton. Such creatures gain the Flexible Quality on their Natural Weapons and +10 to Dodge. A second instance allows them to wrap their flowing limbs around their prey in a stranglehold, granting the Snare Quality to their Natural Weapons. Further instances grant +10 Agility per application.

FOUL AURA (SOPORIFIC)/ FOUL AURA (TOXIC)

The very air surrounding this plant is filled to choking with pollen, spores, or chemical fumes. Breathing the air within five metres of a plant with this Trait requires a **Challenging (+0) Toughness Test t**o avoid suffering the effects of its Foul Aura. Toxic plants cause 1d10 Wounds (ignoring Armour), per round of inhalation, while Soporific plants inflict a level of Fatigue per two Degrees of Failure. Fatigue caused in excess of what is required to render the target unconscious is converted to Wounds that ignore Toughness Bonus and Armour. Each additional instance of this Trait increases the radius of the aura by ten metres and imposes a –10 penalty to the Toughness Test to avoid the effects. If a plant has more than one instance of this Trait, only a full environmental seal provides protection—simply avoiding breathing in the air is not sufficient.

FRICTIONLESS

The xenos has impossibly smooth skin, coats its leaves with an oily residue, or uses some other means to reduce any traction against that surface to almost nothing. Explorers might find themselves helplessly sliding into a digestion maw once they step onto innocuous appearing vegetation, or unable to effectively fight against an attacking predator as they cannot find purchase to hurl it away. Any Tests to Grapple with such a creature suffer a –20 Penalty, and any Damage inflicted on the creature in Melee Combat is reduced by 1d5 as the weapon's impact slips off the surface. Explorers operating on a Frictionless surface must make a **Difficult (–10) Agility Test** or they Fall to the ground. Additional instances of this Trait increases this Test by one Level of Difficulty.

GESTALT

Freakish beasts beyond the nightmares of ordinary Imperial citizens, each Gestalt creature is not one being, but many. They are huge colonies of smaller lifeforms bonded together by some unholy union. This Trait grants +10 Toughness and Willpower but reduces the creature's Intelligence by –10 due to the warring impulses of the gathered minds. Gestalt creatures cannot be Stunned and re-roll all failed Tests to resist psychic influence or other forms of mental control. Multiple instances of this Trait have no effect.

LETHAL DEFENCES

Creatures with this Trait have a defence mechanism to lash out at those who do them harm, whether through a spiny carapace, bio-electric pulses, or acidic blood flowing from their wounds. When such a creature takes Damage past its Toughness Bonus and Armour, its attacker must pass a **Challenging (+0) Dodge Test** or suffer 1d10+3 I Damage. There is a 25% chance this damage possesses either the Toxic or Shocking Qualities (GM's discretion). Each additional instance of this Trait increases the Damage by 1, and makes the Test to avoid it one step harder.

MIGHTY

The muscles of this creature are incomparable, whether they are made of plant fibre, flesh, or living rock. Its attacks land like hammer blows and whatever limbs or tendrils it has could easily crush the life from the unwary. The creature gains +10 Strength. A second instance of this Trait grants Unnatural Strength (x2), and further instances have no effect.

PARALYTIC

The attacks of this creature may drip with a foul slime or inject venom into the bloodstream of those it wounds, but regardless of the vector and appearance of the toxin, the effect is the same. The creature's Natural Weapons gain the Toxic Quality, but do no additional damage. Instead, victims failing the Toughness Test suffer a level of Fatigue per two Degrees of Failure. Each additional instance of this Trait imposes a further –10 penalty to the Test to resist the Toxic effect.

PROJECTILE ATTACK

This Trait can represent a wide variety of attack mediums, from reflex-launched spines or quills to acidic spittle or even gouts of fiery breath. The creature gains a Ballistic Skill of 30, as well as a new ranged attack dealing 1d10+3 Impact, Rending, or Energy damage (determined at the GM's discretion) with a penetration of 0. The attack has a Range of 15 metres and may only fire in single shots. It never needs to reload, as the creature's own metabolic processes provide the necessary fuel or supplies. Each additional instance of this Trait grants +10 Ballistic Skill, +10 metres Range, and +1 Damage and Penetration to the attack.

RESILIENT

Hardy beyond all but the most rugged of lifeforms, this creature is incredibly resistant to damage and illness. It can survive poisons and gunshots with equal tenacity. The creature gains +10 Toughness; a second instance of this Trait grants Unnatural Toughness (x2), and further instances have no effect.

SILICATE

The Magos Biologis hold that all life is made up of the same building blocks—basic chemicals that bind human and xenos alike. Some creatures defy this elementary law, however, and are formed of what amounts to living stone or crystal. Silicate creatures reduce their Agility by –10, and cannot swim under any circumstances. They gain Natural Armour (1d5+1), and the Unnatural Strength (x2) and Unnatural Toughness (x2) Traits. They do not suffer Blood Loss or Suffocation, but their brittle structure doubles any Critical Damage they suffer from attacks that cause Impact or Explosive Damage. Multiple instances of this Trait have no effect.

STEALTHY

A natural ambusher or lurker, this creature may have chameleonic skin or another form of natural camouflage. This Trait grants training in the Concealment, Shadowing, and Silent Move Skills, as well as a +20 bonus to relevant Tests. A second instance of this Trait increases the bonus to +30, and allows failed Tests to be re-rolled. On flora, this Trait allows the plant to keep its original Agility value for purposes of Concealment Tests. Further instances have no effect.

STICKY

The creature exudes a layer of adhesive sap or mucilage on its skin or leaves, which can quickly bind prey as they find themselves stuck to the creature. It is most often found on varieties of carnivorous flora, which feed on the entrapped victim once it eventually perishes. The species itself is immune to these adhesives, but anyone else touching such a creature must pass a **Challenging (+0) Strength Test** to free themselves. Depending on how much of their body is trapped, they might be helpless until they succeed or merely unable to use one limb. Multiple instances of this Trait increase this Test by one Level of Difficulty.

SUSTAINED LIFE

This Trait is common to lifeforms on worlds with weak atmospheres, or ones that lack air altogether. Creatures with this Trait do not need to breathe and are thus immune to Suffocation and inhaled toxins. An additional instance of this Trait indicates a lifeform adapted to the void itself, able to live without air or gravity; while in an airless environment, these creatures gain the Flyer Trait at a value equal to their Agility Bonus.

SWIFT

Creatures with this Trait possess lightning-fast reflexes and speedy locomotion, able to outpace nearly any living thing. This Trait grants +10 Agility. A second instance grants the Unnatural Speed (x2) modifier, while each additional instance increases the multiplier by 1.

THERMAL ADAPTATION (COLD)/ THERMAL ADAPTATION (HEAT)

The extreme temperatures of some environments lead to life uniquely adapted for survival in scorching heat or freezing cold. Thermal Adaptation can reflect one of two similar Traits. All creatures with Thermal Adaptation gain +5 Toughness and the Resistance (Cold) or Resistance (Heat) Talent as appropriate, but suffer −20 to Tests to resist the opposite temperate extreme.

A second instance of Thermal Adaptation (Heat) grants immunity to environmental heat and doubles the creature's Toughness Bonus against heat-based weapons, such as Flame, Melta, and Plasma weapons. However, such a creature suffers one Fatigue for every minute it does not spend in an appropriate environment (as determined by the GM). Further instances of this Trait have no effect.

A second instance of Thermal Adaptation (Cold) grants immunity to environmental cold, but doubles the damage dealt past Toughness and Armour by heat-based weapons against the creature. Such a creature also suffers one Fatigue for every minute it does not spend in an appropriate environment (as determined by the GM). Further instances of this Trait have no effect.

TUNNELLER

Some creatures possess the ability to tunnel through the earth, whether through secreting corrosive slime or tearing at the soil with huge fore-claws. Tunneller creatures gain the Burrower Trait at a value equal to their Strength Bonus. Additional instances of this Trait increase the creature's burrowing speed by 2 per application, and allow the beast to burrow through metal.

UNKILLABLE

There are creatures that just won't die. Whether they draw on the unnatural vitality of the warp or bounce back from grievous wounds due to a hyper-advanced metabolism, the Explorer who tries to put such a beast down is likely to be frustrated in his efforts. This Trait grants +5 Wounds and the Regeneration Trait. Additional instances grant +2 additional Wounds and increase the number of Wounds recovered each round by Regeneration by 1 per application.

UPROOTED MOVEMENT

Flora that have this Trait are not limited to passively waiting for prey to come by, but can actively hunt to feed themselves, or pursue an escaped victim. Such flora strains may uproot themselves as a Half Action, which grants a movement rate appropriate to their Agility Bonus and Size, as well as the ability to use the Dodge Skill (although they do not gain training in it). However, the uprooting process causes 1 Wound, ignoring Toughness and armour, and the flora suffers an additional such Wound at the end of every round it spends uprooted. A plant may become rooted again in any appropriate soil as a Half Action. A second instance of this Trait removes the Damage caused by the uprooting process, and by staying uprooted. Further instances of this Trait have no effect.

VALUABLE

A Rogue Trader is always on the lookout for new sources of profit, and new xenos beings are always worth investigating for the Thrones they might bring to his dynasty. While almost any creature is valuable in some sense (as a basic meat source perhaps, or to burn as fuel), these particular ones have importance to a far greater extent. Their pelts might be part of elite hiveworld fashions, their sap the main ingredient in a powerful (and illegal) drug, their teeth the basis for regicide pieces used in the Tricorn Palace, and so on. The details as to what part of the being is valuable and how much it is worth varies with the creature, but any Valuable being should definitely be worth serious investigation for any profit-minded Explorers. Multiple occurrences of this Trait have no additional game effect.

VENOMOUS

From vines that deliver contact-vector toxins to fangs that inject their lethal payload into the bloodstream and the stingers and mandibles of huge insectoid creatures, poison is used by flora and fauna alike across the galaxy to weaken or slay their enemies. Even some prey animals are known to bristle with poison-coated spines or otherwise use toxins as a defence mechanism. The creature's Natural Weapons gain the Toxic Quality. Each additional instance of this Trait imposes a further –10 penalty to the Test to resist the Toxic effect.

WARPED

The foul touch of Chaos has warped this species, undoing natural evolution and infusing it with the essence of the warp. While some unifying Traits can be found in such species, the power of such unbridled change defies easy classification. Roll once on **Table 14–3: Mutations** (see page 369 of the ROGUE TRADER Core Rulebook) to generate a mutation possessed by all members of the species, and again for each individual of that species encountered. Some thought should be used when applying Mutations—for example, an Enormous creature gaining the "Hulking" Mutation should not lose Size, but might become Massive instead. Each additional instance of this Trait causes an additional roll for individuals of the species, as they become more and more unrecognisable as natural life.

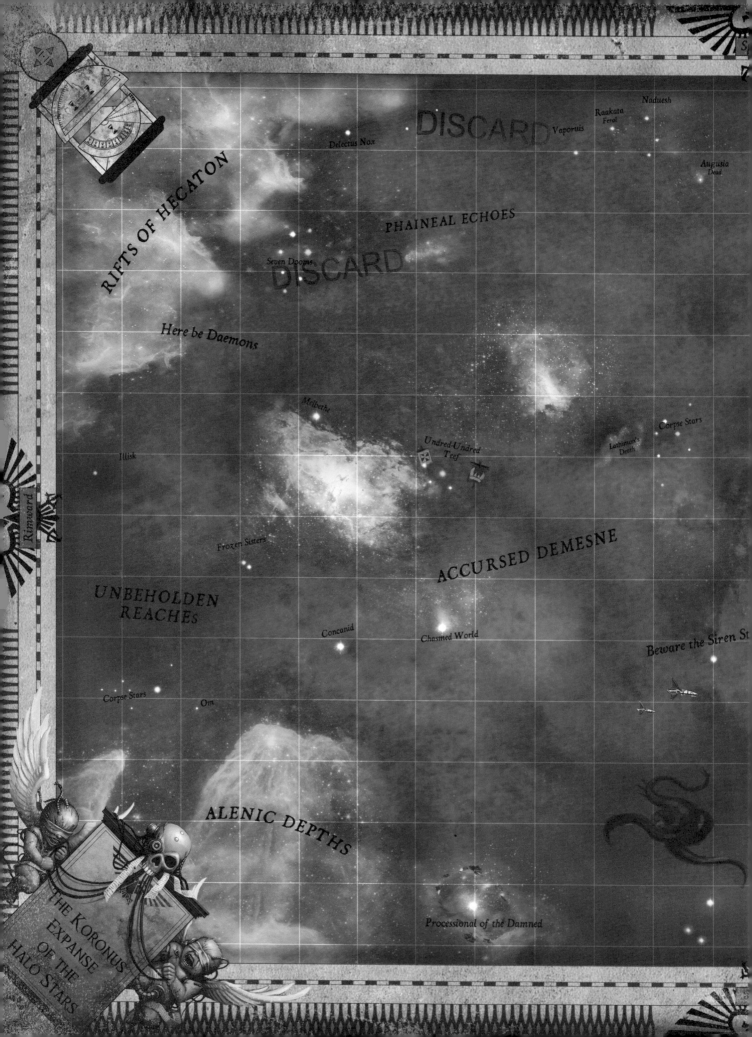

DISCARD

Naduesh

Raakata
Feral

Vaporuis

Delectus Nox

Augusia
Dead

RIFTS OF HECATON

PHAINEAL ECHOES

DISCARD

Seven Dooms

Here be Daemons

Melbethe

Corpse Stars

Undred-Undred
Teef

Lathunox's
Death

Illisk

Rimward

Frozen Sisters

ACCURSED DEMESNE

UNBEHOLDEN
REACHES

Concanid

Chasmed World

Beware the Siren St

Corpse Stars

Om

ALENIC DEPTHS

Processional of the Damned

THE KORONUS
EXPANSE
OF THE
HALO STARS